The
Reference Shelf®

Hate Crimes

The Reference Shelf
Volume 92 • Number 1
H.W. Wilson
A Division of EBSCO Information Services, Inc.

Published by
GREY HOUSE PUBLISHING
Amenia, New York
2020

The Reference Shelf

The books in this series contain reprints of articles, excerpts from books, addresses on current issues, and studies of social trends in the United States and other countries. There are six separately bound numbers in each volume, all of which are usually published in the same calendar year. Numbers one through five are each devoted to a single subject, providing background information and discussion from various points of view and concluding with an index and comprehensive bibliography that lists books, pamphlets, and articles on the subject. The final number of each volume is a collection of recent speeches. Books in the series may be purchased individually or on subscription.

Publisher's Cataloging-In-Publication Data
(Prepared by The Donohue Group, Inc.)

Names: Grey House Publishing, Inc., compiler.
Title: Hate crimes / [compiled by Grey House Publishing].
Other Titles: Reference shelf ; v. 92, no. 1.
Description: Amenia, New York : Grey House Publishing, 2020. | Includes bibliographical references and index.
Identifiers: ISBN 9781642656008 (v. 92, no. 1) | ISBN 9781642655995 (volume set)
Subjects: LCSH: Hate crimes--United States. | Mass shootings--United States. | School violence--United States. | Hate crimes--Government policy--United States. | Hate crimes--Law and legislation--United States. | LCGFT: Reference works.
Classification: LCC HV6773.52 .H38 2020 | DDC 364.150973--dc23

Contents

3

Hate Laws and the Constitution

4

Prevention, Outreach, and Training

5

The Role of the Media and Big Tech

Preface

Places Once Thought Safe

Schools, cafés, shopping malls, churches, and movie theaters were once considered safe places to frequent. Simply listening to news reports has shown that is no longer the case. FBI statistics confirm that most hate crimes occur near an individual's home, on a roadway, and places like those listed above. Reporting of hate crimes is not mandatory, so they may go unreported depending on state law. Official reports, and significant media coverage, show that hate crimes are on the rise.

October 16, 2019, marked the tenth anniversary of the Matthew Shepard and James Byrd, Jr., Hate Crimes Prevention Act (HPCS). Matthew Shepard was a gay University of Wyoming student who was beaten, tortured, and left to die. James Byrd, Jr., was an African American murdered by three white supremacists, who was dragged for three miles behind a pickup truck, These horrific crimes, both in 1998, were the impetus for change in hate crime education and legislation.

Extreme Hate Crimes

Although not defined as hate crimes until recently, persecution has occurred throughout world history. Examples include the genocide of Native Americans in the United States and of Jewish people during the Holocaust. More recently, the Our World in Data listed Iraq and the Central African Republic as areas of active genocides in 2015. Genocides between 1955 and 2014 where death tolls range between 16,000 to 256,000 happened in Algeria, Nigeria, Sudan, Uganda, Angola, Somalia, Iraq, Afghanistan, Pakistan, China, Cambodia, and Indonesia.[1]

An estimated 100,000 Bosnian Muslim and Croatian civilians died during the "ethnic cleansing" by Serbia and Bosnian Serbs between 1992 and 1995. In 1994 approximately 800,000 were slaughtered in Rwanda by Hutu extremists in 100 days with an estimated five million by 2003. Ninety-three people were indicted for these actions, dozens more were convicted of genocide by the UN Security Council and the International Criminal Tribunal, and many more are still awaiting trial.[2]

The rise of hate crimes and anti-Semitism has spurred initiatives in Holocaust education in some states. As of 2019 eleven states participated in Holocaust education: Oregon, California, Connecticut, Florida, Illinois, Kentucky, Michigan, New Jersey, New York, Oregon, Pennsylvania, and Rhode Island.[3] This education is important to dispel the doubt that some have concerning the reality of the Holocaust, doubt that could increase the possibility of it being repeated.

A Look Back

In 1866 Confederate veterans formed the Ku Klux Klan (KKK) in Pulaski, Tennessee, hoping to restore white supremacy and crush political and economic equality for African-Americans. Some KKK members were police officers, so hate crime cases were often overlooked, as in the 1871 case of the lynching of eight black prisoners in South Carolina by the KKK. President Ulysses S. Grant passed the Ku Klux Klan Act of 1871, making depriving citizens of their right to hold office, serve on a jury, and have equal protection a federal offense. In 1915 the KKK was four million strong. They expanded their focus from anti-African-American to include anti-gay, anti-Catholic, anti-immigrant, and anti-organized labor. The KKK disbanded during the Great Depression and regrouped again in 1944, becoming active in the 1960s during the Civil Rights movement, which provoked bombing, shooting, and beating of activists. According to recent statements by Klan members, their goal is to "separate the Whites and Blacks from each other by dividing the country in half."[4]

Native Americans also have reason to be concerned about discrimination and hate crimes that frequently are not prosecuted as hate crimes. In 2015 a park worker shot two sleeping men in an alcohol treatment center in Wyoming, angry for having to clean up after homeless men. A group of whites in a pickup truck waving scalp wigs drove past a 2016 Battle of the Little Big Horn tribal celebration in Montana. In May of 2017 a pick-up truck ran over two members of the Quinault Indian Nation while yelling racial slurs and "war whoops," killing one. None of these were prosecuted as hate crimes. There are concerns that the high rate of suicide among Native youth may be due to this violence.[5]

Race in the Future

U.S. Census Bureau projections show that by the year 2020 more than half of the children in the United States will belong to a minority race or ethnic group. By 2044, there will no longer be a white majority. Minority populations were at 38 percent in 2014 and are expected to rise to 56 percent by 2060. In 2014 people born abroad consisted of 13 percent of the U.S. population and projections show that figure rising to 19 percent by 2060.[6] A number of hate and extremist groups are concerned over these changing demographics.

Rise of the Hate Groups

Despite the KKK making headlines in recent years, the number of chapters has fallen, from 130 in 2016 to 51 in 2018, but other white supremacist groups have formed since President Donald Trump became president. Neo-Nazi group Atomwaffen has grown from one chapter in 2017 to 27 in 2018; white nationalist group Identity Evropa went from one chapter in 2016 to 38 in 2018. Black nationalist groups have also been expanding and increased from 233 chapters in 2017 to 264 in 2018. Heidi Beirich in a Southern Poverty Law Center article, "The Year in Hate," states, "Unlike white hate groups, whose champions found themselves in influential White House positions over the past two years, black nationalists have little or no impact on mainstream politics and no defenders in high office." The number of anti-government groups declined by approximately 12 percent, from 689 chapters in 2017 to 612 in 2018. According to Beirich, "anti-government activists finally have an administration they can believe in . . . and less anger to tap into to build their ranks."

The total number of hate groups rose to 1,020 in 2018 and included white nationalists, neo-Nazis black nationalists, anti-government patriots, and anti-immigrant, anti-LGBT, anti-Muslim, Christian identity, neo-Confederate, and racist skinheads groups.[7]

According to Rachel Frazin of *The Hill*, "FBI Director Christopher Wray said that violent, racially motivated extremists in the U.S. are connecting with foreign extremists, with some traveling abroad to train." Communication via the internet and social media is concerning. U.S. army soldier Jarrett William Smith was arrested in September 2019 for sending bomb-building instructions through social media after reportedly expressing interest in joining Ukraine paramilitary group Azov Battalion.[8]

Why Hate?

Brian Levin and Kevin Grisham of the Center for the Study of Hate and Extremism note that perpetrators often have a "'printed circuit of stereotypes' that label certain groups as inferior, violent, morally deficient, or a threat." Among those who commit hate crimes are young people, prejudiced thrill seekers, and individuals or groups looking for excitement. Some commit hate crimes in response to an extreme incident, such as a terrorist attack; some simply because someone of a different race moved in nearby. Levin and Grisham state that the smallest group are the "mission offenders, the hardcore hatemongers" who may become part of a local or online group. "Defense offenders" may be fueled by "deep-seated fears, anger or a desire for revenge. . . [they] frequently have a violent anti-social predisposition . . . and . . . the switch is always turned on as they view the world through a fanatical and conflictual prism where they are under attack by outgroups." They commit hateful acts against "peers, coworkers, and family members, are the most steeped in hatred and define themselves as warriors for their cause; relying on a defining, often conspiratorial, narrative; history and folklore."

An event or series of events may spur prejudiced individuals to react aggressively or violently. They may be influenced by the spread of negative stereotypes or by conspiracy theorists and are "susceptible to exploitation by the messages and purported facts of those who are bigots . . . who promote a strain of Euro-nationalism, Islamophobia and anti-Semitism as a bulwark against national security threats, demographic change, and a degradation of traditional American culture."[9]

Thomas Brudholm and Birgitte Schepelern Johansen, authors of "Hate, Politics, Law—Critical Perspectives on Combating Hate" cite envy as the emotion driving social conflict rather than hate. They believe understanding envy will provide a better understanding of hate crimes and the underlying humiliation behind them. They ascribe to political scientist Erik Bleich's conclusion that "fighting of hate speech and hate crimes is not 'really' hate, but structures of prejudice, illegitimate power hierarchies and discrimination... Creating hate crimes does not purge society of hate; instead it redirects democratic hatred toward hate crime offenders. Do we in our fighting of hatred risk to hatefully excommunicate the odious others in our midst?"[10]

Accuracy in the Age of Information

The continued occurrences of hate crimes, hate speech, mass shootings, and extremist attacks provide eye-opening and discouraging statistics. FBI and the U.S. Department of Justice have data from the 1990s (FBI) and 2003 (Bureau of Justice Statistics' National Crime Victimization Survey [NCVS]). Reporting is not mandatory or consistent. Some states do not have hate crime laws in place, leaving agencies to determine whether incidents are hate-based or fall under freedom of speech. Training for law enforcement is available through the FBI and the International Association of Chiefs of Police (IACP) but does not ensure individual training at the local level. Many blame the political climate for the rise in prejudice. A number of organizations have stepped forward, tracking and assessing local, county, state, and national media reports to capture unreported incidents. These organizations use polling data, direct questionnaires, and other means to produce in-depth, accurate reports of hate crimes. Some follow internet postings, investigate websites, and track activities of hate groups. However, the media has occasionally fallen victim to reporting hate crimes that later appear to be staged for publicity or not what they seem.

Diversity education has been available since the 1970s, and includes gender sensitivity and ethnic, religious, and sexuality differences as part of affirmative action programs.

The Problem with Guns

Mass shootings have made gun violence the center of a divisive debate. The National Rifle Association (NRA) contends that responsible gun ownership is protected by the Constitution and that passing anti-gun legislation will not stop hate-based shootings. Recent mass and school shootings have resulted in activism and some political support for gun regulation, but there are loopholes in existing gun control law. Examples include the gun show loophole, allowing the sale of firearms at gun shows without background checks, and online sales between private individuals, allowing convicted felons to evade background checks.

One Democrat, Representative Collin Peterson of Minnesota, and 157 Republicans voted against reauthorizing the 1994 Violence Against Women Act (VAWA). The House passed legislation reauthorizing the law for another five years and awaits Senate action. The bill would close the "boyfriend loophole," prohibiting the ownership or sale of guns to those with temporary protective orders and to those convicted of misdemeanor stalking offenses. The NRA gave the GOP congressional candidates $690,950 compared to $19,454 for Democratic candidates, and is thought to be the reason for the 157 Republican votes against reauthorization. The 2016 election received $419 million from the NRA with another $30 million donated to the Donald Trump campaign.[11]

Where We Work and Dine

The Matthew Shepard Foundation started the "Erase Hate in Business" campaign in response to President Donald Trump condoning businesses who put up signs refusing service to the LGBTQ population. The foundation has an #OpenToAll campaign offering a poster: "There is no space for hate within the walls of this business. We Welcome customers of any race, religion, ethnicity, sexuality, gender, disability, or immigration status. We are #OpenToAll."

Bias-related incidents that have occurred in business establishments include a May 2018 confrontation between Waffle House employees and a customer, 22 year-old Anthony Wall, who confronted employees for making homophobic remarks and was later choked by a police officer. Wall was charged with resisting arrest and disorderly conduct; Judge Mario Perez dismissed the disorderly conduct charge but found Wall to be guilty of resisting arrest.

ABC Eyewitness News reported that a settlement had been reached for seven Muslim women who were asked to leave a Laguna Beach Urth Caffe in 2016. The civil lawsuit was found to be in violation of California's Unruh Civil Rights Act, which states that public places are required to provide full and equal services to all regardless of religion. Urth Caffe agreed to ensure its seating policy was available to all customers, and updated their employee handbook to include information on customer diversity. Urth Caffe offered free drinks and dessert for all customers on June 16 in celebration of Eid al-Fitr, the end of the Muslim holy month of Ramadan.

WJTV reported that a deaf women was mocked by KFC employees in Missouri. The employees were not aware she was able to read lips. The *Clarion Ledger* reported on August 9, 2018, that nonprofit Disability Rights Mississippi had reached a nonbinding agreement with the management company of KFC, Pizza Hut, and Taco Bell franchise, who had agreed to offer sensitivity training at all of their 270 locations.[12]

Works Used

Beirich, Heidi. "The Year in Hate: Rage Against Change." Southern Poverty Law Center (SPLC). Feb 20, 2019. https://www.splcenter.org/fighting-hate/intelligence-report/2019/year-hate-rage-against-change.

Bendery, Jennifer. "157 Republicans Just Opposed Renewing the Violence Against Women Act." *Huffington Post*. Updated Apr 5, 2019. https://www.huffpost.com/entry/republicans-oppose-violence-against-women-act.

Brudholm, Thomas, and Birgitte Schepelern Johnansen. "Hate, Politics, Law—Critical Perspectives on Combating Hate." *International Network for Hate Studies (INHS)*. May 12, 2019. https://internationalhatestudies.com/hate-politics-law-critical-perspectives-on-combating-hate/.

Crime Museum. "Ku Klux Klan." https://www.crimemuseum.org/crime-library/hate-crime/ku-klux-klan/.

Frazin, Rachel. "FBI Chief Says Racist Extremists Fueling One Another, Making Connections Overseas." *The Hill*. Oct 30, 2019. https://thehill.com/policy/national-security/468195-wray-domestic-racially-motivated-violent-extremists-are-connecting.

Hilleary, Cecily. "Rise in Hate Crimes Alarms Native American Communities." *VOA News*. Jun 5, 2017. https://www.voanews.com/usa/rise-hate-crimes-alarms-native-american-communities.

Levin, Brian, and Kevin Grisham. "Special Status Report Hate Crime in the United States 20 State Compilation of Official Data." Center for the Study of Hate and Extremism, California State University, San Bernardino, CSUSB. 2016. https://csbs.csusb.edu/hate-and-extremism-center/data-reports/original-reports-hate-and-terrorism-center-staff.

Matthew Shepard Foundation. "Erase Hate in Business." https://www.matthewshepard.org/business-allies/.

Povich, Elaine S. "The Holocaust: States Require Education About It as anti-Semitism, Hate Crimes Surge." *USA Today*. Jul 15, 2019. https://psmag.com/news/a-florida-principals-reassignment-raises-questions-about-the-quality-of-holocaust-education.

Roser, Max, and Mohamed Nagdy. "Genocides in the 20th Century." *Our World in Data*. https://ourworldindata.org/genocides.

"Rwanda Genocide: 100 Days of Slaughter." *BBC News*. Apr 4, 2019. https://www.bbc.com/news/world-africa-26875506.

U.S. Census Bureau. "New Census Bureau Report Analyzes U.S. Population Projections." Mar 3, 2015. https://www.census.gov/newsroom/press-releases/2015/cb15-tps16.html.

Notes

1. Roser and Nagdy, "Genocides in the 20th Century." *Our World in Data*.
2. "Rwanda Genocide," *BBC News*.
3. Povich, "The Holocaust: States Require Education About It as anti-Semitism, Hate Crimes Surge."
4. Crime Museum, "Ku Klux Klan."
5. Hilleary, "Rise in Hate Crimes Alarms Native American Communities."
6. U.S. Census Bureau, "New Census Bureau Report Analyzes U.S. Population Projections."
7. Beirich, "The Year in Hate: Rage Against Change."
8. Frazin, "FBI Chief Says Racist Extremists Fueling One Another, Making Connections Overseas."
9. Levin and Grisham, "Special Status Report Hate Crime in the United States 20 State Compilation of Official Data."
10. Brudholm and Schepelern Johansen, "Hate, Politics, Law—Critical Perspectives on Combating Hate."

11. Bendery, "157 Republicans Just Opposed Renewing the Violence Against Women Act."
12. Matthew Shepard Foundation, "Erase Hate in Business.

1
Hate as Part of Society

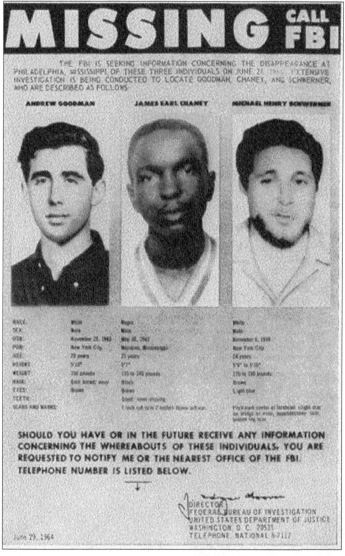

By Federal Bureau of Investigation, via Wikimedia.

The 1964 murders of civil rights workers Andrew Goodman, James Chaney, and Michael Schwerner resulted in the largest federal investigation—Mississippi Burning—ever conducted in the state and led to sustained FBI involvement in civil rights cases. Above is the FBI missing persons poster for these three, whose burned bodies were later found.

Defining Hate

In the present "connected society" social media and news reports are quick to update the public on breaking events as they unfold, the good and the bad. This on-the-spot news reporting begs the question of whether crimes in general, and hate crimes in particular, have always been such a common occurrence in our society. Is it more to do with the speed, quality, and abundance of people reporting events? School bullying, which may be an early warning sign of criminal behavior, is not a new phenomenon. Acts of violence against those that are different, once thought occasional incidents, have suddenly become commonplace, making them the new normal in our society.

In a June 7, 1997, radio address, Bill Clinton announced, "Such hate crimes, committed solely because the victims have a different skin color or a different faith or are gays or lesbians, leave deep scars not only on the victims but on our larger community. They are acts of violence against America itself."[1] Crimes incited by hate were not new in the 1990s; the Federal Bureau of Investigation (FBI) has been looking into what we now refer to as hate crimes dating back to World War I. As the agency responsible for protecting civil rights and freedom of speech, the FBI increased their role in investigating hate crimes with the passage of the Civil Rights Act of 1964. Today, investigating hate crimes is considered a high priority because of their devastating impact, not just on victims, but on communities and victim's families.[2]

FBI Definition of and Role in Hate Crime

The FBI defines a hate crime as "a criminal offense against a person or property motivated in whole or in part by an offender's bias against a race, religion, disability, sexual orientation, ethnicity, gender, or gender identity." Crimes that involve murder, arson, or vandalism are not considered hate crimes unless they are enacted because of bias. The FBI works with local authorities, sharing forensic expertise and other resources, in the investigation of any federal civil rights violations. The FBI gives the results to the U.S. Department of Justice, which decides whether the crime warrants federal prosecution. Training of FBI agents, local law enforcement, and community groups and organizations is offered through seminars and workshops run by the FBI. Local field offices provide public outreach to communities, state and local law enforcement agencies, and religious and community groups in order to address local issues.[3]

Hate Crime in History

The "Freedom Summer" campaign started in June 1964 as a means to register southern black voters. Michael Schwerner, 24, had caught the attention of the KKK because of his role in voter registration and in organizing boycotts of biased businesses. On June 16, the KKK went into a Mississippi church searching for Schwerner; not finding him, they beat the parishioners and burned the church. On June 21 Schwerner, accompanied by volunteers James Chaney and Andrew Goodman, were on their way to investigate the burned building when they were arrested for speeding. They were released, but reported missing on June 22. FBI agents, called in to assist in the search, found the burned car on June 23, and on August 4, the buried bodies of the three men. The case was known as MIBURN. On October 20, 1967, seven of the 18 defendants in the case were found guilty, not of murder, but of conspiring to violate the constitutional rights of the victims. Outrage over the murder resulted in the Civil Rights Act of 1964. Baptist preacher and KKK member Edgar Ray Killen was allowed to go free in 1967, but convicted of manslaughter on June 21, 2005.[4]

The term "hate crimes" was first used after the murder of Michael Griffith by a white mob in Queens, New York, in 1986. While one black man stayed with a disabled vehicle in a predominantly white neighborhood, three other black passengers went for help. They were harassed by whites and Griffith was killed by a car trying to escape. The twelve white youths, who beat the black men with baseball bats and hunks of wood, were charged and convicted of crimes that included murder, manslaughter, riot, criminal facilitation, and assault. That same evening two Hispanic youths were beaten by a gang of white men in nearby South Ozone Park, and another black man was killed by white men. Mayor Koch posted a $10,000 reward and compared the events to "lynching parties that existed in the Deep South" according to the *Daily News*.[5]

On December 19, 2018, the Senate approved the Justice for Victims of Lynching Act introduced by Senator Kamala Harris, Senator Cory Booker, and Senator Tim Scott. According to a 2018 *Smithsonian* article, 4,075 lynchings of African Americans occurred between 1877 and 1950, and 99 percent of the perpetrators went unpunished. Lynching incidents, while uncommon, do continue to happen. In Missouri and Texas in 2016, white students hung nooses around the necks of black classmates, and in 2018 two nooses were found on Smithsonian grounds, one at an exhibit on segregation at the National Museum of African American History and Culture in Washington D.C. The first bill to make lynching a federal crime was introduced in 1918 by Leonidas Dyer, a Missouri Republican. After more than 200 attempts at passage, it was approved in 2018.[6]

The October 6, 1998, murder of a 21-year-old University of Wyoming student and LGBTQ activist Matthew Shepard prompted hate crime reform in the United States. Aaron McKinney and Russell Henderson posed as gay and convinced Shepard to leave a bar with them. He was brutally assaulted and tied to a fence for over 18 hours before being found. His assault received national media coverage and prompted a hospital vigil and visit from Bill Clinton. Shepard died after six days in a coma. McKinney and Henderson were sentenced to life in prison, but not for hate crimes, which were not part of Wyoming law at the time. Shepard's parents created the Matthew Shepard Foundation, advocating hate crime reform and support of LGBTQ individuals.[7]

On June 7, 1998, James Byrd Jr. a 49-year old black man, was beaten, chained to the back of a truck, and dragged to his death by three white men, who left his body in the middle of the road. The Texas crime received international attention, but Texas law did not include hate crime legislation. At the time, Shawn Berry was sentenced to life in prison; Lawrence Russell Brewer was executed; John William King was sentenced to death, and executed in 2019.[8]

At the time of these crimes, federal laws did not include crimes against sexual orientation, and racial violence was only a crime when it happened during federally protected activities, such as during school or voting.

The Matthew Shepard and James Byrd, Jr. Hate Crimes Prevention Act of 2009 allows federal authorities to prosecute crimes based on race, gender, religion, or sexual preference. This law also made funding and assistance available for investigating and prosecuting hate crimes, and criminalized attempts to cause bodily harm because of actual or perceived race, color, religion, national origin, gender, sexual orientation, gender identity, or disability.[9]

The Matthew Shepard and James Byrd, Jr. Hate Crimes Prevention Act (HPCA)

The introduction of hate crime legislation started in 1997 and finally passed the House and Senate and was signed into law in 2009 by president Barack Obama. Crimes are considered hate crimes when the victim is selected because of who they are. The effects of the crime extend beyond the family, affecting the entire community or class of people. The HPCA statutes protect all victims of bias crime where perpetrators intentionally single out victims for violent acts as a way of sending a message to the community and society. The Human Rights Campaign states, "Violent, bias-motivated crimes divide us and devalue lives, not the laws that address the problem." They also state that since the reporting of hate crimes is voluntary, there are many jurisdictions that do not participate.[10]

Statistics and Accuracy of Reporting

The FBI's 2018 annual Hate Crime Statistics Report showed 16,039 agencies that submitted hate crime data with 7,120 hate crime incidents involving 8,496 offences. There were 7,036 single-bias incidents against 8,646 victims and 84 multiple-bias incidents with 173 victims.

Reported motivations for single-bias incidents in 2018:

- 59.6 percent targeted because of race, ethnicity, or ancestry

- 18.7 percent targeted because of religion

- 16.7 percent sexual orientation

- 2.2 percent gender identity
- 2.1 percent disability
- 0.7 percent gender

Race of the 6,266 known offenders:

- 53.6 percent were white
- 24 percent were Black or African American
- 12.9 percent unknown race
- 1.3 percent were Asian
- 1 percent were American Indian or Alaska Native
- 0.3 percent Native Hawaiian or Other Pacific Islander
- 6.9 percent were multirace

During this period there were 2,641 reported hate crimes committed against property that included vandalism, damage or destruction of property, theft of a motor vehicle, and arson.

Congress passed the Hate Crime Statistics Act on April 23, 1990, requiring the attorney general to collect data through the Uniform Crime Reporting (UCR) Program. This data is used to better understand hate crimes and raise public awareness. Twenty-eight states had hate crime laws in 1991, 41 in 2000, and 45 in 2019. The five states still with no hate crime laws or reporting requirements are: Georgia, South Carolina, Indiana, Arkansas, and Wyoming. Gender, LGBTQ, homelessness, and disabled populations are not included in hate crime legislation in some states. Louisiana has added crimes against police to their hate crime statutes.[11]

Adding to the veracity of this data are the following facts: UCR data is submitted voluntarily, and not all agencies take part; determining if a crime's motive was hate-based can be subjective; 39 states have hate crime laws and require data collection and 18 states have hate crime laws but do not require data collection. The five U.S. territories that do not have hate crime laws or require data collection are: American Samoa, Guam, Northern Mariana Islands, and U.S. Virgin Islands.[12]

Statistics and Research Data and Assistance Provided by Others

The lack in uniform official reporting requirements of hate crimes leaves opportunities for significant data gaps when compared to media reporting and polls by private organizations. No one method provides complete or accurate numbers, but a combined view offers a reasonable snapshot of the complexity and extensive reach of the hate crime issue. Some of the private organizations filling data gaps are the Center for the Study of Hate and Extremism, California State University, San Bernardino; Everytown for Gun Safety; the International Network for Hate Studies; the Human Rights Campaign; PEW Research Center; and the Southern Poverty Law Center (SPLC).

Heidi Beirich from SPLC reported that the total number of hate groups rose to 1,020 in 2018, from 954 in 2017. The rise in white nationalist groups alone was close to 50 percent, and, according to a poll by the Public Religion Research Institute, the presidency of Donald Trump is "emboldening white supremacists and helping to grow their ranks." Beirich adds that U.S. Census Bureau projections, that white people will not be a majority by 2044, "helped propel hate to a new high last year." According to Alexa analytics, hate group websites have monthly audiences of 4.3 million (for the neo-Nazi *Daily Stormer*) and 2.2 million (for *Stormfront*).[13]

Jack Levin and Jack McDevitt in their "Hate Crimes" report for the *Encyclopedia of Peace, Violence, and Conflict* further define some common motivations behind hate crimes.

> Defensive hate crimes: offenses aimed at outsiders seen as posing a challenge to a perpetrator triggered by an event that results in defense of their community, school, or workplace.

> Mission hate crimes: offenses committed by a perpetrator on a moral mission as an act of war against a group of people.

> Retaliatory hate crimes: offenses designed to get even for threats, hate crimes, or acts of terrorism, real or perceived.

> Thrill hate crimes: offenses committed by youth harassing those unlike themselves for fun or excitement.

The report also clarifies some of the definitions, statutes, laws, and open-ended standards related to hate crimes. The definition used by the FBI and U.S. law enforcement is "criminal offenses motivated either entirely or in part by the fact or perception that a victim is different from the perpetrator." Other important, widely-accepted points include: (1) the vast majority of hate crime laws do not criminalize any new behavior . . . they increase the penalty for behaviors that are already against the law; (2) racial, religious, ethnic, or other identified differences between victim and offender play at least some role; (3) the definition is intentionally broad and does not identify specific protected groups, allowing for inclusion of groups not yet targeted or reported; (4) a hate crime is unprovoked and sends a message to a group of people that they are not wanted; and (5) a rise in hate crimes is seen when a group feels their position in society is threatened by another group or when there are changing economic or political circumstances.[14]

Works Used

Beirich, Heidi. "The Year in Hate: Rage Against Change." Southern Poverty Law Center (SPLC). Feb 20, 2019. https://www.splcenter.org/fighting-hate/intelligence-report/2019/year-hate-rage-against-change.

Crime Museum. "Matthew Shepard." https://www.crimemuseum.org/crime-library/hate-crime/matthew-shepard.

Federal Bureau of Investigation. "2018 Hate Crime Statistics Released." https://www.fbi.gov/news/stories/2018-hate-crime-statistics-released-111219.

Federal Bureau of Investigation. "A Byte Out of History: Mississippi Burning." https://archives.fbi.gov/archives/news/stories/2007/february/miburn_022607.

Federal Bureau of Investigation. "What We Investigate: Hate Crimes." https://www. fbi.gov/investigate/civil-rights/hate-crimes.

Gearty, Robert, and Don Gentile. "Michael Griffith Dies Fleeing a White Mob in Howard Beach in 1986." *The Daily News*. Dec 21, 1986. https://www.nydai-lynews.com/new-york/nyc-crime/michael-griffith-died-fleeing-white-mob-how-ard-beach-1986-article-1.2917533.

Goodwyn, Wade. "Texas Executes Man Convicted in 1998 Murder of James Byrd Jr." *NPR*. Apr 24, 2019. https://www.npr.org/2019/04/24/716647585/texas-to-execute-man-convicted-in-dragging-death-of-james-byrd-jr.

Human Rights Campaign. "Hate Crimes Timeline." https://www.hrc.org/resources/hate-crimes-timeline.

Human Rights Campaign. "Questions and Answers: "The Matthew Shepard and James Byrd, Jr. Hate Crimes Prevention Act. Hate Crimes." Feb 1, 2010. https://www.hrc.org/resources/questions-and-answers-the-matthew-shepard-and-james-byrd-jr.-hate-crimes-pr.

Katz, Brigit. "The U.S. Finally Made Lynching a Federal Crime." *SmartNews. Smithsonian*. Dec 21, 2018. https://www.smithsonianmag.com/smart-news/af-ter-200-failed-attempts-us-has-made-lynching-federal-crime-180971092/.

Levin, Jack, and Jack McDevitt. "Hate Crimes." In *Encyclopedia of Peace, Violence, and Conflict*. 2nd ed., Academic Press, 2008.   https://jacklevinonvio-lence.com/articles/HateCrimesencyc92206FINAL.pdf.

U.S. Department of Justice. "Hate Crime Laws: About Hate Crimes." https://www. justice.gov/crt/hate-crime-laws.

U.S. Department of Justice. "State Specific Information." https://www.justice.gov/hatecrimes/state-specific-information.

Notes

1. Human Rights Campaign, "Hate Crimes Timeline."
2. Federal Bureau of Investigation, "What We Investigate: Hate Crimes."
3. Ibid.
4. Federal Bureau of Investigation, "A Byte Out of History: Mississippi Burning."
5. Gearty and Gentile, "Michael Griffith Dies Fleeing a White Mob in Howard Beach in 1986."
6. Katz, "The U.S. Finally Made Lynching a Federal Crime."
7. Crime Museum, "Matthew Shepard."
8. Goodwyn, "Texas Executes Man Convicted in 1998 Murder of James Byrd Jr."
9. U.S. Department of Justice, "Hate Crime Laws: About Hate Crimes."
10. Human Rights Campaign, "Questions and Answers: The Matthew Shepard and James Byrd, Jr. Hate Crimes Prevention Act. Hate Crimes."
11. Federal Bureau of Investigation, "2018 Hate Crime Statistics."
12. U.S. Department of Justice, "State Specific Information."
13. Beirich, "The Year in Hate: Rage Against Change."
14. Levin and McDevitt, "Hate Crimes."

What We Investigate

U.S. Department of Justice, 2018

Hate crimes

Hate crimes are the highest priority of the FBI's Civil Rights program due to the devastating impact they have on families and communities. The Bureau investigates hundreds of these cases every year and works to detect and deter further incidents through law enforcement training, public outreach, and partnerships with community groups.

Traditionally, FBI investigations of hate crimes were limited to crimes in which the perpetrators acted based on a bias against the victim's race, color, religion, or national origin. In addition, investigations were restricted to those wherein the victim was engaged in a federally protected activity. With the passage of the Matthew Shepard and James Byrd, Jr., Hate Crimes Prevention Act of 2009, the Bureau became authorized to also investigate crimes committed against those based on biases of actual or perceived sexual orientation, gender identity, disability, or gender.

History

The FBI investigated what are now called hate crimes as far back as World War I. Our role increased following the passage of the Civil Rights Act of 1964. Before then, the federal government took the position that protection of civil rights was a local function, not a federal one. However, the murders of civil rights workers Michael Schwerner, Andrew Goodman, and James Chaney, near Philadelphia, Mississippi, in June 1964 provided the impetus for a visible and sustained federal effort to protect and foster civil rights for African Americans. MIBURN, as the case was called (it stood for Mississippi Burning), became the largest federal investigation ever conducted in Mississippi. On October 20, 1967, seven men were convicted of conspiring to violate the constitutional rights of the slain civil rights workers. All seven were sentenced to prison terms ranging from three to ten years.

Defining a Hate Crime

A hate crime is a traditional offense like murder, arson, or vandalism with an added element of bias. For the purposes of collecting statistics, the FBI has defined a hate crime as a "criminal offense against a person or property motivated in whole or in part by an offender's bias against a race, religion, disability, sexual orientation, ethnicity, gender, or gender identity." Hate itself is not a crime—and the FBI is mindful of protecting freedom of speech and other civil liberties.

> **Outreach is a critical component of the FBI's civil rights program.**

The FBI's Role

As part of its responsibility to uphold the civil rights of the American people, the FBI takes a number of steps to combat the problem of hate crimes.

Investigative Activities: The FBI is the lead investigative agency for criminal violations of federal civil rights statutes. The Bureau works closely with its local, state, tribal, and federal law enforcement partners around the country in many of these cases.

Law Enforcement Support: The FBI works closely with state/local/tribal authorities on investigations, even when federal charges are not brought. FBI resources, forensic expertise, and experience in identification and proof of hate-based motivations often provide an invaluable complement to local law enforcement. Many cases are also prosecuted under state statutes such as murder, arson, or more recent local ethnic intimidation laws. Once the state prosecution begins, the Department of Justice follows the proceedings to ensure that the federal interest is vindicated and the law is applied equally among the 95 U.S. Judicial Districts.

Prosecutive Decision: The FBI forwards results of completed investigations to local U.S. Attorneys Offices and the Civil Rights Division at the Department of Justice, which decide whether a federal prosecution is warranted. Prosecution of these crimes may move forward, for example, if local authorities are unwilling or unable to prosecute a crime of bias.

Public Outreach: Outreach is a critical component of the FBI's civil rights program. The FBI engages with various local and national organizations to identify violations of federal law designed to protect the civil rights of individuals in the United States. Many FBI's field offices participate in working groups with state and local law enforcement partners, as well as community groups within their area of responsibility. These working groups combine community and law enforcement resources to develop strategies to address local hate crime problems.

Training: The FBI conducts hundreds of operational seminars, workshops, and training sessions annually for local law enforcement, minority and religious organizations, and community groups to promote cooperation and reduce civil rights abuses. Each year, the FBI also provides hate crimes training for new agents, hundreds of current agents, and thousands of police officers worldwide.

Print Citations

CMS: "What We Investigate: Civil Rights, Hate Crimes, History, Defining a Hate Crime, FBI's Role." In *The Reference Shelf: Hate Crimes,* edited by Sophie Zyla, 9–11. Amenia, NY: Grey House Publishing, 2020.

MLA: "What We Investigate: Civil Rights, Hate Crimes, History, Defining a Hate Crime, FBI's Role." *The Reference Shelf: Hate Crimes,* edited by Sophie Zyla, Grey Housing Publishing, 2020, pp. 9–11.

APA: U.S. Department of Justice. (2020). What we investigate: Civil rights, hate crimes, history, defining a hate crime, FBI's role. In Sophie Zyla (Ed.), *The reference shelf: Hate crimes* (pp. 9–11). Amenia, NY: Grey Housing Publishing.

FBI Releases 2018 Hate Crime Statistics

U.S. Department of Justice, 2018

The FBI's Uniform Crime Reporting (UCR) Program serves as the national repository for crime data voluntarily collected and submitted by law enforcement. Its primary objective is to generate reliable information for use in law enforcement administration, operation, and management. The 2018 hate crimes data, submitted by 16,039 law enforcement agencies, provide information about

There were 7,120 hate crime incidents involving 8,496 offenses for 2018.

the offenses, victims, offenders, and locations of hate crimes. Of these agencies who submitted incident reports, there were 7,120 hate crime incidents involving 8,496 offenses.

Below are some highlights from the data.

BIAS MOTIVATION CATEGORIES FOR VICTIMS OF SINGLE-BIAS INCIDENTS IN 2018

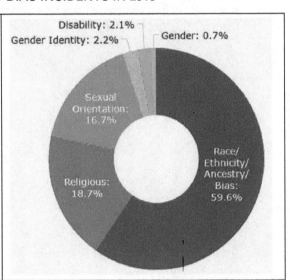

Victims of Hate Crime Incidents

- **7,036** single-bias incidents involved **8,646** victims.
- **84** multiple-bias hate crime incidents, which involved **173** victims

Disability: 2.1%
Gender Identity: 2.2%
Gender: 0.7%
Sexual Orientation: 16.7%
Religious: 18.7%
Race/Ethnicity/Ancestry/Bias: 59.6%

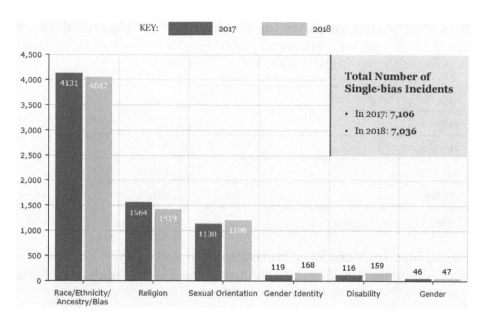

KEY: 2017   2018

Total Number of
Single-bias Incidents

- In 2017: **7,106**
- In 2018: **7,036**

Race/Ethnicity/Ancestry/Bias	Religion	Sexual Orientation	Gender Identity	Disability	Gender
4131 / 4047	1564 / 1419	1130 / 1196	119 / 168	116 / 159	46 / 47

Offenses by Crime Category	Known Offenders	Location Type
Among the 8,496 hate crime offenses reported: • Crimes against persons: 65.5% • Crimes against property: 31.1% • Crimes against society: 3.4%	Of the 6,266 known offenders: • 53.6% were White • 24.0% were Black or African American • 12.9% race unknown • Other races accounted for the remaining known offenders. • Of the 5,349 known offenders for whom ethnicity was reported: • 29.9% were Not Hispanic or Latino • 8.9% were Hispanic or Latino • 1.6% were in a group of multiple ethnicities • 59.5% ethnicity unknown • Of the 5,589 known offenders for whom ages were known: • 84.7% were 18 years of age or older	Law enforcement agencies may specify the location of an offense within a hate crime incident as 1 of 46 location designations. • Most hate crime incidents, 25.7%, occurred in or near residences/homes • 18.7% occurred on highways / roads / alleys / streets / sidewalks • 9.2% occurred at schools/colleges • 5.3% happened in parking/drop lots/ garages • 3.7% took place in churches / synagogues / temples / mosques • The location was reported as other/ unknown of 11.2% of hate crime incidents The remaining 26.1% of hate crime incidents took place at other or multiple locations.

Bias Motivation Categories for Victims of Single-bias Incidents in 2018: This is a pie chart showing the percentage of bias motivation categories for victims of single-bias incidents in 2018. They are as follows:

Race/Ethnicity/Ancestry/Bias	59.6%
Religious	18.7%
Sexual Orientation	16.7%
Gender Identity	2.2%
Disability	2.1%
Gender	0.7%

Single-bias Incident Bias Motivations by Category: Total number of single-bias incidents in 2017: 7,106, in 2018: 7,036. This is a bar chart comparing the 2017 and 2018 data for bias motivation categories for single bias incidents. They are as follows:

Bias Motivation Categories	2017	2018
Race/Ethnicity/Ancestry/Bias	4,131	4,047
Religious	1,564	1,419
Sexual Orientation	1,130	1,196
Gender Identity	119	168
Disability	116	159
Gender	46	47
Total	7,106	7,036

Print Citations

CMS: "FBI Releases 2018 Hate Crime Statistics." In *The Reference Shelf: Hate Crimes*, edited by Sophie Zyla, 12–14. Amenia, NY: Grey House Publishing, 2020.

MLA: "FBI Releases 2018 Hate Crime Statistics." *The Reference Shelf: Hate Crimes*, edited by Sophie Zyla, Grey Housing Publishing, 2020, pp. 12–14.

APA: U.S. Department of Justice. (2020). FBI releases 2018 hate crime statistics. In Sophie Zyla (Ed.), *The reference shelf: Hate crimes* (pp. 12–14). Amenia, NY: Grey Housing Publishing.

Learn More about Hate Crimes

U.S. Department of Justice, 2018

Experts estimate an average of 250,000 hate crimes were committed each year between 2004 and 2015 in the United States. The majority of these were not reported to law enforcement.

What is a hate crime?

In the simplest terms, a hate crime must include both "hate" and a "crime."

Hate

The term "hate" can be misleading. When used in a hate crime law, the word "hate" does not mean rage, anger, or general dislike. In this context "hate" means bias against people or groups with specific characteristics that are defined by the law.

At the federal level, hate crime laws include crimes committed on the basis of the victim's perceived or actual race, color, religion, national origin, sexual orientation, gender, gender identity, or disability.

Most state hate crime laws include crimes committed on the basis of race, color, and religion; many also include crimes committed on the basis of sexual orientation, gender, gender identity, and disability.

Crime

The "crime" in hate crime is often a violent crime, such as assault, murder, arson, vandalism, or threats to commit such crimes. It may also cover conspiring or asking another person to commit such crimes, even if the crime was never carried out.

Under the First Amendment of the U.S. Constitution, people cannot be prosecuted simply for their beliefs. People may be offended or upset about beliefs that are untrue or based upon false stereotypes, but it is not a crime to express offensive beliefs, or to join with others who share such views. However, the First Amendment does not protect against committing a crime, just because the conduct is rooted in philosophical beliefs.

Why Have Hate Crime Laws?

Hate crimes have a broader effect than most other kinds of crime. Hate crime victims include not only the crime's immediate target but also others like them. Hate crimes affect families, communities, and at times, the entire nation.

Why Report Hate Crimes?

The Hate Crimes Reporting Gap is the significant disparity between hate crimes that actually occur and those reported to law enforcement. It is critical to report hate crimes not only to show support and get help for victims, but also to send a clear message that the community will not tolerate these kinds of crimes. Reporting hate crimes allows communities and law enforcement to fully understand the scope of the problem in a community and put resources toward preventing and addressing attacks based on bias and hate.

> **Hate crimes affect families, communities, and at times, the entire nation.**

Terminology

Hate Crime: At the federal level, a crime motivated by bias against race, color, religion, national origin, sexual orientation, gender, gender identity, or disability.

Bias or Hate Incident: Acts of prejudice that are not crimes and do not involve violence, threats, or property damage.

Scenario—Color

Six black men assaulted and seriously injured a white man and his Asian male friend as they were walking through a residential neighborhood. Witnesses stated the victims were attacked because they were trespassing in a "black" neighborhood.

Scenario—Disability

A group home for persons with psychiatric disabilities who were in transition back into the community was the site of a reported arson. Investigation revealed that neighbors had expressed many concerns about the group home in town meetings and were angry that the house was located in their community. Shortly before the fire was reported, a witness heard a man state, "I'll get rid of those 'crazies,' I'll burn them out." Twelve persons, including patients and staff, suffered second and third degree burns.

Scenario—Ethnicity

Two Palestinian university students speaking in Arabic were attending a department reception when another student, a white male, deliberately bumped into one of them. When one Palestinian student said, "Hey, watch where you're going," the white student responded by saying, "I'll go wherever I want. This is my country, you Arab!" The aggressor proceeded to punch the Palestinian student in the face.

Scenario—Gender

A woman took a handgun into a fitness center, entered the men's locker room, and fired numerous shots. Two men were killed and one other man was injured in the shooting. The killer's blog revealed that she had planned the attack for some time and harbored a deep hatred for men for rejecting her all of her life.

Scenario—Gender Identity

A transgender woman was walking down the street near her home when three men walking toward her said, "Hey, what's your problem? Huh?" She kept walking, trying to ignore them. However, as they got close, one yelled "We don't want no queers in this neighborhood!" and a second one knocked her to the ground.

Scenario—Race

In a parking lot next to a bar, a 29-year-old Japanese American male was attacked by a 51-year-old white male wielding a tire iron. The victim suffered severe lacerations and a broken arm. Investigation revealed that the offender and victim had previously exchanged racial insults in the bar. The offender initiated the exchange by calling the victim by a well-known and recognized epithet used against the Japanese and complained that the Japanese were taking away jobs from Americans.

Scenario—Religion

Overnight, unknown persons broke into a synagogue and destroyed several priceless religious objects. The perpetrators drew a large swastika on the door and wrote "Death to Jews" on a wall. Although other valuable items were present, none were stolen.

Scenario—Sexual Orientation

Five gay, male friends, some of whom were wearing makeup and jewelry, were exiting a well-known gay bar when they were approached by a group of men who were unknown to them. The men began to ridicule the gay men's feminine appearance and shouted "Sissy!" "Girlie-men!" and other slurs at them then escalated to physically attacking the victims, rendering them unconscious.

Print Citations

CMS: "Learn More about Hate Crimes." In *The Reference Shelf: Hate Crimes,* edited by Sophie Zyla, 16–18. Amenia, NY: Grey House Publishing, 2020.

MLA: "Learn More about Hate Crimes." *The Reference Shelf: Hate Crimes,* edited by Sophie Zyla, Grey Housing Publishing, 2020, pp. 16–18.

APA: U.S. Department of Justice. (2020). Learn more about hate crimes. (2020). In Sophie Zyla (Ed.), *The reference shelf: Hate crimes* (pp. 16–18). Amenia, NY: Grey Housing Publishing.

The U.S. Finally Made Lynching a Federal Crime

By Brigit Katz
Smithsonian, December 21, 2018

In a legislative victory 100 years in the making, the Senate unanimously approved a bill on Wednesday that declares lynching a federal crime in the United States.

The Justice for Victims of Lynching Act was a bipartisan effort introduced earlier this year by three African-American Senators: California Democratic Senator Kamala Harris, New Jersey Democratic Senator Cory Booker and South Carolina Republican Senator Tim Scott. The bill, according to CNN's Eli Watkins, deems lynching—or mob killings that take place without legal authority—as "the ultimate expression of racism in the United States," and adds lynching to the list of federal hate crimes.

Though the practice existed during the era of slavery in the United States, lynchings proliferated in the wake of the Civil War, when African-Americans began to establish businesses, build towns and even run for public office. "Many whites … felt threatened by this rise in black prominence," according to PBS. In turn, the article reports, "most victims of lynching were political activists, labor organizers or black men and women who violated white expectations of black deference, and were deemed 'uppity' or 'insolent.'"

Lynchings were largely—though not exclusively—a Southern phenomenon. Between 1877 and 1950, there were 4,075 lynchings of African-Americans in 12 Southern States, according to the Equal Justice Initiative. The new bill states that 99 percent "of all perpetrators of lynching escaped from punishment by state or local officials."

Back in 1918, Missouri Republican Leonidas C. Dyer first introduced a bill that would make lynching a federal crime. According to the BBC, the bill passed the House but did not to make it through the Senate. Over the next century, more than 200 anti-lynching bills were introduced to Congress, all of which failed. Filibusters were used three times to block the legislation.

"Excerpts from the Congressional Record show some senators argued that such laws would interfere with states' rights," Avis Thomas-Lester of the *Washington Post* reported in 2005, the same year that the Senate passed a resolution apologizing for its failure to enact anti-lynching legislation. "Others, however, delivered impassioned speeches about how lynching helped control what they characterized as a threat to white women and also served to keep the races separate."

Today lynchings are rare, but their bloody legacy continues to feature in acts of violence against African-Americans. In 2016, as Jaweed Kaleem notes in the *Los Angeles Times*, four

> **Between 1877 and 1950, there were 4.075 lynchings of African Americans in 12 Southern States.**

white high school students in Missouri hung a noose around the neck of a black student and "yanked backward." That same year, a private school in Texas was sued by the family of a 12-year-old black girl, who said that three white classmates had wrapped a rope around her neck and dragged her to the ground. Last year, nooses were found hanging at Smithsonian institutions, including the National Museum of African American History and Culture.

"Lynchings were needless and horrendous acts of violence that were motivated by racism," Senator Harris said after the bill was passed. "And we must acknowledge that fact, lest we repeat it."

Senator Booker acknowledged that the bill "will not undo the damage, the terror, and the violence that has been already done, nor will it bring back the lives that have been brutally taken." But, he added, "it will acknowledge the wrongs in our history. It will honor the memories of those so brutally killed. And it will leave a legacy that future generations can look back on—that on this day, in this time, we did the right thing."

Print Citations

CMS: Katz, Brigit. "The U.S. Finally Made Lynching a Federal Crime." In *The Reference Shelf: Hate Crimes,* edited by Sophie Zyla, 19–20. Amenia, NY: Grey House Publishing, 2020.

MLA: Katz, Brigit. "The U.S. Finally Made Lynching a Federal Crime." *The Reference Shelf: Hate Crimes,* edited by Sophie Zyla, Grey Housing Publishing, 2020, pp. 19–20.

APA: Katz, B. (2020). The U.S. finally made lynching a federal crime. In Sophie Zyla (Ed.), *The reference shelf: Hate crimes* (pp. 19–20). Amenia, NY: Grey Housing Publishing.

Hate-Crime Violence Hits 16-Year High, F.B.I. Reports

By Adeel Hassan

The New York Times, November 12, 2019

Personal attacks motivated by bias or prejudice reached a 16-year high in 2018, the F.B.I. said Tuesday, with a significant upswing in violence against Latinos outpacing a drop in assaults targeting Muslims and Arab-Americans.

Over all, the number of hate crimes of all kinds reported in the United States remained fairly flat last year after a three-year increase, according to an annual F.B.I. report. But while crimes against property were down, physical assaults against people were up, accounting for 61 percent of the 7,120 incidents classified as hate crimes by law enforcement officials nationwide.

State and local police forces are not required to report hate crimes to the F.B.I., but the bureau has made a significant effort in recent years to increase awareness and response rates. Still, many cities and some entire states failed to collect or report the data last year, limiting the conclusions that can be drawn from the F.B.I. report.

In addition, experts say that more than half of all victims of hate crimes never file a complaint with the authorities in the first place.

Even so, the F.B.I. said there were 4,571 reported hate crimes against people in 2018, many of them in America's largest cities, involving victims from a wide range of ethnic and religious backgrounds.

"The trends show more violence, more interpersonal violence, and I think that's probably reliable," said James Nolan, a former F.B.I. crime analyst who helped oversee the National Hate Crime Data Collection Program from 1995-2000.

The F.B.I. defines a hate crime as a "criminal offense against a person or property, motivated in whole or in part by an offender's bias against a race, religion, disability, sexual orientation, ethnicity, gender, or gender identity." Victims of hate crimes can include institutions, religious organizations and government entities as well as individuals.

Here are the biggest takeaways from the report.

Vandalism Is Down, but Assaults Are Up

The 4,571 attacks against people tallied by the bureau for 2018 included aggravated assaults, which were up 4 percent; simple assaults, up 15 percent; and intimidation, up 13 percent.

These trends happened despite a national decline in violent crime in general, and coincided with a 19 percent drop in bias-driven property crimes.

The data points toward a change from young people committing vandalism and other property crimes toward more deliberate attacks on people, said Brian Levin, the director of the Center for the Study of Hate and Extremism at California State University, San Bernardino, who produced an independent analysis of the F.B.I.'s figures

"We're seeing a shift from the more casual offender with more shallow prejudices to a bit more of an older assailant who acts alone," Mr. Levin said. "There's a diversifying base of groups that are being targeted. We're getting back to more violence."

As Immigration Heats Up, Latinos Face More Violence

Immigration has replaced terrorism as a top concern in the United States, according to national surveys. That shift appears to be reflected in the hate-crime data, which shows fewer attacks against Muslims and Arab-Americans in recent years, but more against Latinos.

The F.B.I. said 485 hate crimes against Latinos were reported in 2018, up from 430 in 2017. It said 270 crimes were reported against Muslims and Arab-Americans, the fewest since 2014.

But the Council on American-Islamic Relations, a civil rights group with chapters across the country, said it had recorded 1,664 hate crimes against Muslims in 2018.

Robert McCaw, the group's director of governmental affairs, said that while awareness and reporting of hate crimes have improved, daily acts of bullying or discriminations in schools, workplaces and in public are not included in the F.B.I.'s analysis, which focused on violent crimes.

"We don't know the full scope of anti-Muslim hate crimes and other hate crimes," he said.

Hate crimes against Latinos were at their highest level since 2010, when the unemployment rate and border crossings from Mexico were both peaking. Some advocates placed the blame for the recent rise on President Trump.

"There's a direct correlation between the hate speech and fear-mongering coming from President Trump and the right wing of the Republican Party with the increase in attacks against Latinos," said Domingo Garcia, the national president of the League of United Latin American Citizens.

Mr. Garcia said that immigration had replaced terrorism as the new "bogeyman" for the American right and predicted that the rise in hate crimes would not stop until the harsh rhetoric against Latinos had ended.

Hate Crimes Have Increased in America's Largest Cities

Although nationwide F.B.I. data for all of 2019 won't be available until next November, the Center for the Study of Hate and Extremism examined hate-crime reports so far this year in New York, Los Angeles and Chicago and found that all three

cities—plus the nation's capital—appear to be headed for
decade highs.

As immigration heats up, Latinos face more violence.

Hate crimes against Asian-
Americans, African-Americans
and Muslims are down in New York, the center said, but reports of anti-Semitic
hate crimes are driving the overall total up.

Of the 364 hate crimes reported in New York through Nov. 3, the center said,
148 targeted Jewish people. There were 295 hate crimes reported in the city over
the comparable period in 2018.

"The surge of attacks on the Jewish community, in large cities like New York
and in smaller cities like Pittsburgh and Poway, really has no precedent," said Jona-
than Greenblatt, chief executive of the Anti-Defamation League, referring to deadly
shootings at a synagogue in Pittsburgh last year and one near San Diego in April.

"The severity of these incidents seems to be increasing in both their aggressiveness and physicality," he added.

In Los Angeles, 249 hate crimes were reported in the first nine months of 2019,
up from 217 in the same period last year. And Chicago had 77 reported hate crimes
through early November, compared with 78 for the whole of 2018.

Most Places Reported Zero Hate Crimes to the F.B.I.

The great majority—87 percent—of the 16,039 law enforcement agencies that sent
data to the F.B.I. for 2018 said no hate crimes were reported in their jurisdiction
during the year. Twenty-five cities with populations of more than 150,000 people
reported no hate crimes, including Plano and Laredo, Tex.; Newark; St. Petersburg,
Fla.; and Madison, Wis.

No hate crimes were reported by any law enforcement agency in Alabama or
Wyoming.

Mr. Nolan, the former F.B.I. analyst, said he and his colleagues had sought to
improve the accuracy of hate crime data, but with little success. "It was all lip service; it was never funded," he said.

Compiling crime statistics is not one of the bureau's major priorities, Mr. Nolan
said, though the former director, James Comey, tried to elevate the task, saying in
2014 about tracking hate crimes: "It is not something we can ignore or sweep under
the rug."

Mr. Nolan said the spottiness of the data doesn't invalidate attempts to determine which types of hate crimes are on the rise, though. "All crimes are underreported; it doesn't make them useless that they're underreported," he said. "You
have to be savvy enough to look at the trend lines and see the trends. It tells you
something about what's going on."

Print Citations

CMS: Hassan, Adeel. "Hate-Crime Violence Hits 16-Year High, F.B.I. Reports." In *The Reference Shelf: Hate Crimes,* edited by Sophie Zyla, 21–24. Amenia, NY: Grey House Publishing, 2020.

MLA: Hassan, Adeel. "Hate-Crime Violence Hits 16-Year High, F.B.I. Reports." *The Reference Shelf: Hate Crimes,* edited by Sophie Zyla, Grey Housing Publishing, 2020, pp. 21–24.

APA: Hassan, A. (2020). Hate-crime violence hits 16-year high, F.B.I. reports. In Sophie Zyla (Ed.), *The reference shelf: Hate crimes* (pp. 21–24). Amenia, NY: Grey Housing Publishing.

Mail Bombs, Hate Crimes, and the Meaning of Terrorism

By Bruce Hoffman

Council on Foreign Relations, October 30, 2018

The series of attempted mail bombings and the deadly shooting at a Pittsburgh synagogue this month have once again raised the specter of hate and terrorism in the United States. As public debate intensifies, it is important to understand what the terms "terrorism" and "hate crime" actually mean and why these definitions matter. For instance, both types of crime can carry harsher penalties than other similar violent acts. Both are also symptoms of deep social and political stress, as history has shown. Only once these crimes are appropriately labeled can Americans grapple with their origins.

Terrorism is ineluctably political. It represents an intent to intimidate, coerce, punish, or otherwise influence others by violence or the threat of violence because of their political views, affiliation, or position. Describing terrorism is often complicated by gaps between the strict legal definition and more general societal interpretations.

Many Americans, for instance, were understandably confused when the term was dismissed by authorities in the context of a shooting at a Las Vegas concert last year that killed fifty-eight people, but then invoked in the case of a vehicular assault in New York City that killed eight people last Halloween. The reason is that it is impossible to determine whether Stephen Paddock, the deceased Las Vegas gunman, was motivated by politics. However, the professed allegiance of Sayfullo Saipov, the Uzbek man charged with the Manhattan attack, to the self-proclaimed Islamic State endowed that act with an undeniable political context.

The law enforcement agencies responsible for investigating and prosecuting a violent crime must ensure that it conforms to the definition of terrorism under federal law. In other words, they must be completely confident there is sufficient proof that the act in question was intended "(i) to intimidate or coerce a civilian population; (ii) to influence the policy of a government by intimidation or coercion; or (iii) to affect the conduct of a government by mass destruction, assassination or kidnapping." Hence, until they conclude their investigation, the FBI and police, as well as the relevant prosecuting authority, are understandably constrained from applying the label to an act that may look like terrorism. The difference, therefore, is not in the way that the crime is investigated, but whether it is prosecuted under terrorism or some other violent-crime statute based on the evidence gathered. Terrorism charges can significantly increase the penalties perpetrators face, and the inevitable media coverage can raise public understanding and awareness of what may be a larger, more sustained threat to society.

The terrorism label is just as important to society outside the courtroom, although it can be used in this sphere far more liberally. The term reflects a popular mindset and distinguishes a violent act with political intent and societal messaging from other types of crime. Terrorism, as the title of an important scholarly work explained, is a form of violent communication.

Hate crime has its own definition in U.S. law: It is an offense that "willfully causes bodily injury to any person or, through the use of fire, a firearm, a dangerous weapon, or an explosive or incendiary device, attempts to cause bodily injury to any person," because of actual or perceived race, color, religion, national origin, gender, sexual orientation, gender identity, or disability. What distinguishes hate crimes from other violent offenses are the enhanced penalties. Federal recommendations generally call for hate crime sentences to be some 40 percent longer.

It is not hard to understand why in certain instances terrorism is perhaps the ultimate hate crime.

Terrorism and hate crimes are by no means synonymous, but they do overlap. Indeed, it is not hard to understand why in certain instances terrorism is perhaps the ultimate hate crime, in that it seeks to subjugate, repress, or simply target people because of their race, religion, ethnicity, or national origin.

However, in the U.S. code for terrorism, the perpetrator's intent is the salient definitional consideration. This may not always be immediately apparent and can only be proven after detailed investigation. On the other hand, the main thrust of the U.S. code for hate crimes is the more often readily apparent identity of the perpetrator's target—based on race, religion, ethnicity, nationality, or gender. This distinction does not preclude a hate crime from also being terrorism, but, under U.S. code, determining if a violent act is terrorism entails a higher evidentiary threshold and therefore a more painstaking and prolonged investigative process.

Neither terrorism nor hate crime exists in a vacuum. Both erupt along society's fault lines and reflect the era in which they malignantly surface. They are products of atmospheres of acute contentiousness, profound alienation, increasing polarization, and unbridled enmity.

Unsurprisingly, America's worst periods of violent unrest have occurred at times of great stress, societal fragmentation, and political divisiveness. The era surrounding the Civil War is one such example. Another is the period of industrialization, urbanization, and revolutionary communications changes in the late nineteenth and early twentieth centuries, which gave rise to violent labor disputes, anarchist bombings, and political assassinations that within two decades claimed the lives of two U.S. presidents. The height of the civil rights movement and Vietnam War protests, during the late 1960s and 1970s, brought more unrest. There were 2,500 bombings in the United States during one eighteen-month period between 1971 and 1972, according to the FBI.

Four decades and a global war on terrorism later, one hopes that Americans would better understand what terrorism is and is not—and how, depending on the circumstances, a hate crime can share many

> **Neither terrorism nor hate crime exists in a vacuum. Both erupt along society's fault lines and reflect the era in which they malignantly surface.**

of the same characteristics of terrorism. The public should judiciously use these terms, knowing that their misapplication risks eroding their power to signal crimes with potentially far-reaching sociopolitical implications. Only when a problem is accurately described can its root causes be addressed. With that in mind, there's no doubt that last week's mail bombs and synagogue attack conform to the core elements of terrorism. At the very least, both show that the divisiveness, polarization, and intense anger that has historically fueled terrorism and hate is never far beneath the surface.

Print Citations

CMS: Hoffman, Bruce. "Mail Bombs, Hate Crimes, and the Meaning of Terrorism." In *The Reference Shelf: Hate Crimes,* edited by Sophie Zyla, 25–27. Amenia, NY: Grey House Publishing, 2020.

MLA: Hoffman, Bruce. "Mail Bombs, Hate Crimes, and the Meaning of Terrorism." *The Reference Shelf: Hate Crimes,* edited by Sophie Zyla, Grey Housing Publishing, 2020, pp. 25–27.

APA: Hoffman, B. (2020). Mail bombs, hate crimes, and the meaning of terrorism. In Sophie Zyla (Ed.), *The reference shelf: Hate crimes* (pp. 25–27). Amenia, NY: Grey Housing Publishing.

2
Causes and Responses

The 2018 Tree of Life synagogue shooting in Pittsburgh, which killed 11 people, was the deadliest attack on the Jewish community in the United States. Memorials to the victims are pictured above.

Entering an Era of Rising Hate Crimes

Finding solutions to hate crimes means understanding not only what motivates them but also what discourages them. Diversity and sexual harassment training has been part of business and educational institutions for years. A number of states have also included anti-bullying laws into their statutes, and these programs are being included in business training. Diversity training is designed to address the varied backgrounds, perspectives, and beliefs that make us individuals. Race is a socially developed construct primarily based on physical characteristics, most commonly skin color. Diversity encompasses age, gender, gender identity, race, national origin, work experience, religion, income, political beliefs, and education.[1] The rise in hate crimes indicates that as a nation we have become increasingly less tolerant of those different than ourselves.

Why Violent Hate?

The Center for the Study of Hate and Extremism at California State University has been studying hate and extremism for two decades and independently evaluates trends and compares findings to other statistics. Their recent report, *Global Terrorism: Threats to the Homeland, Part 1,* states that the first nine months of 2019 had more than one mass shooting per day on average with at least four people shot, and that "2018 data showed the majority of the white supremacist homicides clustered roughly before election time." The report goes on, "for today's digital, often loner white nationalist terrorist, internet platforms are force multipliers that record and disseminate not only graphic violence, but narcissistic manifestos as well, in a scripted online folkloric chain of violence." The internet provides a platform for terror groups to recruit members for training or violent activities. The Center's Brian Levin cites a Reuters poll in which 43 percent of respondents believed that whites are under attack. He attributes the spread of white nationalism to "an increasingly fragmented and sometimes violent mainstream sociopolitical landscape." Levin says the major types of violent mass offenders are ideologically motivated, psychologically dangerous, or motivated by revenge or personal benefit.

He states that more people were murdered domestically in 2019 by a handful of white supremacists than all of those killed in all extremist/hate homicide events in 2018. Polls in 2018 indicated a shift in political parties and an increase in hate crimes, the steepest since 2015. November 2016 hit a 14-year record high, as did the time around Barack Obama's election. FBI classifications of domestic terrorism threats are: racially motivated violent extremism; anti-government/antiauthority extremist; animal rights/environmental extremism; and abortion extremism. Currently under FBI investigation are approximately 5,000 terrorism-related incidents, with

850 classified as domestic, 1,000 as ISIS-related, and 1,000 as homegrown violent extremists.[2]

Reaching Across Oceans

The New Zealand mosque shootings, resulting in the deaths of 50 Muslims, were not perpetrated on American soil or by a U.S. citizen, but the motivation and choice of weapons were based on a desired effect in the United States. Perpetrator Brenton Tarrant stated:

> I chose firearms for the affect it would have on social discourse, the extra media coverage they would provide and the affect it could have on the politics of the United States and thereby the political situation of the world." He claimed he was not after fame or the broadcast of his video, but wanted "to create conflict between the two ideologies within the United States on the ownership of firearms in order to further the social, cultural, political and racial divide . . . ensuring the death of the 'melting pot' pipe dream.[3]

Working on Training and Raising Awareness

The FBI is responsible for investigating incidents involving civil rights and cases of hate crime, in the United States and internationally. They work with local, state, tribal, and federal law enforcement to examine criminal violations of federal civil rights statutes, even when federal charges are not brought. The Department of Justice follows state proceedings. The FBI sends completed investigations to the U.S. Attorney's Office and the Civil Rights Division of Department of Justice. The FBI works with state and local law enforcement and community groups in addressing hate crimes, conducting seminars, workshops, and training sessions for local law enforcement, and use their Victim Services Division to inform, support, and assist victims in navigating the aftermath of crime and the criminal justice process with dignity and resilience.[4]

The International Association of Chiefs of Police (IACP) collaborates with community and civil rights organizations, and law enforcement in addressing hate crimes and building trust. Some of IACP's community outreach include: co-hosting community events where individuals can ask questions or raise concerns; creating public awareness campaigns committed to eliminating hate and intolerance; educating the public on hate crime laws and protections; engaging community youth and forming partnerships with universities; partnering with community-based organizations to help address the needs of law enforcement agents and crime victims; and welcoming law enforcement at informal community functions.[5]

Everytown for Gun Safety is an independent and nonpartisan organization that promotes passage of the Disarm Hate Act proposed by Congressman David Cicilline of Rhode Island, which passed the House Judiciary Committee in September 2019. Their research shows more than 10,300 hate crimes involving guns in an average year—28 each day. Everytown for Gun Safety strives for better background checks, red flag laws (temporary removal of firearms from a potentially dangerous individual), increasing school safety, and disarming domestic abusers. They hold the gun industry accountable by repealing gun industry immunity, and recommend the passage of extreme risk state laws to prevent access to guns by those who have exhibited warning signs of bias motivation.[6]

The Human Rights Campaign (HRC), the largest civil rights organization working on LGBTQ equality, address the reasons for the underreporting of hate crimes, including the fact that state and local reporting is voluntary. Some states and large cities report fewer crimes than expected for their populations or crime rates. LGBTQ hate crimes may go unreported due to victim fear or humiliation. For example, the Southern Poverty Law Center (SPLC) disagreed with the FBI number of 8,000 yearly cases, estimating the number closer to 50,000.

In response to the Orlando gay nightclub tragedy in 2016, in which Omar Mateen killed 49 people and injured another 53, HRC president Chad Griffin reminded the public that hate signals come from politicians, extremists groups, and preachers whose words and actions spur hate and bigotry, reinforced by the fact that these crimes happen at churches, mosques, nightclubs, and other public meeting places. Mara Keisling, founder and executive director of the National Center for Transgender Equality stated, "We can no longer have an effective or moral LGBT movement unless it is also an anti-racist movement, anti-poverty movement, a pro-immigrant movement, a pro-disability rights movement, a pro-worker movement, and a pro-women's movement. There are people who want to come for all of us. We have to be standing there together. " Judith Lichtman, National Partnership for Women and Families and Leadership Conference on Civil and Human Rights read the words written during the Holocaust by Martin Niemoller:

> First they came for the socialists, and I did not speak out—because I was not a socialist.
> Then they came for the trade unionists, and I did not speak out— because I was not a trade unionist.
> Then they came for the Jews, and I did not speak out—because I was not a Jew.
> Then they came for me—and there was no one left to speak for me.[7]

The Center for the Study of Hate and Extremism (CSHE) published findings on hate and extremism in July of 2019, with recommendations to political leaders, schools, police agencies, and state legislators for action: making public policy statements on hate crimes. For police officers: instituting department policies and investigating hate crime protocols; making hate crime statistics available on department websites; making materials available in multiple languages; notifying relevant community groups or agencies; employing social media to calm the public and for rumor control; having blueprints of sensitive locations (schools, houses of worship, government offices, etc.) available. For state legislators: expand victim coverage to include gender, gender identity, disability, citizenship/documented status, and homeless status; enact a statue prohibiting private paramilitary training and other activities; make hate crime reporting mandatory; and provide annual statewide totals and breakdowns by known offenders and victims. For political leaders: use

Bully Pulpit Interactive (an online communication platform) to highlight communal values and inclusivity; and condemn prejudice and hate crime.[8]

Plans of the Attorney General and a Presidential Hopeful

Attorney General William P. Barr in his Summit on Combating Anti-Semitism Keynote Speech stated:

> I am deeply concerned about the rise in hate crimes and political violence that we have seen over the past decade. And this trend has included a marked increase in reported instances of anti-Semitic hate crimes. We can all agree this trend is intolerable. We must have zero tolerance for violence that is motivated by hatred for our fellow citizens whether based on race, sex, or creed. Anti-Semitic violence is especially pernicious because it targets both Jewish ethnic identity and religious practice.[9]

The Tree of Life Synagogue in Pittsburgh and the Chabad of Poway in California incidents, which killed and injured worshipers, are two recent examples of anti-Semitic hate crimes. Jewish communities and people are being attacked, and synagogues are being vandalized. Gravestones were desecrated in a Jewish cemetery in Massachusetts. Barr reassured the Jewish community that the federal government will not tolerate these attacks, and discussed the problems of Jewish students targeted and harassed on college compasses.

> My concern today is that under the banner of identity politics, some political factions are seeking to obtain power by dividing Americans. They undermine the values that draw us together, such as shared commitment to our country's success. This is the breeding ground for hatred, and we must reject it…We are a pluralistic Nation composed of very distinct groups, each bound together by ethnicity, race, or religion—each group proud of its identity and committed to its faith and traditions. Yet despite these differences, we can be bound together into a broader community. Not one that seeks to grind away our distinctive identity. Not one that seeks to overbear our religious commitments, which must be paramount. But one that respects, indeed delights in, the freedom of each of us that give meaning to our lives—that help us understand our place and our purpose in this Creation.[10]

Senator Cory Booker feels that white supremacy and racist violence have always been a part of the American story, especially during times of transition and rapid social change:

> We have seen it from the Civil War to the Civil Rights Movement; from the Red Summer of 100 years ago to Charlottesville; From the lynching of people of Mexican descent in Porvenir, Texas 101 years ago to the massacre targeting Latinx people in El Paso, Texas this past Saturday.
>
> To say this, is to speak the truth plainly—because without the truth there can be no reconciliation.

As a candidate for president, Booker's plans for fighting hate crimes include improving federal and local policies; empowering and supporting communities and the victims of hate crimes; and addressing hate online. His outline is detailed and includes addressing underreporting and dealing with white supremacy crimes by improving federal and local response and promoting better communication with impacted communities. He believes that making reporting easier and safer will help prevent the isolation experienced by victims and communities. He wants to ensure the safety of immigrant access to law enforcement and health care without fear of arrest, detainment, or deportation. In addressing social media's use to spread hate, fear, and violence. Booker also plans to improve DoJ resources and efforts relating to white supremacist violence, online threats, and recruitment.[11]

Works Used

Booker, Cory. "Cory's Plan to Confront Hate Crimes and White Supremacist Violence." Cory 2020. https://corybooker.com/issues/national-security/combat-hate/.

Everytown for Gun Safety. "Disarm Hate: The Deadly Intersection of Guns and Hate Crimes." https://everytownresearch.org/wp-content/uploads/2019/05/Disarm-Hate-HATE-CRIMES-FACT-SHEET-051619A.pdf.

Federal Bureau of Investigation. "What We Investigate: Hate Crimes." https://www.fbi.gov/investigate/civil-rights/hate-crimes.

"The History of Diversity Training & Its Pioneers." *Diversity Officer Magazine.* https://diversityofficermagazine.com/diversity-inclusion/the-history-of-diversity-training-its-pioneers/.

Human Rights Campaign. "Civil Rights Leaders Respond to the Orland Nightclub Tragedy." Jun 12, 2016. Video. https://www.hrc.org/videos/civil-rights-leaders-respond-to-the-orlando-nightclub-tragedy.

International Association of Chiefs of Police. "Action Agenda for Community Organizations and Law Enforcement to Enhance the Response to Hate Crimes." Apr 1, 2019. https://www.theiacp.org/resources/document/action-agenda-for-community-organizations-and-law-enforcement-to-enhance-the.

Kirkpatrick, David D. "Massacre Suspect Traveled the World but Lived on the Internet." *New York Times.* Mar 15, 2019. https://www.nytimes.com/2019/03/15/world/asia/new-zealand-shooting-brenton-tarrant.html.

Levin, Brian. "Global Terrorism: Threats to the Homeland, Part 1." Center for the Study of Hate and Extremism, Department of Criminal Justice, California State University, San Bernardino. Sep 10, 2019. https://csbs.csusb.edu/sites/csusb_csbs.

Levin, Brian, and Lisa Nakashima. "Report to the Nation 2019: Factbook on Hate & Extremism in the U.S. & Internationally." Center for the Study of Hate and Extremism, California State University, San Bernardino. Jul 2019. https://www.hsdl.org/c/just-released-report-to-the-nation-on-hate-and-extremism/.

U.S. Department of Justice. "Attorney General William P. Barr Delivers Keynote Speech at the U.S. Department of Justice's Summit on Combatting Anti-Semitism." Jul 15, 2019. https://www.justice.gov/opa/speech/attorney-general-william-p-barr-delivers-keynote-speech-us-department-justices-summit.

Notes

1. "The History of Diversity Training & Its Pioneers," *Diversity Officer Magazine*.
2. Levin, "Global Terrorism: Threats to the Homeland, Part 1."
3. Kirkpatrick, "Massacre Suspect Traveled the World but Lived on the Internet."
4. Federal Bureau of Investigation, "What We Investigate: Hate Crimes."
5. International Association of Chiefs of Police, "Action Agenda for Community Organizations and Law Enforcement to Enhance the Response to Hate Crimes."
6. Everytown for Gun Safety, "How to End Gun Violence, Disarm Hate. Statistics for Every State."
7. Human Rights Campaign, "Civil Rights Leaders Respond to the Orland Nightclub Tragedy."
8. Levin and Nakashima, "Report to the Nation: 2019 Factbook on Hate & Extremism in the U.S. & Internationally."
9. U.S. Department of Justice, "Attorney General William P. Barr Delivers Keynote Speech at the U.S. Department of Justice's Summit on Combatting Anti-Semitism."
10. Ibid.
11. Booker, "Cory's Plan to Confront Hate Crimes and White Supremacist Violence."

Trump and Racism: What Do the Data Say?

By Vanessa Williamson and Isabella Gelfand
Brookings, August 14, 2019

The Brookings Cafeteria podcast last week discussed the role President Trump's racist rhetoric has played in encouraging violence in America. Predictably, some podcast listeners responded skeptically on Twitter, doubting the association between Trump and hateful behavior. It would be naïve to think that data will change many individuals' minds on this topic, but nonetheless, there is substantial evidence that Trump has encouraged racism and benefitted politically from it.

First, Donald Trump's support in the 2016 campaign was clearly driven by racism, sexism, and xenophobia. While some observers have explained Trump's success as a result of economic anxiety, the data demonstrate that anti-immigrant sentiment, racism, and sexism are much more strongly related to support for Trump. Trump's much-discussed vote advantage with non-college-educated whites is misleading; when accounting for racism and sexism, the education gap among whites in the 2016 election returns to the typical levels of previous elections since 2000. Trump did not do especially well with non-college-educated whites, compared to other Republicans. He did especially well with white people who express sexist views about women and who deny racism exists.

Even more alarmingly, there is a clear correlation between Trump campaign events and incidents of prejudiced violence. FBI data show that since Trump's election there has been an anomalous spike in hate crimes concentrated in counties where Trump won by larger margins. It was the second-largest uptick in hate crimes in the 25 years for which data are available, second only to the spike after September 11, 2001. Though hate crimes are typically most frequent in the summer, in 2016 they peaked in the fourth quarter (October-December). This new, higher rate of hate crimes continued throughout 2017.

The association between Trump and hate crimes is not limited to the election itself. Another study, based on data collected by the Anti-Defamation League, shows that counties that hosted a Trump campaign rally in 2016 saw hate crime rates more than double compared to similar counties that did not host a rally.

The data analysis discussed above has centered on correlations; they are suggestive of a link between Trump and racist attitudes and behavior, but do not actually demonstrate that one leads to the other. However, there is also causal evidence to point to. In experiments, being exposed to Trump's rhetoric actually increases expressions of prejudice. In a 2017 survey, researchers randomly exposed some respondents to racist comments by the president, such as: "When Mexico sends its people, they're not sending their best. They're sending people that have lots of prob-

> **There is a clear correlation between Trump campaign events and incidents of prejudiced violence.**

lems… They're bringing drugs. They're bringing crime. They're rapists. And some, I assume, are good people."

Other respondents were exposed to a statement by Hillary Clinton condemning prejudiced Trump supporters. Later in the study, the respondents were asked their opinion of various groups, including Mexican people, black people, and young people. Those who had read Trump's words were more likely to write derogatory things not only about Mexican people, but also about other groups as well. By contrast, those who were exposed to Clinton's words were less likely to express offensive views towards Muslims. Words do matter, and data prove it.

Unfortunately, there is little reason to expect this research to have much impact on public attitudes; increasingly, partisanship skews what Americans think qualifies as racist. But there is no excuse for avoiding clear, accurate descriptions of American political dynamics. When the data show that President Trump's support stems from racist and sexist beliefs, and that his election emboldened Americans to engage in racist behavior, it is the responsibility of social scientists and other political observers to say so.

Print Citations

CMS: Williamson, Vanessa, and Isabella Gelfand. "Trump and Racism: What Do the Data Say?" In *The Reference Shelf: Hate Crimes,* edited by Sophie Zyla, 37–38. Amenia, NY: Grey House Publishing, 2020.

MLA: Williamson, Vanessa, and Isabella Gelfand. "Trump and Racism: What Do the Data Say?" *The Reference Shelf: Hate Crimes,* edited by Sophie Zyla, Grey Housing Publishing, 2020, pp. 37–38.

APA: Williamson, V., & Gelfand, I. (2020). Trump and racism: What do the data say? In Sophie Zyla (Ed.), *The reference shelf: Hate crimes* (pp. 37–38). Amenia, NY: Grey Housing Publishing.

American Islamophobia in the Age of Trump: The Global War on Terror, Continued?

By Tanner Mirrlees
International Network for Hate Studies, **February 7, 2017**

The Global War on Terror and American Islamophobia

Islamophobia has been a problem in the US for a long time, but it grew significantly in response to the terrorist attacks of September 11, 2001, and the US state's subsequent launch of a Global War on Terror across "the Muslim World."

The Global War on Terror has fostered a social milieu in which Islamophobia thrives. Negative stereotypes of Muslims as enemy threats that the US state and its European allies need to closely monitor and neutralize abound, and negative public attitudes toward Muslims are increasing in the US and elsewhere.

American Islamophobia is characterized by hateful ideas about and practices toward Muslims by non-Muslim Americans.

As a system of ideas, American Islamophobia represents Muslim people as an unchanging unity that is radically different from and incompatible with other religious groups in America; Muslims as culturally and intellectually inferior, backwards and barbaric as compared to non-Muslim Americans; and Muslims as a violent and growing threat to America that must be contained, combatted or eliminated in the name of security.

These ideas link with and feed into prejudicial practices such as the discrimination of and hate crimes against Muslims in the US and buttress the US state's ongoing and expanding wars in Muslim countries abroad.

Shaped by the longer history and broader geopolitics of the US-led Global War on Terror, American Islamophobia is not caused by any one politician or party. Nonetheless, the positions taken by politicians and parties can and do play a significant role in strengthening or weakening the grip of this ideology on the public mind.

Trump's Islamophobic Election Campaign

US president Donald J. Trump has energized American Islamophobia and Stephen K. Bannon, the former chief of *Breitbart News* and Chief Executive of Trump's election campaign, had a big hand in this. Bannon, now Trump's chief strategist, is arguably a white supremacist nationalist. He believes that America is on the frontlines of a global "clash of civilizations" between Christianity and Islam. Influenced by Bannon, Trump's campaign communications–press releases, speeches, interviews and tweets—stoked mass fears of Muslims.

Trump routinely exploited instances in which a *few* Muslim Americans inspired by "Islamic extremist" groups committed terrorism against Americans to convey the idea that *all* Muslims are threats to American security.

A few days after the December 2, 2015 San Bernardino terrorist attack by two homegrown terrorists inspired by ISIS, Trump issued a press release called "Donald J. Trump Statement on Preventing Muslim Immigration." Following the Orlando night club shooting of June 13th, 2016, in which a New Yorker killed forty-nine people after swearing his allegiance to ISIS, Trump claimed that more terrorist attacks would happen. In a March 9th 2016 interview with Anderson Cooper on CNN, Trump declared that "Islam hates us."

By failing to make the important distinction between the handful of terrorists that committed violence in the name of Islam and millions of Muslims everywhere, Trump pushed the idea that Muslims are terrorists. Trump promised that if elected president, he would contain or eliminate this Muslim threat with surveillance, travel bans and war.

Islamophobia was integral to Trump's campaign communications, and Islamophobia helped Trump win the White House.

Trump's "Muslim Ban" Cheered by White Supremacists

In the first week of his presidency, Trump delivered on his campaign promise to keep millions of Muslims out of America. On January 27, 2017, Trump signed an executive order called "Protecting the Nation from Terrorist Attacks by Foreign Nationals." Bannon was the main proponent of this order, but he had the support of Trump aide Steven Miller, who shares the Islamophobic worldview of many of Trump's cabinet members.

This "Muslim Ban" stops people hailing from Iraq, Iran, Libya, Somalia, Sudan, Syria and Yemen from entering the US for ninety days. The order also makes it impossible for refugees fleeing the Syrian civil war—a war which the US has played a significant role in shaping—from entering the US for one hundred and twenty days.

Trump's order does not make much strategic sense: since 2001, every deadly jihadist attack inside the US has been carried out by a US citizen or a legal resident, not by a "foreign national" from any of the countries banned. No Muslims from the countries Trump closed the border to have attacked the US. By targeting and banning these countries, Trump makes every Muslim residing in these countries seem like a terrorist threat.

Trump's order is perhaps less about national security and more about pandering to the Islamophobia of his most reactionary constituents. Keeping the most vulnerable Muslims out keeps the white Right seeing in Trump a führer.

The white supremacist Right pushed hard for Trump's election and rejoiced when their man won the White House. After Trump issued the Muslim ban, David Duke, the former Klu Klux Klan grand wizard, tweeted approvingly: "'The Emperor' reigns supreme—back off cucks! President Trump is giving us a chance to undo the decades of demoralization we have suffered under this subversive Marxist agenda. Greatest. Year. Ever. #MuslimBan".

Andrew Anglin, founder of the Daily Stormer and neo-Nazi wunderkind, was impressed as well. In a blog post called "SOMALIANS TO BE BANNED FROM ENTERING AMERICA!!!!!!!111S!", Anglin wrote: "I feel ecstatic joy. I feel admiration for our GLORIOUS LEADER [. . .] God bless you, Donald Trump. May you never die." In another piece titled "Glorious Leader Wreaks Havoc on Filthy Moslem Would-Be Invaders," "Azzmador" calls for Trump to mass murder Muslims in same way that Hitler exterminated six million Jews: "By the end of the month, we should have the rails laid, the camps built, and the gas flowing like Febreze."

The alt-right poster boy Richard Spencer, whose National Policy Institute plots to force all Muslims out of the US, tweeted in support of Trump's order, not because he believed the "security" argument, but because he saw this as a step toward making America white and Christian: "We need an effort across North America and Europe to help Muslims reconnect w/ their roots and families. Yes, Muhammad, you can go home again."

Trump's Muslim ban has galvanized white supremacists and created an enabling context for hate crimes against Muslims.

Countering American Islamophobia (and the Global War on Terror)
The backlash against Trump's "Muslim Ban" has been intense, with protests breaking out across the US, the UK, Canada and elsewhere. Across the US, citizens mobilized at airports and waved placards in defiance of Trump that read: "First they came for the Muslims and We Said: Not Today Motherfucker!" Across the United Kingdom, thousands of citizens rallied against Prime Minister Theresa May's decision to invite Trump to the country and argued that Trump should be banned from the UK until he drops the Muslim ban in America. Canadians united outside of US consulates and chanted: "Freedom for refugees, justice for immigrants!"

The surge of protests against and legal challenges to Trump's executive order highlight how Trump's power to use the presidency to "make America great again" by making it more Islamophobic than ever before is contested.

The Muslim ban was recently halted after a Seattle judge ruled that the order "unlawfully discriminated against Muslims and caused unreasonable harm." But Trump lashed out against the courts on Twitter in response and proceeded to spin the same bogus argument for the ban, again framing every Muslim from every one of the blocked countries as threats: "Radical Islamic terrorists are determined to strike our homeland as they did on 9/11," he said. We cannot let "people who want to destroy us and destroy our country" into the US.

The people that Trump prohibits from entering America hail from the very countries the US-led Global War on Terror has made insecure over the past fifteen years. The US state has been at war—directly or via drones and proxy armies—in all seven of the Muslim countries banned by Trump. All, save Iran, are now "fragile states."

> Anyone committed to countering American Islamophobia and all of the hate and violence unleashed upon Muslim Americans should stand up to the Trump administration and its many white supremacist acolytes.

When at war, states teach their citizens to fear and hate their enemies. By frequently conflating Islam with terrorism and Muslim with terrorist, the US security state and the cultural industries surrounding it have taught many Americans to see Muslims not as human beings, but as enemy threats to the American Way of Life.

In the years ahead, Trump will likely continue the Global War on Terror policies and practices of the previous two US presidencies and adversely impact the lives of millions of Muslims living inside and outside of the US.

The Global War Terror and American Islamophobia march in lockstep, and the Trump team is beating a "war on Islam" drum loudly, spewing anti-Muslim rhetoric, engaging in anti-Muslim practices, and satisfying anti-Muslim bigots.

In this context, anyone committed to countering American Islamophobia and all of the hate and violence unleashed upon Muslim Americans should stand up to the Trump administration and its many white supremacist acolytes.

At the same time, those wishing to counter American Islamophobia should learn from and work with international pacifists to bring the wars in Muslim countries, and all of the hatred and violence they entail, to an end.

As Nikal Saval writes: "There will be no end to the war against Muslims in this country unless there is an end to the war on terror."

Print Citations

CMS: Mirrlees, Tanner. "American Islamophobia in the Age of Trump: The Global War on Terror, Continued?" In *The Reference Shelf: Hate Crimes,* edited by Sophie Zyla, 39–42. Amenia, NY: Grey House Publishing, 2020.

MLA: Mirrlees, Tanner. "American Islamophobia in the Age of Trump: The Global War on Terror, Continued?" *The Reference Shelf: Hate Crimes,* edited by Sophie Zyla, Grey Housing Publishing, 2020, pp. 39–42.

APA: Mirrlees, T. (2020). American Islamophobia in the age of Trump: The global war on terror, continued? In Sophie Zyla (Ed.), *The reference shelf: Hate crimes* (pp. 39–42. Amenia, NY: Grey Housing Publishing.

Steve Scalise: Don't Blame Trump for Mass Shootings

By Kelsey Tamborrino
Politico, August 11, 2019

House Minority Whip Steve Scalise on Sunday called it "a very slippery slope" to blame President Donald Trump's rhetoric for deadly mass shootings in recent weeks.

The Louisiana Republican said on CBS' *Face the Nation* that "there's no place" for attacks based on someone's ethnicity.

"But to try to assign blame to somebody else, I think, is a very slippery slope because the president's no more responsible for that shooting as your next guest, Bernie Sanders, is for my shooting," said Scalise, who was shot in June 2017 during a Republican congressional baseball practice in Alexandria, Va., by a former volunteer for Sanders' 2016 presidential campaign. Sanders condemned the attack as "despicable."

"And he's not, by the way, responsible. The shooter is responsible," Scalise added. Scalise was gravely wounded in the attack but has recovered to return to continue to serve in the House.

Sanders, an independent senator from Vermont seeking the 2020 Democratic presidential nomination, also appeared Sunday on CBS. He said Trump "does not want to see" someone get shot, but he said Trump's rhetoric "creates a climate where we are seeing a significant increase in hate crimes in this country—hate crimes against Muslims, against Mexicans, against Jews."

"He is creating the kind of divisiveness in this nation that is the last thing that we should be doing," Sanders said. "So, he creates the climate. But do I think that he wants to see somebody get shot? Absolutely not."

Several Democratic candidates for president, including former Texas Rep. Beto O'Rourke, have blamed Trump's anti-immigrant rhetoric for two recent shootings.

The suspect in the attack in El Paso, Texas—a 21-year-old white man—is believed to have posted a manifesto online shortly before the shooting, warning of a "Hispanic invasion of Texas."

"What we need to do," Scalise said, "is find out those people that have slipped through the cracks. ... Let's make sure these background check systems work properly and are rooting out the people that shouldn't be able to legally purchase a gun but currently are because the system hasn't worked."

Scalise, asked whether he has advised the president to reconsider some of his words that might be considered inflammatory, said Trump "was very clear just the other day that there's no place for this."

O'Rourke, however, appeared Sunday on CNN where he said the people of El Paso told him "They didn't want to see the president."

> **The president's no more responsible for [mass shootings than] . . . Bernie Sanders is for my shooting.**

They understand Trump is part of the problem, O'Rourke said, citing the president's warnings of infestations and his description of El Paso as one of the most dangerous cities in the United States.

"For him then to focus on comparing political rallies, or on himself or on how much people love him, just shows you how sick this guy is and how unfit for this office," O'Rourke said. "He should be consoling people, bringing people together, focusing on their pain and improving their lives, but instead he is focused on himself."

Print Citations

CMS: Tamborrino, Kelsey. "Steve Scalise: Don't Blame Trump for Mass Shootings." In *The Reference Shelf: Hate Crimes,* edited by Sophie Zyla, 43–44. Amenia, NY: Grey House Publishing, 2020.

MLA: Tamborrino, Kelsey. "Steve Scalise: Don't Blame Trump for Mass Shootings." *The Reference Shelf: Hate Crimes,* edited by Sophie Zyla, Grey Housing Publishing, 2020, pp. 43–44.

APA: Tamborrino, K. (2020). Steve Scalise: Don't blame Trump for mass shootings. In Sophie Zyla (Ed.), *The reference shelf: Hate crimes* (pp. 43–44). Amenia, NY: Grey Housing Publishing.

Did Counties Hosting a Trump Rally in 2016 See a 226% Spike in Hate Crimes?

By Louis Jacobson
PolitiFact, August 12, 2019

At a time of increasing tension over President Donald Trump's rhetoric on un-documented immigrants and people of color, several Democrats have charged that Trump's language is encouraging hate crimes. To make their case, Democrats cite a startling statistic.

"In 2016, counties hosting a Trump rally saw a 226% spike in hate crimes," reads a post on Facebook from the presidential campaign of Bernie Sanders.

A tweet from Rep. Ilhan Omar, D-Minn., makes the same claim.

Rep. Ilhan Omar

@Ilhan

Counties that hosted a 2016 Trump rally saw a 226% increase in hate crimes.

Assaults increase when cities host Trump rallies.

Your rhetoric is directly and indirectly inciting hate, Mr. President. https://twitter.com/nowthisnews/status/1159170592626618368 …

NowThis

@nowthisnews

'[My rhetoric] brings people together.'—Trump rejected a reporter's suggestion that his rhetoric might be fostering hate or domestic terrorism

18.5K people are talking about this

A reader saw the Sanders post on social media and sent it to us, asking whether it was accurate.

We found that the statistic comes from an academic paper. But the Sanders post makes the increase seem dramatic and causal. The findings are actually much more nuanced.

Where the Statistic Comes From

The post cites the *Washington Post* as its source, and we tracked that down to a post on one of the newspaper's blogs, the *Monkey Cage*.

On March 22, the blog published a post titled, "Counties that hosted a 2016 Trump rally saw a 226% increase in hate crimes."

> **Anyone using that data should be aware of the complexity of extremist actions and their connection to rhetoric.**

The post summarized a paper written by three academics: Ayal Feinberg, an assistant professor of political science at Texas A&M University-Commerce; Regina Branton, a professor of political science at the University of North Texas; and Valerie Martinez-Ebers, a professor of political science at the University of North Texas. (Sanders' campaign did not respond to an inquiry.)

The authors told *PolitiFact* that the paper is currently under peer review for publication in an academic publication. The authors presented it in 2019 at meetings of both the Southern Political Science Association and the Western Political Science Association.

Here's how the authors summarized their work in the *Post*:

Using the Anti-Defamation League's Hate, Extremism, Anti-Semitism, Terrorism map data (HEAT map), we examined whether there was a correlation between the counties that hosted one of Trump's 275 presidential campaign rallies in 2016 and increased incidents of hate crimes in subsequent months.

To test this, we aggregated hate-crime incident data and Trump rally data to the county level and then used statistical tools to estimate a rally's impact. We included controls for factors such as the county's crime rates, its number of active hate groups, its minority populations, its percentage with college educations, its location in the country and the month when the rallies occurred.

We found that counties that had hosted a 2016 Trump campaign rally saw a 226% increase in reported hate crimes over comparable counties that did not host such a rally.

How the Social Media Posts Characterized the Finding

In their posts, Sanders (and Omar) referenced the headline in the *Monkey Cage* blog post almost verbatim. But there's a discrepancy between the headline's phrasing and what the researchers' academic paper looked at.

The phrasing used by Sanders implies that hate crimes spiked in one jurisdiction, jumping from one level before the rally to a rate three times higher afterward. That's not the case. As the study summary says, the 226% difference compares Trump-rally counties to non-Trump rally counties with similar demographics.

So a more accurate phrasing might be: "Counties that hosted a 2016 Trump rally had 226% more hate crimes than counties that did not."

There are other nuances that aren't captured by the statistic Sanders posted, experts told *PolitiFact*.

Challenges Affecting All Research of This Type

In an interview, Feinberg, one of the coauthors of the study cited in the *Post* article, noted a few general challenges facing the field of hate-crime studies.

First, he said, there are limitations in "how extremist incidents, events motivated by hate, and hate crimes lack a cohesive definition" under the law. What constitutes a hate crime in one state may not in another. Also, some of the data is self-reported, making it hard to tell how many hate crimes in a given jurisdiction are unreported.

In addition, Feinberg said, "not all police departments investigate hate crimes or perceive incidents motivated by prejudice" with the same degree of aggressiveness.

Feinberg said that these caveats are always top of mind for hate-crimes researchers.

He added that a 2018 research project he collaborated on did not find that the inclusion of far-right parties in governing coalitions in Europe had an effect on reported anti-Semitic incidents. So when starting work on the Trump paper, he came in to the research with an open mind.

Before undertaking the study, he said, "I was not sure that Trump rhetoric would have any impact on reported extremist events, hate incidents, anti-Semitism, or hate crimes."

Other Methodological Unknowns

Meanwhile, Brian Levin, Kevin Grisham, and John Reitzel, three of the contributors to a California State University-San Bernardino study of hate crime trends in recent years, told *PolitiFact* that it's hard to know whether other factors could have played a role in boosting hate crimes in the counties with a Trump rally.

"It is hard to untangle all these relationships without some interviews and in-depth qualitative data," Grisham said. "I think the data is fascinating and may be the first step in a larger and more in-depth project. But, we cannot say with absolute certainty that hate follows the rallies."

For instance, Grisham said, it could be that the rallies may be a contributing cause rather than a dominant one. "Anyone using that data should be aware of the complexity of extremist actions and their connections to rhetoric. Like anything with human beings, nothing is black and white."

Another potential problem: A 226% difference sounds massive, but in many locales, that may mean only a small numerical difference, especially the types of low-population counties that tended to host Trump rallies. The difference between one hate crime and three is 200%, but with numbers like that, a small difference in the reporting of crimes or police investigations could cloud the question of whether Trump's rallies had an effect.

There is "statistical noise" when raw numbers are small, Reitzel said. Focusing on percentage changes, "even where the numbers are true, can still distort interpretation," he said.

Overall, the study is "certainly interesting and suggestive," Levin said. "But I would have preferred to see a comparison that's apples to apples."

Our Ruling

Sanders' post said, "In 2016, counties hosting a Trump rally saw a 226% spike in hate crimes."

This is from an academic study. However, it's worth noting some caveats—that the data can be subject to "statistical noise" and jurisdictional differences in hate crime definitions and police aggressiveness, and that cause and effect are hard to pinpoint.

Perhaps most important is that Sanders' wording implies that the 226% jump stems from comparing hate crimes before and after a Trump rally within the same county, when in fact it's a comparison from Trump rally counties to similar counties that did not host a Trump rally.

The statement is partially accurate but leaves out important details, so we rate it Half True.

Print Citations

CMS: Jacobson, Louis. "Did Counties Hosting a Trump Rally in 2016 See a 226% Spike in Hate Crimes?" In *The Reference Shelf: Hate Crimes,* edited by Sophie Zyla, 45–48. Amenia, NY: Grey House Publishing, 2020.

MLA: Jacobson, Louis. "Did Counties Hosting a Trump Rally in 2016 See a 226% Spike in Hate Crimes?" *The Reference Shelf: Hate Crimes,* edited by Sophie Zyla, Grey Housing Publishing, 2020, pp. 45–48.

APA: Jacobson, L. (2020). Did counties hosting a Trump rally in 2016 see a 226% spike in hate crimes? In Sophie Zyla (Ed.), *The reference shelf: Hate crimes* (pp. 45–48). Amenia, NY: Grey Housing Publishing.

"We Need to Evolve": Police Get Help to Improve Hate Crime Tracking

By Hannah Allam and Marisa Peñaloza
NPR, May 28, 2019

For the picturesque college town of Durham in southeastern New Hampshire, a reckoning came in 2017.

That was the year a complaint about the cultural appropriation of Cinco de Mayo spiraled into weeks of racial unrest, a boiling over of tensions that had simmered for years at the University of New Hampshire. Students who called out racist incidents faced a backlash of online bullying, swastikas and slurs, and the vandalism of sculptures that symbolized their cause.

Student activists blamed UNH leadership for allowing the problem to fester. Their criticism was backed up by news reports that showed the university hadn't reported a single hate incident for more than a decade before—an oddity for a campus its size. "That time was sad," UNH Police Chief Paul Dean said. "But there were opportunities."

Dean was speaking from a campus auditorium this month as he welcomed guests to one of those opportunities: a hate-crime training for the university police and the Durham Police Department.

Dean and Chief Dave Kurz of Durham, N.H., where the college is located, were among the latest chiefs to enlist the help of a traveling workshop organized by two advocacy groups, the Matthew Shepard Foundation and the Lawyers' Committee for Civil Rights Under Law. In the daylong workshop, the officers learned about state and federal laws related to bias crimes, heard from black and Jewish activists who've had firsthand experience with hate incidents, and debated whether certain scenarios had all the legal requirements of a hate crime.

Dean said the workshop is one of many ways he's trying to make good on a promise to students to be more responsive to bias-motivated incidents.

"Just because something has always been the way it is doesn't necessarily mean that's the right way. We need to evolve," Dean said. "I just don't like the idea of somebody feeling uncomfortable in my community."

The idea for the mobile trainings came a couple of years ago, when FBI data showed a sharp increase in reported hate crimes—and that's with only spotty, voluntary reporting from law enforcement agencies around the country.

The trainers are former senior Justice Department prosecutors and agents with years of experience in bias-motivated crimes. They go from city to city teaching police about hate-crime laws in their states—not always an easy task given the debate in law enforcement circles over whether such laws are necessary or even constitutional.

"There's one set of the population that looks at hate crimes and sees laws that were passed to protect certain people. And why were those certain people more special than somebody else?" said trainer Cynthia Deitle, a former FBI special agent who was in charge of the bureau's Civil Rights Unit and is now with the Matthew Shepard Foundation.

The workshop materials list some of the most common arguments of skeptical officers: *Laws are already in place for crimes, so it's a waste of time and resources to add an extra charge for bias. Hate crimes aren't a major problem in our area. These laws are an exercise in political correctness.*

The trainers don't shy away from the tough conversation; they open with it. In New Hampshire, trainer Albert Moskowitz, a former senior Justice Department prosecutor, stood before roughly 50 officers and posed the big question about hate-crime laws.

"Do we need them?" Moscowitz asked. "What do you think?"

At first, nobody responded. Then one officer said he supports the approach New Hampshire takes now—no state hate-crime law, but prosecutors can seek tougher sentencing when bias is a motivation.

"So you're saying that somehow these crimes are more serious than they'd otherwise be," Moscowitz said, prodding the officer to explain his thinking.

"I didn't say more serious," the officer said. "An assault is an assault no matter how you look at it."

"Because an assault against anybody is a serious crime, right?" Moscowitz said. "So why would it be more serious if the assault is substantially motivated by the person's race or religion?"

"It should be enhanced as far as penalties," the officer replied. "But as far as seriousness? No."

Supporters of hate-crime laws say the idea is to acknowledge the sweeping impact of targeting someone simply for who they are. The torching of a mosque is felt by the larger Muslim community, for example, just like the murder of a trans woman sends a message to others who identify as LGBT.

Strafford County Attorney Thomas Velardi, who oversees Durham and the surrounding area, says he sees hate-crime laws as restorative.

"There are some people that are being singled out, and in some instances hurt, and we need to do something about that. We're sort of struggling with how to respond to that—what do we do and how do we do it?"

The trainers are careful about the framing, stressing how it's just good police work to stay on top of hate incidents that might point to a trend or signal the formation of groups like the ones that wreaked havoc in Charlottesville, Va.

"None of us want you to be the next Charlottesville or the next Charleston or the next Pittsburgh," Deitle said, referring to cities where deadly hate-inspired attacks took place. "We don't want you to be that. But we don't know. And you need to be prepared."

During the training, few of the New Hampshire officers volunteered their thoughts, but they opened up a little more over lunch. The chiefs asked that the officers not be identified by name because of the sensitive nature of the topic and because some work undercover.

> **The trainers are former senior Justice Department prosecutors and agents with years of experience in bias-motivated crimes.**

Sitting around a table in the campus cafeteria, the officers used some of the language of hate-crime skeptics. There's not an increase, it's just that there's more reporting now, they argued, or the media are quick to call something a hate crime without knowing the facts. Still, the officers said, they see the training as helpful even if they're still conflicted about the purpose of hate-crime laws.

"If we don't train, if we don't stay on top of the current changes and laws and the attitudes and the climate, then we're going to pay a big price for that," one veteran officer said, as others nodded in agreement. "We'll lose the trust of the community, and we can't do that."

Print Citations

CMS: Allam, Hannah, and Marisa Peñaloza. "'We Need to Evolve': Police Get Help to Improve Hate Crime Tracking." In *The Reference Shelf: Hate Crimes,* edited by Sophie Zyla, 49–51. Amenia, NY: Grey House Publishing, 2020.

MLA: Allam, Hannah, and Marisa Peñaloza. "'We Need to Evolve': Police Get Help to Improve Hate Crime Tracking." *The Reference Shelf: Hate Crimes,* edited by Sophie Zyla, Grey Housing Publishing, 2020, pp. 49–51.

APA: Allam, H., & Peñaloza, M. (2020). "We need to evolve:": Police get help to improve hate crime tracking. In Sophie Zyla (Ed.), *The reference shelf: Hate crimes* (pp. 49–51). Amenia, NY: Grey Housing Publishing.

The F.B.I.'s New Approach to Combating Domestic Terrorism: Straight Talk

By Adam Goldman

The New York Times, November 10, 2019

OAKWOOD VILLAGE, Ohio—As a group of prominent black pastors listened, the top federal prosecutor in northern Ohio, Justin E. Herdman, spoke recently at Mount Zion church about the prospect that a gunman could target one of their congregations.

The subtext was clear. Mr. Herdman is among a group of federal law enforcement officials who have begun speaking more forthrightly about fighting domestic terrorism from the front lines. They want to reassure a skeptical public that the Justice Department is forcefully combating racist and politically motivated violence in the Trump era, amid their own mounting concerns about a possible surge in attacks sparked by the 2020 election.

"When I sit in church," Mr. Herdman told the pastors, "I have one eye on what's going on at the altar, and I have got one eye on the entrance to the sanctuary."

"Mm-hmm," the pastors responded in unison.

The community relations effort is the most visible of several aggressive steps by federal prosecutors and F.B.I. agents to combat domestic terrorism. The bureau has about 850 open investigations across the United States. Prosecutors have backed rewriting the laws on domestic terrorism. And in northern Ohio, Mr. Herdman has encouraged his investigators to use wiretaps, one of their most intrusive tools, in such cases.

A spotlight on the people reshaping our politics. A conversation with voters across the country. And a guiding hand through the endless news cycle, telling you what you really need to know.

Their efforts show how federal law enforcement officials are fighting domestic terrorism and its underlying ideologies, including white nationalism and neo-Nazism, as they navigate not only demands to do more to stop high-profile mass shootings but also limits on their power, like First Amendment protections for hate speech.

At the church in Oakwood Village, a middle-class suburb southeast of Cleveland, Mr. Herdman was joined by the area's top F.B.I. agent, Eric B. Smith, who expressed concern that the bitter divisions that have colored the nation's political discourse will only worsen in an election year and could stoke more violence.

"One of the great concerns for us in the upcoming year is this domestic terrorism threat," Mr. Smith said. "People are simply conducting acts of terror because it's their side."

Mr. Herdman, a career prosecutor and former intelligence officer in the United States Navy Reserve, gained attention recently for his performance at a news conference announcing charges against a white nationalist suspected of threatening the Jewish Community Center of Youngstown, about 60 miles from Cleveland.

Investigators discovered an AR-15 military-style assault rifle, World War II-era Nazi propaganda and a Hitler Youth knife in the basement of the suspect, 20-year-old James P. Reardon of New Middletown.

Evoking recent mass shootings, Mr. Herdman denounced Mr. Reardon and his toxic views, describing Nazism and racial superiority as failed ideologies.

"Threatening to kill Jewish people, gunning down innocent Latinos on a weekend shopping trip, planning and plotting to perpetrate murders in the name of a nonsense racial theory, sitting to pray with God-fearing people who you execute moments later — those actions don't make you soldiers, they make you criminals," Mr. Herdman said.

His words resonated. Letters, phone calls and emails poured in. "Thank you for so accurately describing the limits of fanaticism," wrote Larry Schwarz, who is Jewish and lives in Hatboro, Pa. "I have never heard the case made so eloquently and so cogently."

Mr. Herdman explained in an interview why he was compelled to speak out. "I wanted to lay down the marker," he said. "I couldn't let it go unsaid what the position of our office is."

Mr. Reardon's case is one of dozens that Mr. Herdman's office has pursued in recent months. The F.B.I.'s Cleveland field office, which has a dedicated domestic terrorism squad, plans to add more investigators soon.

Mr. Herdman has encouraged his investigators to work aggressively, including using wiretaps to thwart domestic terrorists. Investigators must clear a high bar to start a wiretap; it requires the approval of a federal judge, and prosecutors must show that less invasive methods have failed or likely would.

Mr. Herdman's office has charged others with making threats against federal law enforcement officers and against Representative Alexandria Ocasio-Cortez, Democrat of New York and a frequent target of conservative criticism.

Those arrests came after a man opened fire in August in a nightclub on the other side of the state, in Dayton, gunning down nine people and wounding 19. The gunman possibly embraced troubling beliefs, including anti-government, racist and misogynist views, according to a law enforcement official.

Civil liberty and Muslim advocacy groups have accused the government of being slow to recognize the deadly threat as investigators focused heavily on Islamic terrorists.

"For too long, the F.B.I. was myopically targeting Muslims as potential terrorists," said Faiza Patel, co-director of the Liberty and National Security Program at the Brennan Center for Justice at the New York University Law School. "It is now feeling pressure from Congress and the public to address white nationalist violence, so we are seeing a wave of investigations and prosecutions."

Around the country, federal law enforcement officials have vocally taken on domestic terrorism. Thomas T. Cullen, the top prosecutor in the Western District of Virginia and a Trump appointee, has moved aggressively to convict white supremacists who break the law.

He prosecuted James Fields Jr., the avowed white supremacist from Ohio who steered his Dodge Challenger into a crowd of protesters near a white nationalist rally in Charlottesville, Va., in 2017, killing a young woman and injuring dozens. As Mr. Fields was sentenced in June to life in prison, Mr. Cullen said his attack was "motivated by this deep-seated racial animus."

Mr. Cullen has targeted local members of a Southern California-based violent white supremacist group, the Rise Above Movement. Two regions of growing concern are the West Coast and the states around the Great Lakes, where the F.B.I. has seen more arrests than in other parts of the country.

Other prosecutors in Virginia as well as in Florida and Los Angeles have also targeted white supremacists.

Agents have also ramped up activity against members of Atomwaffen, one of the most violent extremist groups in the country, arresting suspected members on gun charges and asking a local judge to seize the weapons of one in the Seattle area because he was a risk to the public.

The group, which has dozens of members across the country, wants to start a race war in the United States, according to the F.B.I. The bureau is also concerned about an Atomwaffen offshoot, Feuerkrieg Division.

Federal prosecutors have backed a domestic terrorism bill that they say could aid in investigations, but the effort has stalled at the White House, a Justice Department official said.

Any legislation also would probably face stiff resistance from civil rights activists over its First Amendment implications. An existing federal statute defines domestic terrorism roughly as people trying to use political violence to intimidate others but carries no penalties.

The F.B.I. made 107 domestic terrorism-related arrests in the fiscal year that ended in September, a total roughly consistent with recent years.

"Certainly, the most lethality in terms of terrorist attacks over the recent years here in the homeland has been on the domestic terrorism side," Christopher A. Wray, the F.B.I. director, told lawmakers last month. Just days after his testimony, the F.B.I. charged a white supremacist in Colorado with plotting to blow up a synagogue.

Though he and other senior law enforcement officials have spoken out about the rise of hate crimes and political violence, including Attorney General William P. Barr, who condemned both in a July speech on combating anti-Semitism, they stand out somewhat in terms of how the politics of fighting domestic terrorism have played out in Washington.

President Trump has stoked race-based fears and praised "both sides" after the deadly Charlottesville attack. He also continues to lend credibility to white nationalists and anti-Muslim bigots by amplifying suspect accounts on Twitter, according to an investigation by the *New York Times*.

After years of prodding, the Department of Homeland Security finally affirmed in September that domestic terrorism was a national security threat.

But after years of prodding, the Department of Homeland Security finally affirmed in September that domestic terrorism was a national security threat while earlier this year, the F.B.I. established a domestic terrorism-hate crimes fusion cell.

The Justice Department should also craft and make public a strategy to combat white nationalist violence, Ms. Patel said, adding that the government does not necessarily need new laws to fight domestic terrorism, just new priorities.

In Ohio, Mr. Herdman expects extremism to persist. "Just based on the trend line, I don't see where it goes down," he said.

He has prosecuted cases associated with a mixed bag of ideologies, including anarchists, people obsessed with mass killings and sovereign citizens, who view government as illegitimate.

The F.B.I. late last year arrested Damon M. Joseph, a white supremacist-turned-aspiring-jihadist who was planning to attack a synagogue in the Toledo area. The arrest came weeks after the mass shooting at a Pittsburgh synagogue that killed 11 worshipers, an attack that Mr. Joseph had praised.

That same week, agents arrested a Toledo couple, Elizabeth Lecron and Vincent Armstrong, both 23, on charges of planning to blow up a bar there. Investigators said Ms. Lecron consumed Nazi literature and was infatuated with mass killers, posting photographs and comments on social media glorifying the Columbine school shooters, who killed 13 and wounded 21 in Littleton, Colo., in 1999, and the man convicted in the killing of nine black worshipers at a church in Charleston, S.C., in 2015.

In a journal, Mr. Armstrong wrote: "I have a vision. A vision to kill. To hunt the unwilling."

Ms. Lecron pleaded guilty in August to providing material support to terrorists, a crime frequently charged in international terrorism cases—but not domestic ones. Mr. Armstrong also pleaded guilty to his role in the thwarted attack.

At the church, Mr. Herdman, who has given the same sober talk to Muslim and Jewish religious leaders, offered a reminder about why the Justice Department was founded after the Civil War: to fight the Ku Klux Klan, whose members have historically terrorized black people and targeted churches.

"We're here for you," he told the pastors.

Print Citations

CMS: Goldman, Adam. "The F.B.I.'s New Approach to Combating Domestic Terrorism: Straight Talk." In *The Reference Shelf: Hate Crimes,* edited by Sophie Zyla, 52–56. Amenia, NY: Grey House Publishing, 2020.

MLA: Goldman, Adam. "The F.B.I.'s New Approach to Combating Domestic Terrorism: Straight Talk." *The Reference Shelf: Hate Crimes,* edited by Sophie Zyla, Grey Housing Publishing, 2020, pp. 52–56.

APA: Goldman, A. (2020). The F.B.I.'s new approach to combating domestic terrorism: Straight talk. In Sophie Zyla (Ed.), *The reference shelf: Hate crimes* (pp. 52–56). Amenia, NY: Grey Housing Publishing.

Congressman Serrano and Senator Casey Introduce the Stop HATE Act to Address the Rise in Hate Crimes through Social Media

New York State Government, March 28, 2019

Washington, D.C.—Today, Congressman José E. Serrano (D-The Bronx) and Senator Bob Casey (D-PA) introduced the Stop Harmful and Abusive Telecommunications Expression (HATE) Act, legislation to address how social media and other forms of electronic communication have helped spread hate speech and fuel the rise in hate crimes against minority groups.

"Hate speech online is directly related to the rise of hate crimes in the U.S. and worldwide. As an avid user of Twitter, Facebook, and Instagram to communicate with my constituents, I've witnessed firsthand the rise in hate speech online in recent years. Many times, I've been the target of hateful rhetoric on these platforms," said Congressman Serrano. "Given the devastating attacks in Pittsburgh, Charleston, New Zealand, and elsewhere, countering hate crimes must be a priority in this Congress. The Stop HATE Act will help us better understand the role of social media, which has become ingrained in our daily lives, [and] plays in aiding the spread of hate speech and crimes. It will also help us understand what we can do to prevent the First Amendment from being weaponized in order to hurt other Americans because of their race, ethnicity, national origin, gender, or sexual orientation."

"The rapid development of media platforms and technology has outpaced our understanding of how they can be used to disseminate hate," said Senator Casey. "We need to examine how these platforms and technologies have been used to facilitate the commission of hate crimes so we can take appropriate steps to prevent another tragedy. I hope my colleagues in Congress will join in this effort to help address hate-based violence in the United States and around the world."

In 1993, the Department of Commerce's National Telecommunications and Information Administration (NTIA), the principal adviser on telecommunications policies and regulations for the federal government, released a report entitled *The Role of Telecommunications in Hate Crimes*. The report examined how telecommunications of that era played in the rise of hate crimes and recommended ways the government and private citizens could combat these growing threats. The Stop HATE Act would direct the Departments of Commerce and Justice to update its

1993 report by analyzing all new forms of electronic communications that have since been developed; issue a new report to Congress including recommendations, consistent with the First Amendment, to

> **The Stop HATE Act will help us better understand the role of social media, which has become ingrained in our daily lives, [and] plays in aiding the spread of hate speech and crimes.**

address these threats; and require the NTIA to periodically report to Congress with its assessment of new forms of media that emerge.

House cosponsors include Reps. Ro Khanna, Gwen Moore, Eleanor Holmes Norton, Steve Cohen, Val Demings, Nydia M. Velázquez, Alcee L. Hastings, Brenda L. Lawrence, and Yvette D. Clarke. Senate cosponsors include Senators Bernie Sanders, Chris Van Hollen, Bob Menendez, Amy Klobuchar, Kamala Harris, Doug Jones, and Cory Booker. The bill is supported by the National Hispanic Media Coalition, Free Press Action Fund, the Anti-Defamation League, and Color of Change.

Print Citations

CMS: "Congressman Serrano and Senator Casey Introduce the Stop HATE Act to Address the Rise in Hate Crimes through Social Media." In *The Reference Shelf: Hate Crimes,* edited by Sophie Zyla, 57–58. Amenia, NY: Grey House Publishing, 2020.

MLA: "Congressman Serrano and Senator Casey Introduce the Stop HATE Act to Address the Rise in Hate Crimes through Social Media." *The Reference Shelf: Hate Crimes,* edited by Sophie Zyla, Grey Housing Publishing, 2020, pp. 57–58.

APA: New York State Government. (2020). Congressman Serrano and Senator Casey introduce the stop HATE act to address the rise in hate crimes through social media." In Sophie Zyla (Ed.), *The reference shelf: Hate crimes* (pp. 57–58). Amenia, NY: Grey Housing Publishing.

3

Hate Laws and the Constitution

Photo by Anthony Crider, via Wikimedia.

The 2017 Unite the Right rally, pictured above, brought together extremist groups like the KKK, neo-Nazis, and neo-Confederates. The rally turned deadly when a white supremacist drove his car into a group of counter-protestors, killing one. The public backlash resulted in only 20–30 protestors attending Unite the Right II in 2018, compared to thousands of counter-protestors.

The Limits of Free Speech

Efforts have unquestionably been made by state and federal authorities to protect the rights of citizens and address social issues, however, states are inconsistent in implementation of hate crime protections. Most have anti-discrimination, hate crime, bullying, and equal employment laws, ensuring equal treatment for protected classes. Teaching tolerance, diversity training, affirmative action, equal employment opportunity, and sexual harassment training has become mandatory in many state agencies, educational institutions, and businesses. Initiatives regarding discrimination and protected classes are based on the Civil Rights Acts of 1964 and 1991.

Hate Crime Laws

In 1968 President Lyndon Johnson signed the first federal hate crime statute into law. It criminalized threats and force against a person based on race, religion, or national origin, targeting bias in schools, the workplace, and other public places. The same protections were also afforded to housing rights that same year. In 1988, protections on the basis of familial status and disability were added. In 1996 the Church Arson Prevention Act was passed by Congress, criminalizing defacement, damage, or destruction of religious property because of the race, color, or ethnicity of associated persons as well as interference with a person's religious practice.[1]

Brian Levin in his 2019 report *Global Terrorism: Threats to the Homeland, Part 1* says "the domestic terror threat is a fluid one, with increasingly transnational and internet dimensions. The societal and international divisions that fuel extremism will likely be further exacerbated by a highly charged political season and increasing international instability." While he does not recommend making major changes to the statutes, he supports the following:

Enacting HR 3106, the Domestic Terrorism DATA Act, to improve the availability and production of timely government data on terrorism and the Jabara-Heyer NO HATE Act;

Enhancing both statutory and administrative provisions to counter the growing threat against public officials and elected office holders;

Amending 18 USC §231 to punish not only trainers, but trainees in violent methods designed to foment civil disorder;

Improving background checks and closing loopholes on firearms purchases, as well as the placement of restrictions on semiautomatic rifles, and extended magazines inter alia;

Providing greater funding and resources to enhance interagency coordination to combat the threat that white supremacist /far right extremism poses to the homeland.

Levin attributes extreme misogyny as the cause of the November 2018 Tallahassee, Florida, yoga studio attack that left two dead and five injured before the perpetrator killed himself.[2]

While the FBI defines a hate crime as a criminal offence against gender, misogyny has not been added to the list. In the UK, British Labour's Melanie Onn argued for its inclusion: "Hate crime law was designed to combat crimes that deny equal respect and dignity to people who are seen as other. . . . That violence is a consequence of sex inequality. . . .That inequality undermines the ability of targeted people to feel safe and secure in society." All-Party Parliamentary Groups in the UK Parliament on domestic violence found that there is a clear link between low-level incidents of harassment towards women and more serious forms of violence and sexual crime. Misogyny has since been added to the list of hate crimes in the UK.[3]

Hate Crimes, Hate Speech, and the First Amendment

Hate alone—expressed as dislike, anger, or even rage—is not a crime. Prejudice or bias without accompanying threats, violence, or property damage is not a crime. People cannot be prosecuted for their beliefs, even if those beliefs are offensive or upsetting. The First Amendment states: "Congress shall make no law respecting an establishment of religion, or prohibiting the free exercise thereof; or abridging the freedom of speech, or of the press; or the right of the people peaceably to assemble, and to petition the Government for a redress of grievances."[4]

The Matthew Shepard and James Byrd, Jr. Hate Crimes Prevent Act (HCPA) of 2009 does not punish thought, speech, or criticism of another nor does it prohibit lawful expression of one's beliefs. According to the Human Rights Campaign, the HCPA does not punish violent thoughts or beliefs. In the early 1990s, *R.A.V. v. City of St. Paul* and *Wisconsin v. Mitchell* demonstrated that a criminal statute may consider bias motivation when that motivation is directly connected to a defendant's criminal conduct. The Supreme Court, in *Wisconsin v. Mitchell,* clarified that "the First Amendment . . . does not prohibit the evidentiary use of speech to establish the elements of a crime or to prove motive or intent." HPCA language specifically states:

- Nothing in this division shall be construed to allow a court, in any criminal trial for an offense described under this division or an amendment made by this division, in the absence of a stipulation by the parties, to admit evidence of speech, beliefs, association, group membership, or expressive conduct unless that evidence is relevant and admissible under the Federal Rules of Evidence. Nothing in this division is intended to affect the existing rules of evidence.

- This division applies to violent acts motivated by actual or perceived race, color, religion, national origin, gender, sexual orientation, gender identity, or disability of a victim.

- Nothing in this division, or an amendment made by this division, shall be construed or applied in a manner that infringes any rights under the First Amendment to the Constitution of the United States.[5]

The HCPA is also written in a way that it is in compliance with the Commerce Clause, "that the government allege and prove beyond a reasonable doubt that there is an explicit and discrete connection between a prohibited act (a hate crime based on religion, national origin, gender, sexual orientation, gender identity or disability) and interstate or foreign commerce. Thus, the HCPA is clearly within Congress's power to legislate." Sexual orientation includes homosexuality, bisexuality, or heterosexuality and, in the Hate Crimes Statistics Act of 1990, consensual homosexuality or homosexuality is included in the definition. Gender identity is covered under the HCPA as "actual or perceived gender-related characteristics." The HCPA does not have sentencing authority. The Violent Crime Control and Law Enforcement Act of 1994 under the Hate Crimes Sentencing Enhancement Act allows for harsher penalties against hate crime perpetrators. Hate crimes continue to be prosecuted at the state level with federal prosecution only if:

- the state does not have jurisdiction;

- the state has requested that the federal government assume jurisdiction;

- the verdict or sentence obtained pursuant to state charges left demonstratively un-vindicated the federal interest in eradicating bias-motivated violence;

- a prosecution by the United States is in the public interest and necessary to secure substantial justice

While the majority of hate crimes are prosecuted at a state level, HCPA allows for states to enlist the assistance of federal authorities for investigation and prosecution, including those crimes that cross state lines.[6]

Recent Federal Laws and Proposals

The Center for the Study of Hate & Extremism "Report to the Nation: 2019 Factbook on Hate & Extremism in the U.S. & Internationally" provides updates on recent state reforms, federal laws and proposals and individual state reforms, and includes the following.

The Protecting Religiously Affiliated Institutions Act of 2018. Enacted in September 2018. This act expands on the law protecting houses of worship to include real property owned or leased by a nonprofit or religiously affiliated organization.

The Matthew Shepard and James Byrd, Jr. Hate Crimes Prevention Act of 2009. Signed by President Obama in 2009. This law extended the civil rights statute by adding gender, gender identity, disability, and sexual orientation. These categories are protected when the crimes also affect interstate commerce because of the requirements of the Constitution's Commerce Clause. The Act punishes violence and attempts involving bodily injury through firearms, fire, explosives, and other dangerous devices.

The Hate Crime Sentencing Enhancement Act. Enacted in 1994. This penalty enhancement law increased the sentence for underlying federal offenses when the target is intentionally selected because of race, color, religion, national origin, ethnicity, gender, disability, or sexual orientation.

The Hate Crime Statistics Act (HCSA). Signed into law by president George H.W. Bush in April 1990. The act required the attorney general to collect data on crimes motivated by race, religion, sexual orientation, and ethnicity submitted voluntarily by states. It was amended in the 1990s to include disability, in 2013 to include gender and gender identity, and in 2017 to include religious and ethnic subcategories.

Khalid Jabara and Heather Heyer National Opposition to Hate, Assaults, and Threats to Equality (NO HATE) Act of 2019. Proposed July 2019. This bill would provide incentives for state and local jurisdictions to improve their hate crime reporting and data collection systems.

Never Again Education Act. Proposed July 2019 This act would establish a grant program enabling teachers to access resources and training for Holocaust education. The act was first introduced by Representative Carolyn Maloney in 2018 and reintroduced in 2019.[7]

Hate Groups Sites and Their Hosts

Levin's report also lists six Russian-sponsored Facebook pages that promoted fake news and hate speech, which have since been removed: Blacktivits with 103.8M followers; Txrebels with 103.0 million followers; MuslimAmerica with 71.4 million followers; Patriototus with 51.1 million followers; Secured Borders with 5.6 million followers; and Lgbtun with 5.2 million followers. A July 2019 *Gizmodo* report lists 151 tech companies that provide service for 391 websites run by white supremacists, neo-Nazis, the Ku Klux Klan, new-Confederates, black nationalists, and racist Odinists (white supremacist philosophy based on an ancient Nordic religion). Google, GoDaddy, Endurance International Group, Cloudflare, DNC Holdings, Microsoft, and Squarespace are among the thirteen host sites for six of the top white nationalist podcasts. Google is listed as the host for three Combat 18 neo-Nazi sites involved with mail-bomb attacks in non-white UK neighborhoods. GoDaddy has two sites for neo-Nazi group Blood & Honour, members of which have been convicted of murdering homeless people. GoDaddy representatives responded that "while we detest the sentiment of such sites, we support a free and open Internet and, similar to the principles of free speech, that sometimes means allowing such tasteless, ignorant content." A Cloudflare representative stated, "It's easy to point at sites you don't like and make a single decision. . . .But to come up with a consistent policy you can apply to the 16 million websites that use us for various services in a predictable and consistent way is very difficult."[8]

Revisiting the Past to Educate the Future

A mandate was in place in 1994 in Florida to ensure that the Holocaust was "taught as a uniquely important event in modern history, emphasizing the systemic and state-sponsored violence, which distinguish it from other genocides."[9] Spanish River Community High School principal William Latson, however, was removed from his position for stating, "Not everyone believes the Holocaust happened" and for his belief that courses on the Holocaust should not be forced upon all students.[10] In response, Senator Marco Rubio filed the Never Again Education Act in the Senate in 2019. With only eleven states participating in Holocaust education, many feel more needs to be done. A Schoen Consulting study for the Conference on Jewish Material Claims Against Germany shows that 49 percent of Millennials cannot name a concentration camp, and 41 percent believe two million or less died.

The Schoen study also states that 70 percent of people polled care about the Holocaust and 58 percent believe something similar can happen again. In contrast, 11 percent of adults and 22 percent of Millennials either were not sure if they had heard, or did not know, of the Holocaust. Approximately 68 percent of Americans believe anti-Semitism exists in the United States; 34 percent believe there are many neo-Nazis and 17 percent acknowledge "a great deal" of Neo-Nazis in the United States.[11]

Thoughts on Censorship

Randall Kennedy's review of Nadine Strossen's *Why We Should Resist It with Free Speech, Not Censorship* summarizes Strossen's perspective on censorship and hate speech, based on her personal experience with anti-Semitic slurs. She asserts that Nazism hangs over hate speech censorship debates but laws would not have prevented or stopped the Holocaust from their "hateful, tangible crimes." Strossen writes, "For our own well-being we should develop relatively thick skins, so that our own sense of self-confidence is not threatened by hateful words." She was president of the American Civil Liberties Union from 1991 to 2008, and feels that forceful government intervention to eliminate hate speech is a mistake, unless in an emergency situation without preventative intervention options. "Even worse than speech's potential power to harm individuals and society is government's potential power to do likewise by enforcing hate speech laws. Predictably, this elastic power will be used to silence dissenting ideas, unpopular speakers, and disempowered groups." Strossen's research of hate speech repression at institutions in the United States showed that it was "ineffective or even counter productive, giving rise to suppression of some groups that these instruments of mandatory civility were intended to assist."[12]

Works Used

First Amendment. National Constitution Center. https://constitutioncenter.org/interactive-constitution/amendment/amendment-i.

Human Rights Campaign. "Questions and Answers: The Matthew Shepard and James Byrd, Jr. Hate Crimes Prevention Act. Hate Crimes." Feb 1, 2010. https://www.hrc.org/resources/questions-and-answers-the-matthew-shepard-and-james-byrd-jr.-hate-crimes-pr.

Kennedy, Randall. "Is the Cure of Censorship Better Than the Disease of Hate Speech?" *Knight First Amendment Institute.* Apr 9, 2018. https://knightcolumbia.org/content/cure-censorship-better-disease-hate-speech.

Levin, Brian. "Global Terrorism: Threats to the Homeland, Part 1." Center for the Study of Hate and Extremism, Department of Criminal Justice, California State University, San Bernardino. Sep 10, 2019. https://csbs.csusb.edu/sites/csusb_csbs/files.

Levin, Brian, and Lisa Nakashima. "Report to the Nation: 2019: Factbook on Hate & Extremism in the U.S. & Internationally. Center for the Study of Hate and Extremism, California State University, San Bernardino. Jul 2019. https://www.hsdl.org/c/just-released-report-to-the-nation-on-hate-and-extremism/.

Mervosh, Sarah. "Principal Who Tried to Stay 'Politically Neutral' about Holocaust Is Removed." *New York Times,* Jul 8 2019. https://www.nytimes.com/2019/07/08/us/spanish-river-william-latson-holocaust.html.

Onn, Melissa. United Kingdom Parliament, House of Commons Hansard. "Misogyny as a Hate Crime." Vol. 637. Mah 7, 2018. https://hansard.parliament.uk/Commons/2018-03-07/debates/92236C51-2340-4D97-92A7-4955B24C2D74/MisogynyAsAHateCrime#contribution-452DE3BC-B238-48C0-8D21-0198B5348C5B.

Povich, Elaine S. "The Holocaust: States Require Education about It as Anti-Semitism, Hate Crimes Surge." *USA Today.* Jul 15, 2019. https://psmag.com/news/a-florida-principals-reassignment-raises-questions-about-the-quality-of-holocaust-education.

Schoen Consulting. "The Conference on Jewish Materials Claims Against Germany." Feb 23-27, 2018. http://www.claimscon.org/wp-content/uploads/2018/04/Holocaust-Knowledge-Awareness-Study_Executive-Summary-2018.pdf.

United Kingdom Parliament, House of Commons Hansard. "Misogyny as a Hate Crime." Volume 637. Mar 7, 2018. Retrieved from: https://hansard.parliament.uk/Commons/2018-03-07/debates/92236C51-2340-4D97-92A7-4955B24C2D74/MisogynyAsAHateCrime#contribution-452DE3BC-B238-48C0-8D21-0198B5348C5B

Notes

1. Human Rights Campaign, "Questions and Answers: The Matthew Shepard and James Byrd, Jr. Hate Crimes Prevention Act."
2. Levin, "Global Terrorism: Threats to the Homeland, Part I."

3.   Onn, "Misogyny as a Hate Crime."
4.   First Amendment, National Constitution Center.
5.   Human Rights Camaign, "Questions and Answers: The Matthew Shepard and James Byrd, Jr. Hate Crimes Prevention Act."
6.   Ibid.
7.   Levin and Nakashima, "Report to the Nation: 2019: Factbook on Hate & Extremism in the U.S. & Internationally."
8.   Ibid.
9.   Povich, "The Holocaust: States Require Education about It as Anti-Semitism, Hate Crimes Surge."
10. Mervosh, "Principal Who Tried to Stay 'Politically Neutral' about Holocaust Is Removed."
11. Schoen Consulting, "The Conference on Jewish Materials Claims Against Germany."
12. Kennedy, "Is the Cure of Censorship Better Than the Disease of Hate Speech."

Is the Cure of Censorship Better Than the Disease of Hate Speech?

By Randall Kennedy
Knight First Amendment Institute at Columbia University,
April 9, 2018

In *HATE: Why We Should Resist It with Free Speech, Not Censorship* (Oxford University Press), the constitutional scholar Nadine Strossen recalls the first time she was subjected to an anti-Semitic slur. Although she was "a well-educated young adult" when targeted, she was nonetheless "stunned into silence." That did not last long. Strossen later became a leading champion of freedom of expression. She has served as president of the American Civil Liberties Union (1991 to 2008) and has persistently propounded the key tenet of engaged pluralism—*More speech!*—against the reflexive upshot of fear and disgust—*Ban it!* Now she has come forward with a splendid, accessible, instructive book that could not be more timely.

Strossen argues that, except in tightly defined circumstances, it is a mistake to attempt to deploy the coercive force of the government to eliminate so-called "hate speech"—speech that expresses hostility, detestation, contempt, or any related animus against individuals or groups. She accepts governmental suppression of this category of speech in an emergency, when there is no opportunity for deliberation or counter-speech, or when a speaker is directly threatening or harassing an individual. She resists suppression, however, when the basis for it is a conclusion that the type of speech in question is too hurtful, too vicious, or too loathsome to allow.

She acknowledges, quoting the Supreme Court, that "speech is powerful," that it "can stir people to action" and "inflict great pain." She concedes that malevolent expression can scald sensibilities and intimidate the vulnerable. She insists, however, that the cure of censorship is worse than the disease of hate speech. "Even worse than speech's potential power to harm individuals and society," she maintains, "is government's potential power to do likewise, by enforcing 'hate speech' laws. Predictably, this elastic power will be used to silence dissenting ideas, unpopular speakers, and disempowered groups."

In advancing her argument, Strossen introduces readers to the canonical doctrines and rhetoric of jurists who have forged the speech-protective architecture of First Amendment jurisprudence. She invokes with special affection writings by Justices Oliver Wendell Holmes, Louis Brandeis, and William Brennan. But she also invokes Thurgood Marshall, "Mr. Civil Rights," noting his insistence that equal treatment of protest by government is and should be an essential feature of First Amendment jurisprudence.

"There is an 'equality of status in the field of ideas,'" Marshall wrote, when the Supreme Court ruled in favor of a white defendant prosecuted for picketing against what he viewed as an anti-white hiring policy: "Government must afford all points of view an equal opportunity to be heard." Strossen's suggestion that Mr. Civil Rights was also Mr. Civil Liberties underscores one of her central claims: struggles for racial justice are typically reinforced, not impeded by, struggles for freedom of expression. That includes expression that is vicious, racist, or otherwise hateful. Equal-rights advocates, she maintains, should rally around her capacious concept of free speech because, among other things, their own views are often disparaged, feared, and targeted for censorship.

Though Strossen relates the key constitutional arguments surrounding the hate-speech debate, a notable virtue of her book is its attentiveness to what wisdom counsels, beyond what the law allows. To determine whether repression in the service of protecting vulnerable groups might be a wise policy, she appraises the record of institutions in America, such as public universities, that have deployed hate-speech prohibitions and the experience of nations across the globe that have turned to censorship to repress group vilification. Almost without exception, she finds that these efforts, even when made in good faith, turn out to be ineffective or even counterproductive, giving rise to suppression of some groups that these instruments of mandatory civility were intended to assist.

The specter of Nazism hovers over any debate over censorship of hate speech. Strossen faces that baleful fact with characteristic directness. "Given the horrors of the Holocaust," she writes, "even die-hard free speech stalwarts [such as herself, the daughter of a Holocaust survivor] would support 'hate speech' laws if they would have averted that atrocity." She argues, however, that Germany's prosecutions of Nazis in the 1930s for group vilification actually helped them gain attention and support. The problem with the response to the rise of Nazism, she avers, is not that the National Socialists enjoyed too much free speech but that they were allowed, literally, tragically, to get away with murder. The problem was their hateful, tangible crimes, not their hateful speech. The ineffectiveness of censorship to facilitate social decency, she declares, is oft-repeated and oft-ignored. Quoting Human Rights Watch, Strossen maintains that investigations around the world have revealed consistently that "there is little connection in practice between draconian 'hate speech' laws and the lessening of ethnic and racial violence or tension."

By contrast, Strossen praises the potential of what she terms ""non-censorial strategies": holding peaceful but vigorous counterdemonstrations when bigots stage their prejudice; deliberately ignoring obnoxious provocateurs since "silence can convey implicit messages of disdain, while at the same time denying hateful speakers the attention they seek and often get from sparking controversy"; encouraging public education, since bigotry so often feeds off ignorance; and inculcating habits of stoical and self-reliant articulateness, so that individuals develop a capacity to address cruel tormentors in an effective way. A feature of governmental hate-speech suppression that Strossen sees as profoundly bad is its tendency to weaken putative beneficiaries. "For our own well-being," she writes, "we should develop relatively thick skins, so that our own sense of self-confidence is not threatened by hateful words."

> **The problem with the response to the rise of Nazism is not that the National Socialists enjoyed too much free speech, but that they were allowed, literally, tragically, to get away with murder.**

Struggles will continue over the appropriateness of governmental censorship of speech that many deem to be hateful and dangerous. For a guide through the labyrinthine byways of this conflict one cannot do better than Strossen's book. She illuminates this topic with hard-won knowledge and disciplined conviction.

Print Citations

CMS: Kennedy, Randall. "Is the Cure of Censorship Better Than the Disease of Hate Speech?" In *The Reference Shelf: Hate Crimes,* edited by Sophie Zyla, 68–70. Amenia, NY: Grey House Publishing, 2020.

MLA: Kennedy, Randall. "Is the Cure of Censorship Better Than the Disease of Hate Speech?" *The Reference Shelf: Hate Crimes,* edited by Sophie Zyla, Grey Housing Publishing, 2020, pp. 68–70.

APA: Kennedy, R. (2020). Is the cure of censorship better than the disease of hate speech? In Sophie Zyla (Ed.), *The reference shelf: Hate crimes* (pp. 68–70). Amenia, NY: Grey Housing Publishing.

The Limits of Free Speech for White Supremacists Marching at the Unite the Right 2, Explained

By Alexia Fernandez Campbell
Vox, August 12, 2018

You may have heard that white supremacists are marching through the nation's capital this weekend. Their rally, Unite the Right 2, is sort of a sequel to the violent neo-Nazi march they held a year ago in Charlottesville, Virginia, that ended with the death of a counterprotester and multiple people sent to the hospital.

Sunday's festivities, organized by Jason Kessler, will culminate outside the White House in a rally for "white civil rights." Despite the public backlash to last year's event, white nationalists still feel emboldened by President Trump's administration to take their racist views from the dark corners of the internet into the mainstream. And any time they face criticism or opposition, members of the alt-right assert their free speech rights.

Even the mayor of the District of Columbia, who is overseeing the police and emergency response for the rally, merely referred to the event in an official memo as a series of "First Amendment activities."

There is no question that all Americans, including white supremacists, have a constitutional right to publicly express racist, offensive, unpopular views under the First Amendment. That right has been repeatedly upheld by the US Supreme Court. But what's often left out of the current defense of racist speech is that the First Amendment does not protect people from saying just any vile, racist thing that comes to mind.

The First Amendment would not, for example, protect any rallygoers this weekend who hurl threatening racial slurs to specific people during their march, as many of them did in Charlottesville. These could be considered "fighting words," a category of speech that the Supreme Court has said has no value to American democracy. In 1942, the Court defined fighting words as "those which by their very utterance inflict injury or tend to incite an immediate breach of the peace."

Considering the violence that broke out in Charlottesville last year, and the anxiety about potential clashes in the nation's capital this weekend, it's important to analyze the role that language may play in sparking the violence, and whether it's protected by the First Amendment.

The "fighting words" doctrine represents a gray area of constitutional law, but several legal experts I talked to last year said that many white supremacists in Charlottesville crossed that line when they began chanting racial and homophobic slurs to specific people on the streets.

Generic Racist Chants Are Protected, but Not Slurs Aimed at Specific People

The images of white men draped in swastikas and carrying lit torches in Charlottesville last year were disturbing, as were many of their chants, like "Jews will not replace us."

Yet these generic anti-Semitic and anti-immigrant rants are protected under the First Amendment, especially when they are part of a political rally. (Political speech is highly protected under the Constitution.)

While these chants don't rise to the level of fighting words, free speech experts believe right-wing demonstrators may have gone too far when they called specific people the n-word or a gay slur. These could be interpreted as fighting words because they are profanities directed at certain individuals that would lead a reasonable person to retaliate.

However, some legal experts think it would be hard to prove whom the slurs were aimed at, since the demonstrators were part of a political rally.

"The most extreme of [Unite the Right's] outrageous utterances in Charlottesville would be easy to deem unprotected," said Robert O'Neill, a well-known First Amendment scholar and former director of the Thomas Jefferson Center for the Protection of Free Expression at the University of Virginia (the campus where demonstrators rallied last year).

When Demonstrators Went Too Far

Last year, media outlets reported a few repeated chants heard during the Unite the Right rally, including, "One people, one nation, end immigration," "Jews will not replace us," "White lives matter," and "Blood and soil."

These white supremacist slogans clearly offended many counterprotesters, but the courts have generally interpreted such broad statements as protected forms of speech.

As the rally grew more heated, though, demonstrators directly disparaged specific people and groups of people. *Huffington Post* reporter Christopher Mathias tweeted a video of demonstrators yelling, "Fuck you, faggots," at counterprotesters:

(video from twitter here/in article)

A few hours later, *Washington Post* reporter Joe Heim said he heard demonstrators chanting, "Go the fuck back to Africa," and shouting the n-word at a black woman across the street.

Constitutional law experts say these last two examples are not protected forms of speech.

"You could make the case that it was an insulting epithet, obviously a slur and racist comment that would provoke someone to retaliate," said Caroline Mala Corbin, a constitutional law professor at the University of Miami.

When "fighting words" became exempt from protection under the *Chaplinsky v. New Hampshire* Supreme Court ruling, it was based on the idea that such language did nothing to further public discourse and instead inflicted harm on people. Based on that, Corbin says the use of the gay slur and the n-word at demonstration would clearly fit this category of unprotected speech.

But over the years, Supreme Court justices have shown an aversion to the "fighting words" doctrine, out of concern that it might be used to suppress protected political speech. So they've drastically narrowed their interpretation of fighting words to insults directed on the personal level.

In the landmark 1971 case *Cohen v. California*, the Court overturned the conviction of an antiwar protester who was charged with disturbing the peace in a public courthouse for wearing a jacket that said "Fuck the draft."

In a 5-4 decision, the justices said the law, which banned offensive language in public, was too broad and trampled the protester's First Amendment rights. In their opinion, they ruled out the argument that the phrase on his jacket involved fighting words, because "no individual actually or likely to be present could reasonably have regarded the words on appellant's jacket as a direct personal insult."

The case essentially created three hurdles for someone to prove that certain speech is constitutionally unprotected under the "fighting words" doctrine: First, they would have to show that the language is, in fact, an insulting epithet. Second, that it's uttered directly to an individual. Third, that it's likely to provoke someone to retaliate and breach the peace.

The fighting words doctrine was later tested by the justices in the 1992 case *RAV v. City of St. Paul*, in which a Minnesota teen was convicted under a hate crime ordinance for burning a cross on the front lawn of a black family. The Supreme Court agreed that such an action met all three hurdles and constituted fighting words, but they overturned his conviction anyway. They said the ordinance was unlawful because it restricted speech based on the content of the words, instead of the context in which they were expressed. (The law banned offensive speech related to someone's race, gender and religion.)

In the context of the Charlottesville demonstration, most experts I spoke to agreed that slurs such as the n-word and "faggot" would probably clear the first two hurdles: They are serious personal insults and they were directed at a specific person or group of people. What is unclear is whether their words were likely to spark imminent violence.

Considering that the black woman was across the street from demonstrators, and that counterprotesters were separated by barricades, lawyers could argue that it's unlikely their words would trigger immediate violence.

David Hudson, a First Amendment expert and law professor at Vanderbilt University, said the context of a political rally adds another layer of complexity. "Most fighting-words cases involve one-on-one, face-to-face insults," Hudson wrote in an email. Demonstrators might say that their slurs weren't directed at anyone in particular.

What the Lower Courts Think

While the Supreme Court tends to side with free speech arguments in such cases, lower courts have upheld many rulings that certain language is unprotected under the First Amendment. And some of those rulings involved similar racist slurs.

Here are some examples Hudson points to when state courts have found certain language not protected under the fighting words doctrine:

In 1999, a Minnesota appeals court found that a black man who called a police officer a white racist "motherfucker" and wished his mother would die was not protected by the First Amendment.

In 2001, a Minnesota appeals court upheld a ruling in *State v. Hubbard* that a man who repeatedly flashed lewd hand signals to a young female driver was not expressing protected speech. That same year, an appeals court in Arizona found that it was not free speech when a white man called two black women the n-word and threw an empty can of Mountain Dew at them on the street.

In 2003, a Wisconsin appeals court ruled that calling a nude woman on the beach a "whore," "harlot," and "Jezebel" were fighting words.

In 2010, a North Dakota court upheld a ruling against a white teen who called a black girl the n-word at a teen dance and then again at a restaurant. The defendant's attorney argued that saying the n-word is not a crime. The court said that while the First Amendment does protect the use of the slur, "an objectively reasonable person would find the totality of [the defendant's] statements constituted explicit and implicit threats that were likely to incite a breach of the peace or violent reaction and alarm the listener."

Kessler and other Unite the Right organizers are now embroiled in their own legal battle. Victims who were injured in the first rally are suing them for conspiracy to commit violence against Jews and people of color. The organizers tried to use the free speech defense, but a federal judge rejected it.

"The First Amendment does not protect violence," Judge Norman Moon wrote in his July ruling, allowing the lawsuit to proceed.

That's probably why Kessler has been so worried about discussing the chance of violence breaking out again at the rally this weekend, telling participants that such talk doesn't help with his legal situation. It might also help to remind his fellow "white rights" activists that they don't have a right to spew every hateful thought that comes to mind when marching through the nation's capital.

> While the Supreme Court tends to side with free speech arguments in such cases, lower courts have upheld many rulings that certain language is unprotected under the First Amendment.

Print Citations

CMS: Campbell, Alexia Fernandez. "The Limits of Free Speech for White Supremacists Marching at the Unite the Right 2, Explained." In *The Reference Shelf:
Hate Crimes,* edited by Sophie Zyla, 71–75. Amenia, NY: Grey House Publishing, 2020.

MLA: Campbell, Alexia Fernandez. "The Limits of Free Speech for White Supremacists Marching at the Unite the Right 2, Explained." *The Reference Shelf: Hate
Crimes,* edited by Sophie Zyla, Grey Housing Publishing, 2020, pp. 71–75.

APA: Campbell, A.F. (2020). The limits of free speech for white supremacists
marching at the Unite to Right 2, explained. In Sophie Zyla (Ed.), *The reference
shelf: Hate crimes* (pp. 71–75). Amenia, NY: Grey Housing Publishing.

Hate Speech and Hate Crime

By the American Library Association
December, 2017

The First Amendment to the United States Constitution protects speech no matter how offensive its content. To be clear, the First Amendment does not protect behavior that crosses the line into targeted harassment or threats, or that creates a pervasively hostile environment. But merely offensive or bigoted speech does not rise to that level, and determining when conduct crosses that line is a legal question that requires examination on a case-by-case basis.

Hate Speech in the Law and the Courts

Speech that demeans on the basis of race, ethnicity, gender, religion, age, disability, or any other similar ground is hateful; but the proudest boast of our free speech jurisprudence is that we protect the freedom to express "the thought that we hate." (Matal v. Tam, 2017)

"Hate speech" doesn't have a legal definition under U.S. law, just as there is no legal definition for rudeness, evil ideas, unpatriotic speech, or any other kind of speech that people might condemn. Generally, however, hate speech is any form of expression through which speakers intend to vilify, humiliate, or incite hatred against a group or a class of persons. (*Free Speech and the Development of Liberal Virtues: An Examination of the Controversies Involving Flag Burning and Hate Speech*, 1998)

In the United States, hate speech enjoys substantial protection under the First Amendment. This is based upon the belief that freedom of speech requires the government to strictly protect robust debate on matters of public concern even when such debate devolves into distasteful, offensive, or hateful speech that causes others to feel grief, anger, or fear. Under current First Amendment jurisprudence, hate speech can only be criminalized when it directly incites imminent criminal activity or consists of specific threats of violence targeted against a person or group.

In 1969, the Supreme Court protected a Ku Klux Klan member's hateful and disparaging speech directed towards African-Americans, holding that such speech could only be limited if it posed an "imminent danger" of inciting violence. The court ruled in *Brandenburg v. Ohio* that a state could only forbid or proscribe advocacy that is "directed to inciting imminent lawless action and is likely to incite or produce such action."

In 1978, the Supreme Court upheld an appellate court decision that allowed a group of neo-Nazis to march on the streets of an Illinois suburb housing a substantial Jewish population that included Holocaust survivors. (*Collin v. Smith, 1978*).

It 1992, the the Supreme Court overturned the conviction of a teenager convicted of burning a cross on the lawn of an African American family's home (*R.A.V. v. City of St. Paul, 1992*).

In 2011, the Supreme Court set aside a civil judgment that punished a church group, the Westboro Baptist Church, for picketing a military funeral with signs displaying messages disparaging the dead officer, LGBTQ persons, and the U.S. government (*Snyder v. Phelps, 2011*). Many Americans found the signs hateful and offensive, but the Supreme Court's decision re-confirmed the Supreme Court's historically strong protection of freedom of speech that does not promote imminent violence.

According to the Supreme Court, we "must tolerate insulting, and even outrageous, speech in order to provide adequate 'breathing space' to the freedoms protected by the First Amendment." (*Boos v, Barry, 1988*). Tolerance of hate speech not only protects and upholds everyone's right to express outrageous, unorthodox or unpopular speech; it also allows society and the targets of hate speech to know about and respond to racist or hateful speech and protect against its harms.

Hate Crime

Hate itself is not a crime. For the purposes of collecting statistics, the FBI has defined a hate crime as a "criminal offense against a person or property motivated in whole or in part by an offender's bias against a race, religion, disability, sexual orientation, ethnicity, gender, or gender identity." Hate crimes, which can also encompass color, or national origin, are overt acts that can include violence against persons or property, violation of civil rights, conspiracy, or certain "true threats," or acts of intimidation. The Supreme Court has upheld laws that either criminalize these acts or impose a harsher punishment when it can be proven that the defendant targeted the victim because of the victim's race, ethnicity, identity, or beliefs.

For Libraries

Libraries are sanctuary spaces for First Amendment ideals. There is no "hate speech" exception to the First Amendment.

Symbols of hate are also constitutionally protected if worn or displayed in a public place. Libraries should comply with the ideals and legal requirements of the First Amendment. We make room for offensive, bigoted, and biased speech in the libraries if that speech is simply that: just speech.

Hate speech stops being just speech and becomes conduct when it targets a particular individual and includes behavior that interferes with a patron's ability to use the library.

Directed Action + Hate Speech = Hateful Conduct

All patrons are wel-come and have the right to use the library free of discrimination and loss of individual safety. Hateful conduct is not tolerated in the library and must be ad-dressed as a behavioral issue or a violation of a library's Code of Conduct. We can-not limit speech on the basis of its content alone, but we can address inappropriate or illegal behavior.

> **The First Amendment does not protect behavior that crosses the line into targeted harassment or threats, or that creates a pervasively hostile environment.**

A hate crime, however, is about more than speech or conduct. It is about specific criminal behavior. Examples include:

- Defacement or vandalization of library property in a way that includes lan-guage or symbols that target specific groups. This would include racial epi-thets or swastikas, for instance, as we have seen in Kansas City, Mo. and Evanston, Ill.

- Harassment or assault. Here the behavior is meant to physically injure, or threaten to injure, people because of their membership in a specific group (typically religious, racial, cultural, sexual, or disability). If someone says, "stop stealing our jobs!" that's an unpleasant confrontation, but it's not a hate crime. On the other hand, if someone shouts, "your days are numbered!" that's a threat. If someone touches, strikes, or might reasonably be construed as getting ready to physically intimidate someone else because that person is a member of a diverse group, that is a hate crime

Responding to Hateful Speech and Hate Crime

Reports of hateful speech and hate crimes in libraries is escalating. The Ameri-can Library Association's Office for Intellectual Freedom and Office for Diversity, Literacy and Outreach Services have prepared a white paper, Hateful Conduct in Libraries: Supporting Library Workers and Patrons to provide additional guidance for librarians struggling with issues of hate and intolerance.

ALA Statements and Policies

Equity, Diversity, Inclusion: An Interpretation of the Library Bill of Rights (2017)
Libraries are essential to democracy and self-government, to personal development and social progress, and to every individual's inalienable right to life, liberty, and the pursuit of happiness. To that end, libraries and library workers should embrace equity, diversity, and inclusion in everything that they do.

Libraries Respond: Hate Crimes in Libraries (2017)
ALA's Office for Diversity, Literacy, and Outreach Services (ODLOS) works in close coordination with the Office for Intellectual Freedom (OIF) to respond to incidents that have been reported, as well as units across the Association and its

affiliates as needed. However, if library staff have encountered hate speech that may not be defined as a crime, we acknowledge that the impact can be traumatizing. We encourage you to reach out to ODLOS at diversity@ala.org, or directly contact ODLOS Director Jody Gray.

Libraries Respond: Hate Groups and Violence in Libraries (2017)
This resource focuses on responding to and preventing violence in libraries.

The Universal Right to Free Expression: An Interpretation of the Library Bill of Rights (2014)
There is no good censorship. Any effort to restrict free expression and the free flow of information through any media and regardless of frontiers aids discrimination and oppression. Fighting oppression with censorship is self-defeating.

Diverse Collections: An Interpretation of the Library Bill of Rights (2019)
Collection development should reflect the philosophy inherent in Article I of the Library Bill of Rights: "Books and other library resources should be provided for the interest, information, and enlightenment of all people of the community the library serves. Materials should not be excluded because of the origin, background, or views of those contributing to their creation." A diverse collection should contain content by and about a wide array of people and cultures to authentically reflect a variety of ideas, information, stories, and experiences.

"Under our system of government, people have the right to use symbols to communicate. They patriotically wave the flag or burn it in protest; they may reverently worship the cross or burn it as an expression of bigotry,' said Justice Donald W. Lemons."

Hate crimes can be reported on the OIF Challenge Reporting form.

Resources and Publications

Perspectives on Harmful Speech Online (2017)
Essays published by Berkman Klein Center for Internet and Society
This collection of essays includes perspectives on and approaches to harmful speech online from a wide range of voices that highlights diverse views and strands of thought on the subject.

Defining Hate Speech (2016)
A paper by Andrew Sellars published by Berkman Klein Center for Internet & Society
A longer, in depth discussion that examines the various attempts to define hate speech and explores the tensions between hate speech and principles of freedom of expression.

How Federal Law Draws a Line Between Free Speech and Hate Crimes (2015)
An article published by PBS
Brief, general overview of how federal law establishes a line between protected speech and a hate crime, with links to historic and more recent high-profile cases regarding freedom of speech.

Speech on Campus
Resource by ACLU
Although targeted to universities and student led speech and invited speakers, the positions hold consistent with library programs and collection of materials.

"Bigoted speech is symptomatic of a huge problem in our country. Our schools, colleges, and universities must prepare students to combat this problem. That means being an advocate: speaking out and convincing others. Confronting, hearing, and countering offensive speech is an important skill, and it should be considered a core requirement at any school worth its salt.

When schools shut down speakers who espouse bigoted views, they deprive their students of the opportunity to confront those views themselves. Such incidents do not shut down a single bad idea, nor do they protect students from the harsh realities of an often unjust world. Silencing a bigot accomplishes nothing except turning them into a martyr for the principle of free expression. The better approach, and the one more consistent with our constitutional tradition, is to respond to ideas we hate with the ideals we cherish."

Social Tolerance and Racist Materials in Public Libraries (2010)
By Susan K. Burke published in ALA Reference & User Services Quarterly
RUSQ summarizes three areas of thought to form a framework from which to examine the concept of books with racist content in public libraries. First is an introduction to the concept of intellectual freedom in libraries. This is followed by a brief review of library and information studies (LIS) literature concerning racism in library books. Most of this literature has concerned children's materials, although children's materials are not the focus of this study. Last is a brief introduction to scholarly thought from different disciplines concerning racist speech or hate speech and whether such speech should be controlled.

Assistance and Consultation

The staff of the Office for Intellectual Freedom is available to answer questions or provide assistance to librarians, trustees, educators and the public about hate speech and hate crimes. Areas of assistance include policy development, First Amendment issues, and professional ethics. Inquiries can be directed via email to oif@ala.org or via phone at (312) 280-4226.

Print Citations

CMS: "Hate Speech and Hate Crime." In *The Reference Shelf: Hate Crimes,* edited by Sophie Zyla, 76–81. Amenia, NY: Grey House Publishing, 2020.

MLA: "Hate Speech and Hate Crime." *The Reference Shelf: Hate Crimes,* edited by Sophie Zyla, Grey Housing Publishing, 2020, pp. 76–81.

APA: American Library Association. Hate speech and hate crime. (2020). In Sophie Zyla (Ed.), *The reference shelf: Hate crimes* (pp. 76–81). Amenia, NY: Grey Housing Publishing.

The El Paso Shooting Revived the Free Speech Debate. Europe Has Limits

By Melissa Eddy and Aurelien Breeden
The New York Times, August 6, 2019

The massacre of 22 people in El Paso, an attack announced in a hate-filled manifesto about an immigrant "invasion," has revived debate about the limits of free speech, protected by the First Amendment in the United States.

But in Europe, where history has proved that domestic threats can be as devastating to democracy as those from abroad, freedom of speech, while a constitutional right, comes with certain caveats. Restricted in scope and linked to specific threats, these limitations are based on the premise that protecting certain ideals, such as the public good or human dignity, can justify curbing what individuals are allowed to say.

A Constitutional, but Limited, Right

Free speech is constitutionally enshrined in both Germany and France, as it is in the United States. But there is an important difference.

"The big nuance between the First Amendment and the European texts is that the European texts allow for possible limitations" on speech, said Emmanuel Pierrat, a French lawyer who specializes in publishing and free speech issues.

Freedom to express an opinion in "speech, writing and pictures" is guaranteed under Article 5 of the German Constitution, alongside freedom of the press. But the same article warns that this freedom can be limited by "general laws, in provisions for the protection of young persons, and in the right to personal honor."

In France, Article 10 of the Declaration of Human and Civic Rights guarantees that no one can be "disturbed on account of his opinions, even religious ones," as long as they do not trouble public order. Article 11 calls the freedom to communicate thoughts and opinions "one of the most precious rights of man," but adds that the law can determine cases in which that freedom is abused.

Even in the United States, First Amendment protections, while vast, are not without any restriction. Journalists, for instance, must routinely work within the bounds of libel and defamation laws and, as the famous example goes, people are not necessarily free to falsely yell "fire" in a crowded theater.

Historical Necessity

The restrictions in France and Germany are partly linked to traumatic experiences suffered by both countries in the bloody wars of the 20th century. Other historical trends, and more recent threats, especially violent Islamic extremism and the expansion of the internet and social media, have also shaped legislation.

"Incitement to hatred" is a crime in Germany that refers to any form of violence or defamation against parts of the population, including assaults on human dignity. The law is often used to punish acts that in the United States would be protected by the First Amendment, such as denial of the Holocaust or promoting far-right ideology. In recent years, the law has been used against people posting hateful comments about Jews or foreigners over social media.

German law also prohibits the public display of symbols from banned organizations, such as the Nazi swastika or the stiff-armed Hitler salute. These laws date back to the founding of the country's democracy after World War II. Recent disputes have raised the issue of whether they can be displayed, even when crossed out.

In France, the act of publicly denying the Holocaust is also an offense, as is the act of publicly denying other crimes against humanity. French laws punish defamation or provocation to hatred or violence on the basis of race, religion and other factors.

"Disseminating" messages that are "violent" or that could "seriously harm human dignity" and that could be seen by a minor is also an offense. The far-right leader Marine Le Pen is being prosecuted on that charge, after she posted pictures of Islamic State violence on Twitter.

Terrorist attacks over the past decade have also shaped attitudes toward free speech in France and elsewhere in Europe, with some recent laws punishing the incitement to terrorism, or even the public justification of terrorism.

The manifesto published shortly before the El Paso shooting—which praises a gunman who killed 51 people at two mosques in New Zealand—would in France probably be considered defamatory on the basis of race, an incitement to racial hatred and violence, and an incitement to and justification of terrorism. In Germany, it would likely be seen as incitement and therefore be against the law.

More broadly, France's laws can be restrictive of free speech in cases of defamation, libel, slander and privacy. That is in part because of the historical context of the French Revolution, according to Mr. Pierrat.

"We were coming out of the absolute monarchy, so there needed to be a liberation of speech," he said, a concern shared both in 18th-century France and America. But the proliferation in France of anonymous incendiary

> In Europe, where history has proved that domestic threats can be as devastating to democracy as those from abroad, freedom of speech, while a constitutional right, comes with certain caveats.

pamphlets made the French much more wary of unfettered free speech than the framers of the American Constitution, Mr. Pierrat said.

In Norway, where a gunman killed 77 people in a 2011 attack that he defended in a 1,500-page manifesto against what he viewed as the Muslim takeover of Europe, freedom of expression is also enshrined in the Constitution, but hate speech or incitement to violence is a crime.

In 2015, the government, realizing that hate speech was curbing public discourse, created a strategy for various ministries to combat its rise.

Reining in Social Media

European nations, and the European Union more broadly, have been more willing to regulate what is said over social media and other internet platforms that are mostly the creation and domain of powerful American tech companies.

Worried that social media platforms were becoming a breeding ground for hate speech, Germany passed a law in 2017 that required companies operating social media platforms to remove illegal, racist or slanderous comments or posts within 24 hours of their appearance online. Violators faced fines of up to $57 million.

Heiko Maas, Germany's justice minister at the time the law was drafted, described it as "not a limitation, but a prerequisite for freedom of expression," by ensuring that "everyone can express their opinion freely, without being insulted or threatened."

In a broad policy speech earlier this year, the head of Germany's domestic intelligence agency, Thomas Haldenwang, called for increased patrolling of digital communication, including social media. German law permits officials to search through data in the digital sphere in the face of certain threats, including domestic terrorism.

Partly inspired by Germany's social media hate speech law, France's Parliament recently started debating a similar bill.

"There is no reason that comments that would not be tolerated on a bus, in a cafe or in school—basically, in 'real life'—should be tolerated on a website or network," Laetitia Avia, a member of France's lower house of Parliament who is sponsoring the bill, said in June.

Boundaries Are Not Always Clear

Freedom of artistic expression is also a constitutional right, one that has been used repeatedly to test the limits of how far an individual can go. Most recently, satire has proved a stage for a debate around the boundaries of what is acceptable and what is hurtful.

In Germany, a poem laced with profanity making fun of President Recep Tayyip Erdogan of Turkey landed the comic Jan Böhmerman in a courtroom and provoked a diplomatic dispute between Berlin and Ankara. Although Mr. Böhmerman was prevented from repeating certain lines of his poem, prosecutors dropped charges against the satirist of insulting a foreign leader, on the grounds that hyperbole was allowed in the name of art.

In France, while limits on hateful speech are broadly favored, there is also robust support for open public debate and biting satire, as shown by public outpouring of support for free expression after the attacks on the satirical weekly newspaper Charlie Hebdo in 2015.

But that balance is sometimes hard to find. The French comedian Dieudonné M'bala M'bala, for instance, has repeatedly run afoul of France's anti-hate speech laws, but his case has also set off debates over whether some of the provisions—in some cases, the authorities went as far as to pre-emptively ban his shows—were counterproductive and overreaching.

In France, Mr. Pierrat said, "Freedom of expression stops where it starts to encroach upon the freedom of others."

Perhaps aware of the cultural and legal differences that exist between France and the Anglo-Saxon world regarding free speech, the French government published in 2015 an English-language guide called "Everything you need to know about freedom of expression in France."

Freedom of expression, the guide says, is one of France's highest values. "But this freedom has limits," it adds. "Racism, anti-Semitism, racial hatred and justification of terrorism are not opinions. They are offenses."

Print Citations

CMS: Eddy, Melissa, and Aurelien Breeden. "The El Paso Shooting Revived the Free Speech Debate: Europe Has Limits." In *The Reference Shelf: Hate Crimes*, edited by Sophie Zyla, 82–85. Amenia, NY: Grey House Publishing, 2020.

MLA: Eddy, Melissa, and Aurelien Breeden. "The El Paso Shooting Revived the Free Speech Debate: Europe Has Limits." *The Reference Shelf: Hate Crimes*, edited by Sophie Zyla, Grey Housing Publishing, 2020, pp. 82–85.

APA: Eddy, M., & Breeden, A. (2020). The El Paso shooting revived the free speech debate: Europe has limits. In Sophie Zyla (Ed.), *The reference shelf: Hate crimes* (pp. 82–85). Amenia, NY: Grey Housing Publishing.

Portland Considers Antimask Law
Aimed at Antifa Violence

By Zusha Elinson
The Wall Street Journal, July 18, 2019

City leaders in Portland, Ore., are considering making it illegal for protesters to wear masks in an attempt to address violent clashes between left-wing and right-wing activists, the latest of which occurred a few weeks ago.

Police Chief Danielle Outlaw first called for an antimask law after dueling protests on June 29, where a conservative writer said he was assaulted by members of the left-wing group Antifa, who frequently wear masks. Demonstrators from Antifa, short for antifascist, were among those countering a march by the Proud Boys, which calls itself a "Western Chauvinist Group" and is designated as a hate group by the Southern Poverty Law Center.

"A lot of people are emboldened because they know they can't be identified," Ms. Outlaw said at a news conference.

A spokeswoman for Portland Mayor Ted Wheeler said city officials have had initial discussions about outlawing the wearing of a mask to commit a crime or escape identification in the commission of a crime. Mr. Wheeler "wants to weigh his options thoroughly and hear concerns from community leaders before making a decision," said Eileen Park, the spokeswoman.

The idea received a swift rebuke from the American Civil Liberties Union of Oregon.

"A policy that prohibits wearing a mask to a protest not only risks chilling First Amendment-protected activities, particularly for those who wear 'masks' for political and religious reasons, it misses the issue entirely," spokeswoman Sarah Armstrong said in an email. "Behavior is the issue, not the mask."

About 15 states and some counties and cities have some sort of antimask legislation. Many date to the middle of the last century when states and cities sought to target the Ku Klux Klan, but in recent years the laws have been passed amid activism by left-wing groups. Last year, police in Georgia invoked an antimask law passed in the 1950s to arrest antiracism protesters. North Dakota passed an antimask law in 2017 in response to protests over an oil pipeline. A federal version called the "Unmasking Antifa Act" was introduced in Congress last year but failed to make it out of committee.

While violent conflicts between White supremacists and left-wing groups like Antifa have been rare in the U.S. since a large and deadly clash in 2017 in

> **About 15 states and some counties have some sort of antimask legislation.**

Charlottesville, Va., the two sides have remained active in Portland. The Pacific Northwest has long been home to a volatile combination of white supremacist and militia groups on the right and militant antiracist groups like Antifa on the left, experts say.

The election of Donald Trump, viewed as an ally by some white supremacists, has only fueled both sides, said Joseph Lowndes, an associate professor of political science at the University of Oregon who has studied race and social movements.

A member of an Antifa chapter in Portland said his group's goal is to disrupt fascist and white supremacist organizing, which has grown since Mr. Trump's 2016 election as president. He said an antimask law would unfairly target Antifa.

Joey Gibson, who heads the far-right Patriot Prayer Group, cheered the talk of an antimask law. He began holding rallies in Portland and other cities in 2016 because he felt that police weren't protecting Trump supporters from counterprotesters.

"The second the mask come off, they even act polite," said Mr. Gibson. "If Ted Wheeler is tired of the national attention, all they have to do is enforce a no-mask law."

Howard Jordan, a retired police chief from Oakland, Calif., where political demonstrations are frequent, said that the first goal for law enforcement should be to keep warring groups separated. Because that isn't always possible, however, he said an antimask law could be useful. "It's a good tool for officers," he said.

Mr. Jordan said that Oakland police rarely enforced that city's antimask ordinance, which was adopted in 1922 in response to KKK activity. However, he said it could be more useful in Portland if it is implemented to address a current problem.

Print Citations

CMS: Elinson, Zusha. "Portland Considers Antimask Law Aimed at Antifa Violence." In *The Reference Shelf: Hate Crimes,* edited by Sophie Zyla, 86–87. Amenia, NY: Grey House Publishing, 2020.

MLA: Elinson, Zusha. "Portland Considers Antimask Law Aimed at Antifa Violence." *The Reference Shelf: Hate Crimes,* edited by Sophie Zyla, Grey Housing Publishing, 2020, pp. 86–87.

APA: Elinson, Z. (2020). Portland considers antimask law aimed at Antifa violence. In Sophie Zyla (Ed.), *The reference shelf: Hate crimes* (pp. 86–87). Amenia, NY: Grey Housing Publishing.

Free Speech Can Be Messy, but We Need It

By Lee Rowland
American Civil Liberties Union, March 9, 2018

The year 2017 was a hell of a year for the First Amendment. Nowhere was more central to this culture war than the campuses of universities across America—including right here at the University of Nevada, Reno.

Two students found themselves embroiled in the biggest free speech controversies of recent years. Peter Cytanovic became the face of white nationalism when a picture of him snarling, holding a tiki torch at the Unite the Right Rally in Charlottesville went viral. On the opposite end of the political spectrum, graduate Colin Kaepernick went on to the NFL and used his position to highlight police brutality and racial injustice by taking a knee during the national anthem. Both men became incredibly controversial for their speech. There were calls and campaigns for them to be expelled for their opinions.

But regardless of whether you agree with one of them, both of them, or neither, the First Amendment protects both of those men and their opinions from censorship and retaliation by the government.

That's a good thing. Let me tell you why.

It's becoming more common to call for lower legal protections for speech—specifically, that we should criminalize "hate speech." I hear this from the left a lot. I think many on the left would love a world where Mr. Kaepernick could take a knee without any worry the government would force the NFL to fire him, but where a government school would still have the power to expel Mr. Cytanovic. This is a dangerous proposition.

I'm a progressive. It's not hard for me to choose between white nationalism and racial justice. The first is abhorrent and racist. The other is a demand for equal rights. But what if we gave the government the power to decide which of those men was too hateful to speak? Look at our current president—he called Charlottesville marchers "very fine people," while reserving his ire for Black NFL players, whom he called "sons of bitches." Your idea of "hate speech" may not be the government's idea of "hate speech." I know mine isn't. But even if you agree with Trump—are you sure our next president will agree with your worldview? You shouldn't be.

That's why I'm a true believer in the First Amendment. I am an anti-authoritarian. And I know that the government has historically wielded its raw power to silence those who speak truth to power. And because I want students everywhere to be able to take a knee without fear of government censorship, I know we have to cherish our robust First Amendment—even for speech that is hateful.

But even though I'm a free speech attorney, I find many of the common tropes and myths about free speech unsatisfying. I'm going to explain why I'm a true believer by debunking three of these common myths, and, in the process, hopefully reveal three practical tips for exercising your free speech rights powerfully and strategically.

Let's start with one myth we all learned in kindergarten:

Sticks and Stones May Break my Bones, But Words Will Never Hurt Me

Does anyone as an adult actually believe this? It's manifestly untrue. I'm a free speech attorney precisely because I believe that words matter. We cannot protect free speech by denying its power.

So why on earth do we teach this obvious lie to kids? Because humans can be vicious. And when kids are at the receiving end of taunts, we want them empowered, not diminished, in the face of that injustice.

In February, notorious troll Milo Yiannopoulos had a planned speech at the University of California, Berkeley. Students and others in the community went nuts. There were protests. There were riots. Things were set on fire. The administration canceled his talk.

In April, there was a repeat—except this time it was Ann Coulter. She was going to speak, school officials said there would be riots, and they canceled her talk. Both of these individuals then spent 2017 identifying as victims of liberal censorship. And my god the media ate it up—they got more attention for being silenced than they did for trying to peddle actual substantive views.

A goal of professional provocateurs is to provoke the campus community into trying to silence them. Think of campus trolls as schoolyard bullies. Oh, their words definitely hurt. But the real question is: How do we respond to that hurt? A troll wants you to censor them. It feeds into their power and gives them something to sell. You don't have to play that role.

Yes, there is power in hateful words. But there is also power in sass—in unwillingness to be goaded into a fight or to play the role of censor.

But not all words wound in the same way. That brings us to our second myth:

Hate Speech Isn't Protected by the First Amendment

I often hear younger people say that hate speech isn't protected by the First Amendment. But that's untrue. As President Trump's views of Mr. Kaepernick should make plain, "hate speech" is a flexible concept. Just this week, the Spanish government arrested and charged a man with "hate speech" for calling cops "slackers" on Facebook. That's what criticizing the government looks like without a First Amendment. "Hate speech" can easily be redefined as speech that threatens the state.

But we shouldn't only protect speech out of paranoia—there's an upshot here, too. Our history shows the same First Amendment that protects hateful, racist speech can be and has been used by civil rights advocates to protect historically vulnerable communities.

Charles Brandenburg was an avowed racist convicted of "incitement to violence" for holding an Ohio Ku Klux Klan rally in the late 1960s. The KKK's lawyers took it all the way up to the Supreme Court, arguing his hateful ideas were protected by the First Amendment. The Supreme Court agreed with Brandenburg that his vicious, genocidal talk about Jews and Black people was constitutionally protected because it only fantasized about future violence. The court decided that before the government can punish speech, there has to be an immediate and specific risk of actual violence to a real person.

In a vacuum, that result might upset you. But at around the same time, NAACP leader and civil rights icon Charles Evers gave a passionate speech advocating a boycott of racist, white-owned businesses. He promised that he'd "break the damn neck" of any activist who broke the boycott. White business owners sued Evers and the NAACP for—you guessed it—"incitement," arguing that his violent language had led to riots. But the NAACP looked to that Brandenberg case. Those civil rights leaders appealed all the way to the Supreme Court, to be sure that Mr. Evers benefitted from the same rights as a KKK member. And they succeeded.

The court boiled it down to this question: Are we talking about theoretical future violence, or is there an immediate risk of harm to a real person? And while there is nothing equivalent about the KKK and the NAACP, from that point of view, these cases looked the same.

There is reason to be skeptical that the rights extended to a KKK member will actually trickle down to someone like an NAACP leader. The hard truth is that every right in our society first gets distributed to the privileged and powerful. Americans did not get the right to vote at the same time regardless of sex or race. Today, your rights during an arrest—or your right to carry a gun—do not look the same for all races.

But would you say the answer to that uneven distribution of rights is to eliminate the very constitutional protections that enable us to fight the government when it violates them? No. Distributing our constitutional rights equally is a process. The First Amendment is no different.

It's our job to ensure that everyone benefits from the same level of constitutional protection, that our free speech rights are truly "indivisible." Our First Amendment is necessary to ensure that those who challenge the government are not silenced—but that's not sufficient to ensure justice. We have to do the rest of the work.

So, are today's students up for it? That brings us to our third and final myth:

Students Today Are Snowflakes

Public schools and universities are governed by the First Amendment. That means they can't just keep hateful people off campus because of their views. That means Black and Jewish students have had to face white supremacists on campus; immigrant students have been demonized; women have had to endure campus speakers calling feminism a cancer. I guarantee you that most adults don't have to pass by a group of people calling for their extermination on their walk into work. I don't think students are snowflakes. I think you're badasses.

> **If you want to keep having conversations that can change the world, you should embrace the First Amendment too—messiness and all.**

When I tell you trying to silence or censor political enemies is wrong, it's not because I think it's weak. It's because I think it's unstrategic and strengthens the force of your opponents. But if silencing hateful speech isn't an option, what does it look like to be empowered in the face of hate?

Sometimes the answer will be in your numbers. In August 2017, a group of alt-right protesters planned a gathering at Boston Common, labelling it the "Free Speech Rally." Only dozens of the permit holders showed up. But ringing the Common were 40,000 people standing strong against racism. That huge counter-protest sent a powerful message of resistance: a blizzard of snowflakes. And it made clear the foolishness of one group trying to own the brand of "free speech."

Sometimes all it takes is a single person to make a powerful statement. A few years ago, a musician, appalled by a KKK rally in his hometown of Charleston, didn't bother to try to refute the racist ideas—he just followed them around with a sousaphone, loudly oompah-oompahing along. His message of protest was clear—without a single word. The marchers disbanded in short order when forced to peddle their message of hate over a goofy tuba line.

I believe in the First Amendment because it is our most powerful tool to keep the government from regulating the conversations that spark change in the world. If you want to keep having conversations that can change the world, you should embrace the First Amendment too—messiness and all.

I hope unpacking these myths has helped reveal some truths about how we can strategically exercise our powerful First Amendment rights:

Know your history. Know that the same high-water mark that has protected the most vile and hateful speakers has also protected civil rights and anti-war advocates.

Don't silence your way out of a debate. Remember that a provocateur wants you to play censor. If you know that a speaker you disagree with—or one you believe is dangerous—is coming to your campus, remember how counterproductive silencing tactics can be.

Dance to your own tune. You can decide when to counter-protest, when to stage an alternative event, and when to ignore ideas unworthy of debate. The very choices you make for confronting—or ignoring—speech you abhor can become benchmarks for how you handle conflict throughout your life.

Print Citations

CMS: Rowland, Lee. "Free Speech Can Be Messy, but We Need It." In *The Reference Shelf: Hate Crimes,* edited by Sophie Zyla, 88–92. Amenia, NY: Grey House Publishing, 2020.

MLA: Rowland, Lee. "Free Speech Can Be Messy, but We Need It." *The Reference Shelf: Hate Crimes,* edited by Sophie Zyla, Grey Housing Publishing, 2020, pp. 88–92.

APA: Rowland, L. (2020). Free speech can be messy, but we need it. In Sophie Zyla (Ed.), *The reference shelf: Hate crimes* (pp. 88–92). Amenia, NY: Grey Housing Publishing.

Should We Treat Domestic Terrorists the Way We Treat ISIS?: What Works—and What Doesn't

By Daniel Byman
Foreign Affairs, October 3, 2017

The mass shooting in Las Vegas on Sunday night has again raised fears about terrorism. There's much we don't yet know. The Islamic State (ISIS) has claimed the attack, but the FBI claims that there is no international terrorism link. The attacker, Stephen Paddock, was 64 years old and white, fitting a stereotype of a right-wing terrorist more than a jihadist one. And he may just be a crazy nut. But regardless of Paddock's particular pathology, the situation highlights how the United States treats similar forms of violence differently depending on the nature of the perpetrator.

Almost two months before, on August 12, 2017, James Alex Fields Jr. drove his car into a crowd of peaceful demonstrators in Charlottesville, killing Heather Heyer, one of the demonstrators. Heyer's death came after a day of demonstrations in which armed neo-Nazis and Klansmen, including Fields, who bore the symbols of Vanguard America (a white supremacist, neo-Nazi organization), marched ostensibly to protest the removal of a statue of Confederate Civil War hero Robert E. Lee but really to trumpet their hateful ideas.

Fields' act was treated as the crime it was: he was charged with second-degree murder and hit-and-run, along with several crimes related to the injuries of other victims. Yet given the political nature of the violence, and given the power of terrorism as a label, many have called for treating Heyer's death as terrorism. Indeed, Fields' use of a car to drive through a crowd resembles nothing more than the vehicle attacks that we've seen in Barcelona, Berlin, London, Nice, and other cities in the past two years. In turn, U.S. Attorney General Jeff Sessions labeled Field's attack "domestic terrorism," which federal law defines as trying to intimidate a civilian population or affect government policy through violence in an area of U.S. territorial jurisdiction.

Fields' attack is not the first time right-wing violence has raised questions about the terrorism label. After the 2015 attacks on a Planned Parenthood Clinic and a black church in Charleston, demands to treat right-wing violence as terrorism were loud. A December 2015 YouGov poll found that 52 percent of Americans thought the Planned Parenthood attack was terrorism, and civil rights activists widely criticized the fact that few media outlets were calling Dylann Roof, the perpetrator of the Charleston massacre, a terrorist.

Words matter, but deeds matter more. It is all well and good to label left- and right-wing violence at home as terrorism, but what if the U.S. government went beyond rhetoric and truly treated these groups as it treats Americans suspected of being involved with jihadist organizations like ISIS?

The differences would be profound. Not only would the resources that law enforcement devotes to non-jihadist groups soar, but so too would the means of countering those groups. The legal toolkit would grow dramatically. Perhaps as important would be the indirect effects: banks, Internet companies, and other organizations vital to any group's success would shy away from anything smacking of domestic terrorism. Nonviolent groups that share some of the radicals' agenda would also face pressure, and many would feel compelled to change, often in ways that go against U.S. ideals of free speech and free assembly.

Taken to its logical conclusion, this thought experiment makes clear that treating domestic extremism just like foreign terrorism would be a mistake, but moving a bit in that direction would be desirable. Federal law enforcement in the United States should have the legal authority to take on more responsibility for addressing domestic terrorism. However, given the power of many terrorism-related laws and the political connotations, the terrorism label should be used sparingly, and the new authorities should be tightly defined and monitored.

Independent of greater federal legal authority, the resources allocated to countering domestic terrorism in general and right-wing violence in particular should increase given the danger these groups pose. Counterterrorism and law enforcement officials should also focus on the violent elements within radical groups, using the law to move them away from the line that separates legitimate (if deplorable) protest and violence. In addition, officials should use the law more aggressively to stop potentially violent situations, such as when armed protestors show up at a legitimate march. Finally, legitimate mainstream groups that share part of the radicals' agenda have a responsibility to report suspects and otherwise police their ranks—just as the United States expects other communities, like American Muslims, to do.

What Does It Mean to Be a Terrorist?

Although many definitions of terrorism exist, the most prominent make little differentiation between violent individuals like Fields and jihadists who pledge their allegiance to ISIS. However, both the political baggage that comes with the terrorism label and American public perceptions make it far easier to use the t-word when discussing foreign groups than when describing domestic ones.

Bruce Hoffman, one of the world's foremost experts on terrorism, defines terrorism as organized political violence (or the threat of it) by a substate group with a goal of having a broader psychological impact. U.S. government definitions follow a similar logic. The State Department contends that terrorism is "the unlawful use of force and violence against persons or property to intimidate or coerce a government, the civilian population, or any segment thereof, in furtherance of political or social objectives." Whether aiming to kill non-Muslims or non-whites is not relevant—it is the nature of the act, not the particular agenda behind it, that matters.

With images of 9/11 dominating the thinking on terrorism, some might dismiss white supremacist and like-minded violence as a lesser threat unworthy of the terrorism label, but in post-9/11 United States, non-jihadist terrorists are as dangerous as jihadists. Although the right-wing category encompasses many disparate groups—including white nationalists, neo-Nazis, neo-Confederates, Sovereign Citizens, anti-abortion zealots, anti-Muslim and anti-immigrant groups, Christian Identity believers, and related fanatics—they collectively form a serious threat to Americans. Treating domestic extremism just like foreign terrorism would be a mistake, but moving a bit in that direction would be desirable.

Since 9/11, right-wing groups killed 68 people compared to 95 for jihadist groups; the jihadist figure would be more than halved (and lower than right-wing murders) if the 2015 shooting of 49 people at a gay night club in Orlando were excluded. The year 2016 was the bloodiest year for domestic extremists since 1995, when the right-wing radical Timothy McVeigh killed 168 people when he bombed a federal building in Oklahoma City. Since the election as president of Donald Trump, right-wing violence has soared. In the 34 days following the vote, the Southern Poverty Law Center documented 1,094 bias related incidents, and 37 percent of incidents involved Trump or his campaign slogans. (If the Las Vegas attack is determined to be done by a terrorist group that will have a big impact on the overall numbers.)

What about the political impact of domestic terrorism? We often evoke the days after September 11 as a time of national unity in the face of horror. But left- and especially right-wing violence is driving us apart. On the left, the killing is minimal, but images of Antifa and other violence is used to bolster the perception that Trump's opponents are extreme and committed to stopping legitimate speech and protest. The impact is far greater on the right because of the scope and scale of the violence. Right-wing violence is usually in the name of a cause—racism, anti-abortion, gun rights, opposition to migrants, and so on—that at least some Americans support, even if the more mainstream groups vehemently reject violence. Over 15 percent of Americans believe that abortion should be illegal in all cases, for example. But very few have ever taken up arms in support of that cause. In 2016 polls, meanwhile, most white people believed that anti-white bias was a bigger problem than anti-black bias, despite outcomes for white Americans exceeding those of black Americans on almost every metric. Violent white supremacists thus poke at bigger political wounds than do jihadists, with many Americans sympathizing for the cause but rejecting the killing.

That problem is compounded by the fact that Americans are much more comfortable calling some types of political violence "terrorism" than others because the terrorism label carries normative weight. It suggests that both the person's actions and cause is beyond the pale. The definitions and laws above are all about actions, not the ideology behind it, but most non-experts lump the two together. As terrorism analyst Brian Jenkins observed many years ago, "terrorism is what the bad guys do."

There are also the legal complications to contend with. Although the United States does have a federal definition of domestic terrorism, domestic terrorism is not an independent federal crime. The U.S. State Department maintains a list of

"Foreign Terrorist Organizations," and this list is necessary so law enforcement, businesses, and ordinary citizens can know which groups are illicit even if they agree with the cause as a whole. To treat domestic terrorism like international terrorism, the United States would need a separate "Domestic Terrorist Organization" list, presumably compiled by the Department of Homeland Security and the Federal Bureau of Investigation with input from other agencies. Who is on that list would be tricky, though, as many "radical" activities such as encouraging hateful beliefs are protected free speech. Also, the government would have to disentangle the domestic and foreign lists if there are groups at home that have no real foreign links but are fanboys of foreign groups such as ISIS. Making this more complex, some states do have domestic terrorism laws. Alabama, Arizona, and New York have prosecuted ISIS cases as state terror cases because the feds either didn't want to or didn't have enough evidence.

Even if the United States developed a federal statute, there is no immediate legal reason to use a terrorism charge unless other legal means do not offer sufficient prosecutorial power, resources, or other advantages. In general, the U.S. system gives the states, not the federal government, responsibility for punishing violent crimes. There is no general federal murder statute, for example. To qualify as federal, the issue must be a national one, requiring cross-state authority and federal resources. For example, when a U.S. citizen abroad might be a victim of terrorism, the FBI investigates.

In addition, several laws enable the federal government to play a role in terrorism-like cases without calling it terrorism. The Fair Access to Clinic Entrances Act, for example, gives the FBI some responsibility for securing abortion clinics, enabling them to investigate potential threats. Federal hate crime statutes can be invoked against violent white supremacists. These laws can be as tough as anything we'd see if terrorism were made a crime, with some carrying the federal death penalty. Dylann Roof, who murdered nine black churchgoers in Charleston, South Carolina in 2015 was convicted of 33 federal charges, including hate crimes, but not terrorism. Nevertheless, he is on death row.

New Rules

What if the United States changed the rules anyway? Treating domestic groups the way we do American individuals tied to designated foreign groups would make a profound difference. Consider, notionally, an individual suspected of ties to ISIS and one suspected of ties to the National Socialist Movement, the organization of American Nazis, (or, if it suits your predilections, say Antifa). In addition to action against ISIS abroad, the response to the ISIS suspect at home would be characterized by a mix of the following:

First, there would be early action and monitoring. The government would move quickly to address the terrorism threat. Depending on the opinion of the Department of Justice and FBI, a confidential informant might be used to befriend the suspect and gather evidence. A gentler approach might be a knock on the door by local law enforcement, working closely with federal officials, to assess the situation or possibly an attempt to work with relatives and community leaders to move the individual away from violence.

Second, there would be far more resources. The anti-ISIS counterterrorism budget is robust. Much of the funding goes to intelligence, including electronic surveillance, human sources, and other means. As of 2016, the United States had spent $6.2 billion in the fight against ISIS, and the Trump administration's budget proposal requested another $2 billion flexible fund for fighting the group.

There is no neo-Nazi or Klan proto-state comparable to what ISIS has carved out in Iraq and Syria, and thus no need for expensive air and ground operations or satellite intelligence on suspected facilities. However, the numbers above are roughly the same as the FBI's entire budget, which includes cyber defense, white collar crime, and other concerns. Of the small slice of the FBI budget that goes to counterterrorism, a tiny portion specifically goes to activities focused on right-wing extremist organizations. Indeed, domestic terrorism gets normalized into the FBI's, DHS', and the Department of Justice's regular budgets in part because many of the tools used to address domestic terrorism closely resemble what is done in the name of "ordinary" law enforcement.

Third, there would be no tolerance for violence. When the individual seemed to be acquiring firearms, let alone materials for a bomb, law enforcement officials would swoop in. It is hard to imagine concerns about First Amendment rights leading the government to allow a group of armed protestors to march through a town chanting slogans extolling the virtues of shari'a.

Fourth, treating domestic extremist violence like ISIS-linked terrorism would open up broad use of the power of the law. The statutes about providing material support for terrorism are incredibly powerful, enabling prosecutors to nab suspected terrorists for even limited support, including simply joining a group (and thus giving one's own person to the cause). According to the Center on National Security at Fordham Law, in 2016, 80 percent of ISIS-related prosecutions involved a material support charge. Suspected jihadists are often convicted of lesser charges just to get them off the streets.

For terrorists without a foreign link, the rules are different. Fewer law enforcement resources coupled with a cautious government response out of fear of violating First and Second Amendment rights offers domestic terrorist groups more space to operate, organize, and preach without heavy surveillance or government interference. The United States does not have an existing infrastructure for preemptive disruption, like with the anti-ISIS campaign, and the law is applied more carefully than it is with regard to suspected jihadists. The FBI and other U.S. government organizations do try to preempt right-wing as well as jihadist attacks at home, of course. For ISIS, however, a few tweets may be enough to get the FBI to act; the bar for non-jihadist organizations is much higher. Violent white supremacists poke at bigger political wounds than do jihadists, with many Americans sympathizing for the cause but rejecting the killing.

In short, a change in domestic terrorism policy would result in huge legal and political shifts. If right-wing and the smaller left-wing groups received similar attention as jihadists, the halls of the FBI and DHS would be bursting with new employees. Intelligence penetration of the right-wing community (and any relevant left-wing groups) would soar. This would range from monitoring phones and electronic communications of individuals with possible links to terrorists to planting informers in right-wing radical groups, regular police check-ins with leaders of legitimate right-wing causes to encourage them to provide information on potentially violent members, and trying to "turn" current group members to inform on their comrades. The public social media accounts of potential radicals would also be scrutinized. Affected communities would hate this. Many American Muslims believe that U.S. counterterrorism programs single out Muslims unfairly, and expanding the use of informants and surveillance would increase the numbers under the microscope.

Because of the greater intelligence coverage—and lower regard for the privacy of the affected citizens—the amount of information on right-wing groups and individuals would skyrocket. Using link-analysis software, metadata, and greater information gathering, the government would know not only suspected right-wing terrorists, but also their friends, family members, and other parts of their network. The amount of analysis of groups, causes, and individuals would also grow exponentially. The expansion would seek to uncover heretofore unknown connections and otherwise anticipate and disrupt problems before they manifest.

Informants would play a particularly large role. With suspected jihadists, the FBI often uses undercover agents and informants who claim to be members of a foreign terrorist organization. They engage individuals they feel have radical ideas and then encourage them to take prosecutable actions. A man named Antonio Martinez, for example, posted messages endorsing violent jihad on Facebook. An FBI informant then began to interact with Martinez posing as a jihadist. The agent gave him a fake bomb, which Martinez then tried to set off. Sting operations are used on right-wing groups, but far less frequently. If we treated right-wing radicals as we do jihadists, government officials would scan Facebook for individuals posting messages embracing violence against Jews or African Americans and then providing them with fake bombs in order to prosecute them. Social media sites contain a staggering number of anti-Semitic and racist threats, and the FBI would have its hands full. Given the politicized nature of America today, if an administration focused largely on right or left-wing groups, it would be accused of suppressing opposition, not fighting terrorism

Past experience is useful. In the early 1990s, the FBI conducted the PATCON (Patriot Conspiracy) program. FBI agents posed as members of a fictional right-wing extremist group and collected information on real like-minded groups by attending conventions and other gatherings as well as reporting on private conversations. Analyst J.M. Berger found that the investigation produced little that could be used for criminal prosecution because it did not meet a high evidentiary bar, but it did provoke paranoia in the groups being monitored, with some members being removed as suspected spies. It's hard to feel sorry for these individuals, but the result—that individuals not guilty of any crime found it harder to exercise freedom of assembly and speech—should trouble everyone.

The counterterrorism microscope would also reveal numerous minor but prosecutable offenses not related to terrorism. As investor guru Warren Buffett noted, "If a cop follows you for 500 miles, you're going to get a ticket." Arresting such individuals would send a message that the police were watching. Credit card fraud, drug use, and other minor crimes would serve as justification to arrest and disrupt suspected terrorists and as leverage to convince them to cooperate in other investigations of their associates. Indeed, the government at times does not pursue criminal charges if the offense is deemed minor or resources are needed elsewhere, but this would be far less likely if there was a perceived terrorism link. For example, Virginia allows its residents to openly carry a firearm. However, the law stipulates that a non-Virginian from a state where open carry is illegal cannot carry a firearm—a seemingly obscure technicality. Police, however, did not check to make sure all the marchers in Charlottesville—many of which were from other states—met this criterion. (Part of the reason was that the protesters were better armed than the police.) If the marchers were perceived as having potential ties to designated terrorist groups, then law enforcement would likely take extra precautions to ensure they abide by the law—and to have more firepower at hand. Using such a standard would allow protest, but it would make it harder for at least some participants to do so while armed.

Another change would be that government lawyers would use the material support laws to go after domestic terrorists. Under the material support statue, providing money, weapons, or even a person's time to a designated terrorist group is a felony. Civil rights advocates have criticized the scope and breadth of these laws for years. In 2011, David Cole, now the National Legal Director for the ACLU, argued that the laws even create risk for nongovernmental organizations that might advise designated terrorist groups on how to begin peace negotiations to end conflict.

Causes linked to domestic terrorist groups domestic would have to eliminate any ambiguity in their actions for fear it could result in their arrest or be used against them in court.

For those linked to a group but not convicted of any crime, the consequences could still be dire and should trouble many Americans. In 2011, the FBI declared all Juggalos, the fans of the hip-hop group Insane Clown Posse, which has both violent and nonviolent members, to be a criminal street gang. The designation means that some Juggalos and Juggalettes (female fans) have lost custody battles, jobs, and otherwise suffered as their employers and the courts treated them as gang members. Juggalos staged several protests against the FBI designation and many describe its effects as discrimination.

Beyond changing the groups and those pursuing them, treating right-wing violence as terrorism would affect the broader community that might sympathize with the cause but not the violence. Doing business with a declared terrorist organization would create legal liability and would damage a firm's reputation, which every financial institution would seek to avoid. A U.S. bank, for example, held up money going from a legitimate U.S. charity to provide supplies for hospitals in Syria in order to ensure that the money did not end up the hands of terrorists. One can imagine legitimate charities operating in poor areas with a large Klan or Sovereign Citizen presence facing financial problems because banks fear the money could end up in the wrong hands.

The government would also try to shut down the virtual presence of suspected terrorists. After the killing in Charlottesville, GoDaddy, a website hosting company, refused to allow the American neo-Nazi news and commentary site the Daily Stormer to use its platform even though GoDaddy had hosted the site since 2013. When its webmasters went to Google for hosting, they were also turned down. Facebook banned links to the site on its platform. Rather than drawing on the law to justify their actions, these sites said that the Daily Stormer violated their terms of service because it could incite violence. Government scrutiny would make far more companies willing to purge themselves of anything that could be linked to terrorism and eager to create service terms that enable them to do so. Although these companies already take steps to mitigate extremism—Facebook recently announced an initiative to use more artificial intelligence to screen content for extremist material—they would have to apply those steps to the specific needs of right and left-wing extremism if there was a change to the law. Suspected domestic terrorists would be treated similar to suspected child pornographers: if companies had any doubt, they would shun the group.

Counter-messaging programs—just say no to jihad—would be far more robust, targeting the community in the hopes of reducing support for radicals within it. The Obama administration funded these poorly, and the Trump administration appears even more skeptical. The Department of Homeland Security gives out $10 million each year in Countering Violent Extremism Grants to organizations that work to develop resilience to extremism. Under the Trump administration, the program has focused almost wholly on jihadism. But similar programs to target non-jihadist domestic extremism would logically follow a change to the laws although, of course, it remains politically easier to focus on jihadists, which both the right and left agree are dangerous, than extremists on either end of the U.S. political spectrum.

Nonviolent groups that share part of the radicals' agenda would also be viewed differently. Many Sovereign Citizens share the NRA's pro-gun agenda; eco-terrorists' goals overlap with those of the Sierra Club. Today, such nonviolent political mobilization is not just protected under freedom of speech and freedom of assembly: it is considered vital to democracy, which requires citizens to express their views in the marketplace of ideas and to inform their elected officials. But with a change to the treatment of domestic terrorists, peaceful organizations might become considered "feeders" of the violent organizations. At the very least, they would be suspected of creating a conducive environment to radicalism. Saudi Arabia, for example, funds an array of mosques, textbooks, and extremist preachers for Muslim communities around the world and is often blamed when young men take up arms in the service of these ideas. Domestic nonviolent groups would have an incentive to distance

themselves from violent individuals, with the added
benefit of helping to make
sure that extremists do not
slip through the cracks by
hiding among a more mod-
erate cohort. This would

> **The right-wing threat in particular is comparable to that of jihadist violence at home, and similar resources should be allocated to addressing it.**

have a chilling effect on organizations as many would avoid links to individuals who
might have links to violence, however defined.

Any terrorist seizure of territory, meanwhile, would be viewed as particularly
dangerous. When terrorists control territory, they can create training camps that
indoctrinate new recruits and provide training on bomb-making, document forgery,
assassination, and other dangerous tactics. In addition, controlling territory gives
the group legitimacy and undermines the authority of the state. Even small safe
houses are dangerous. In 2016, Ammon Bundy and several followers seized control
of the headquarters building in the Malheur National Wildlife Refuge in Oregon,
claiming that federal land should be turned over to the states to manage. The result
was a siege that lasted more than a month, with the participants eventually being arrested—and one killed when he resisted. Under the new system, the radicals would
still be given a chance to surrender, and if the police and FBI could arrest them
without risk, they would do so. But the situation would not be allowed to persist
for days, let alone weeks. In addition, if the danger were deemed high, then taking
domestic terrorists out via snipers, drones, or other standoff means would be considered acceptable.

Finally, public perception would change. Using the terrorism label carries normative force and would change how these fringe groups are viewed. It would also
indirectly shape causes seen as linked to a terrorist group. Before 9/11, a handful of
Americans favored a government ruled under Islamic law; after 9/11, the number
of supporters remains a handful, but fear concerning this issue became a major
political issue in some states. In 2017 alone, 13 states have introduced anti-sharia
legislation; Texas and Arkansas passed such laws. This public perception would give
any government crackdowns legitimacy and, at the same time, put pressure on companies, local police departments, and others if they do not act decisively.

Proceed with Caution

This thought exercise shows how profoundly things might change if the terrorism
label were applied more broadly—and that's probably why we should do so cau-
tiously. Many of the current measures to fight domestic terrorists, such as arrests,
work well. In addition, most Americans probably don't want their government to be
treating legitimate political movements with suspicion or making banks or Internet
companies suppress free speech.

U.S. law enforcement, intelligence, and counter-messaging professionals should
apply the law aggressively to prevent and disrupt violent activity while leaving individuals espousing the same ideas to protest in peace. History professor and former

senior government official Philip Zelikow calls for shutting down groups that seek to create private militias—that is, the ones that are not "well-regulated" by the states. The Charlottesville marchers, for example, are more like an organized rival to the state rather than individuals acting on their own because they involve organizations with membership rolls, leaders, and even uniforms responding to a common call. This approach balances public safety concerns and First Amendment protections. This standard also works well for domestic Islamist groups, even if they champion ideas most Americans find objectionable.

If the non-jihadist terrorism problem continues to grow, the United States should also consider having a carefully worded domestic terrorism statute at the federal level along with an associated list of designated organizations. This would enable the federal government to step in more effectively, using its resources and legal power, if a group becomes a greater danger. Many of the measures described above would represent too much of a change, and any legislation should factor in counterterrorism measures we don't want as well as ones we do. Suspicion of authority is at a high point, and even the perception that the government might abuse new powers could worsen this even more. The language should be tightly worded and subject to regular legislative oversight—the definition of a foreign terrorist organization is broad, and any domestic legislation should focus heavily on the threat or use of violence and be regularly reviewed to ensure that changes in group behavior are reflected.

Even without such a legislative change, the government must allocate an appropriate level of funding and manpower to domestic terrorism. The right-wing threat in particular is comparable to that of jihadist violence at home, and similar resources should be allocated to addressing it. The FBI and DHS should create larger offices dedicated to domestic groups and otherwise develop their intelligence presence. Some of the resources used for jihadist violence could be transferred with little loss.

Finally, Americans should recognize the responsibilities of nonviolent organizations that contain radical members or cross paths with them. Just as Muslim-Americans are a vital source of information on suspected ISIS supporters, so too should other mainstream communities and organizations feel compelled to point out the few troublemakers in their midst. Nonviolent pro-life advocacy groups should, for example, monitor comment threads on forums for indicators of violent activity. We want the line between violence and nonviolence to be bright, but this puts some moral onus on legitimate groups to police themselves rather than shrug off violence as the work of a few bad actors.

Print Citations

CMS: Byman, Daniel. "Should We Treat Domestic Terrorists the Way We Treat ISIS?: What Works—and What Doesn't." In *The Reference Shelf: Hate Crimes*, edited by Sophie Zyla, 93–103. Amenia, NY: Grey House Publishing, 2020.

MLA: Byman, Daniel. "Should We Treat Domestic Terrorists the Way We Treat ISIS?: What Works—and What Doesn't." *The Reference Shelf: Hate Crimes*, edited by Sophie Zyla, Grey Housing Publishing, 2020, pp. 93–103.

APA: Byman, D. (2020). Should we treat domestic terrorists the way we treat ISIS?: What works—and what doesn't. In Sophie Zyla (Ed.), *The reference shelf: Hate crimes* (pp. 93–103). Amenia, NY: Grey Housing Publishing.

4
Prevention, Outreach, and Training

Photo by Carol M. Highsmith, Library of Congress Prints and Photographs division.

Wall of Remembrance at the U.S. National Holocaust Museum, Washington, D.C. Several U.S. states have laws requiring Holocaust education to ensure that students are taught the facts about the genocide that occurred in Nazi Germany.

Schools as Safe Places for Learning

The challenges facing our schools today are wide-ranging, from bullying and racism to drugs and gun violence. Fire drills have become lockdown exercises. Cell phones and tablets have introduced the challenges of social media into the school day. Metal detectors, armed guards and arming teachers are topics of discussion. The safety of being in school, at work, and in social and recreational places has been compromised.

Political Influences and Consequences

Discord resulting from Donald Trump's presidency has found its way into schools. A March 2019 survey of 500 high school principals by the Institute for Democracy, Education, and Access found rising political incivility and division. Students are now learning in an "environment marked by fear, distrust, and social isolation" while experiencing anxiety and stress.

Principals voiced several concerns: hostility toward immigrants; derogatory remarks about other racial or ethnic groups; hostile exchanges outside of class; and hateful remarks over political views. Other issues are use of social media to share hateful posts, cyberbullying, and increased access by students to unfiltered and untrustworthy information. Gun violence is reported to be cause of the most stress and area of greatest concern in schools across the nation.[1]

After the 2016 election, incidents at the mostly white, affluent Philadelphia Council Rock High School prompted a letter to parents from the principal addressing homophobic notes, swastikas in restrooms, comments of "If Trump wins, watch out" and "I Love Trump," and a note in a student's backpack telling her to "go back to Mexico." The school, one of many facing similar problems, formed a council to provide diversity training for school staff which, some argued, was not enough to stop racist views from being expressed. *ProPublica* and *Education Week* partnered in a project of the research of three years of media and school reports involving hate and bias incidents. Most of the 472 accounts showed that black, Latino, Jewish, or Muslim individuals were the main targets, but that bodily harm was rare. The day with the most hate reports was the day after Trump's election. Spreading hate messages on social media has become widespread, forcing parents to monitor their children's social media accounts.

Child Trends director Deborah Temkin, who oversaw antibullying efforts during the Obama administration, stated: "There is usually never just one cause of bullying, so if we scapegoat it on the president, we are overlooking the broader climate issues that were there before and will likely continue if not directly addressed." Identifying the causes behind acts of hate would help in establishing multicultural programs offering solutions. The response of adults and discipline of school administrators also affect the behavior of students. Aprile Benner, a professor and researcher of the development of low-income and race/ethnic minority youth at the University of Texas at Austin, notes that evidence shows that peer discrimination affects social and emotional well-being while educator discrimination influences learning. Both parents and teachers feel that increasing diversity in teachers would benefit all races of students.[2]

The Role of Teachers

Christina Torres, an eighth-grade teacher in Honolulu, Hawaii, and an *Education Week* journalist, believes that: "Until we provide focused education about the history and current iterations of racist beliefs at the root of this hatred, we cannot claim we are actively working to solve the problem in our classrooms. . . . Mass shooters were once students sitting in our classrooms. . . . It is essential to understand racism outside our classroom."[3]

Educational Organizations, Hate Issues, and Reporting

Learning First Alliance lists a number of resources addressing hate and harassment in schools. "Our schools reflect our society's strengths, hopes, aspirations and many challenges—challenges that range from the fact that some don't have a home or enough to eat to others who don't know where they fit in or whose anger has become aggression." They also remind us that hate speech is not new. In 1999 the U.S. Department of Education issued a guide to schools on how they could protect students from harassment and hate crimes. In 2001 Learning First Alliance produced a guide on how to make schools safe and supportive.[4]

The Southern Poverty Law Center's 2019 *Hate at School* report shows that of news-reported hate incidents: 63 percent were racial or ethnic, 18 percent were anti-Semitic, 10 percent were anti-LGBTQ, 4 percent were anti-immigrant, 3 percent were anti-Muslim, and 2 percent were other. In comparison, educator-reported incidents showed: 33 percent were racial or ethnic, 25 percent were anti-LGBTQ, 18 percent were anti-immigrant, 11 percent were anti-Semitic, 6 percent were anti-Muslim, and 7 percent were other.

Incidents of hateful actions recently posted to social media include Wisconsin prom students giving a Nazi salute, Idaho teachers dressed as Mexicans carrying a cardboard "border wall" for Halloween, and New York sixth-graders dressed in blackface mimicking apes. These viral images find their way to national news and organizations tracking such incidents, even if they are not included in FBI statistics.

Incidents not directly reported to the FBI are not included in yearly statistics. SPLC reports that while the FBI identified 821 school incidents in 2018, their questionnaire responses from K-12 educators showed 3,265 incidents during the fall season alone. Even though two-thirds of the 2,776 educators in their report witnessed a hate or bias event, fewer than 5 percent were reported in the media and no disciplinary action was taken in 57 percent of cases.[5]

The Hate Crime Victimization 2004-2015 Special Report published in June 2017 by the U.S. Department of Justice shows that between 2011-2015 racial bias accounted for 48 percent of hate crimes, and 54 percent of hate crimes were not reported to the police. Hispanics experienced the highest rate of violent hate crimes. While percentages of these crimes have changed over the years, reasons for not reporting them most likely have not: 23 percent felt law enforcement would not help or would make matters worse; 19 percent felt the incident was not important enough to report.[6]

Educators report that current events or political discussions in classrooms are resulting in heated discussions or conflicts. The *Hate at School* 2018 report lists the following incidents reported by educators:

- In New York, a middle-school student writes in a textbook that he will lynch the black husband of a white teacher;

- In Illinois, white elementary students call black students apes and monkeys;

- In Minnesota, a middle-school student tells a Latino child that his mother should be in jail with all the illegal immigrants;

- In Massachusetts, a 10-year-old Muslim girl gets a note saying, "You're a terrorist. I will kill you";

- In Oklahoma, a fifth-grader draws a swastika and writes "white power" on his hand.[7]

A 2019 Anti-Defamation League article recommends talking to students about gun violence and mass shootings. Incidents resulting in four or more deaths are typically considered a mass shooting. Between 1982 and 2012, 78 mass shootings involving guns occurred and between 2000 and 2013 the FBI identified 160 incidents. The rate of mass shootings has tripled since 2011.[8]

In 2019, the Center for the Study of Hate and Extremism (CSHE) listed recommendations for schools (many would also apply to business): reinvigorate civic education relating to pluralism and the U.S. Constitution; streamline the process for minors to report hate crime incidents; photograph vandalism and preserve evidence; report hate crimes to police and incidents to human relations agencies; and implement tolerance education into curriculum and events.[9]

Works Used

ADL. "Gun Violence and Mass Shootings." Updated Aug 2019. ADL website. https://www.adl.org/education/resources/tools-and-strategies/table-talk/gun-violence-mass-shootings.

Costello, Maureen, and Coshandra Dillard. "Hate at School Report." *Teaching Tolerance.*: https://www.tolerance.org/magazine/publications/hate-at-school-report.

Institute for Democracy, Education, and Access. "Executive Summary—School & Society in the Age of Trump." *UCLA/IDEA Publications.* Mar 2019. https://idea.gseis.ucla.edu/publications/files/executive-summary-school-and-society-in-the-age-of-trump/view.

Learning First Alliance. "Resources Addressing Hate and Harassment in Schools." https://learningfirst.org/page/resources-addressing-hate-and-harassment-in-schools.

Levin, Brian, and Lisa Nakashima. "Report to the Nation 2019: Factbook on Hate & Extremism in the U.S. & Internationally." Center for the Study of Hate and Extremism, California State University, San Bernardino. Jul 2019. https://www.hsdl.org/c/just-released-report-to-the-nation-on-hate-and-extremism/.

Southern Poverty Law Center. "Hate at School: Something Ugly Is Happening in America's Schools. And It's Not Going Away." May 2, 2019. https://www.splcenter.org/20190502/hate-school.

Torres, Christina. "The Urgent Need for Anti-Racist Education." *Education Week Teacher*. Aug 14, 2019. https://www.edweek.org/tm/articles/2019/08/14/the-urgent-need-for-anti-racist-education.html.

U.S. Department of Justice. Office of Justice Programs, Bureau of Justice Statistics. "Special Report: Hate Crime Victimization, 2004-2015." Jun 2017. https://www.bjs.gov/content/pub/pdf/hcv0415.pdf.

Vara-Orta, Francisco. "Swastikas on Bathroom Stalls. Chants of 'Build the Wall.' Notes That Say 'Go Back to Mexico.'" *Education Week*. Aug 6, 2018. https://www.edweek.org/ew/projects/hate-in-schools.html.

Notes

1. Institute for Democracy, Education, and Access, "Executive Summary—School & Society in the Age of Trump."
2. Vara-Orta, "Swastikas on Bathroom Stalls. Chants of 'Build the Wall.' Notes That Say 'Go Back to Mexico.'"
3. Torres, "The Urgent Need for Anti-Racist Education."
4. Learning First Alliance, "Resources Addressing Hate and Harassment in Schools."
5. Southern Poverty Law Center, "Hate at School: Something Ugly is Happening in America's Schools. And It's Not Going Away."
6. U.S. Department of Justice. "Special Report: Hate Crime Victimization, 2004-2015."
7. Costello and Dillard, "Hate at School Report."
8. ADL, "Gun Violence and Mass Shootings."
9. Levin and Nakashima, "Report to the Nation 2019: Factbook on Hate & Extremism in the U.S. & Internationally."

The Urgent Need for Anti-Racist Education

By Christina Torres
Education Week, August 14, 2019

Lately, when I open my phone to read the day's news, I'm reading not just with curiosity, but with fear. Our newsfeeds are filled with horrible stories of mass shootings and hate crimes that make many Americans feel unsafe and out of control.

Many of the recent shootings—including in El Paso, Texas; Pittsburgh; potentially Gilroy, Calif.—are linked to white supremacist hatred. And hate crimes have been on the rise nationwide for three consecutive years, according to FBI data released last year.

This growing hatred seeps into our classrooms. Like many teachers, I read these stories and statistics and wonder: What can I do to help my students feel safe and ensure that the next generation no longer operates from a place of hatred and fear?

These mass shooters were once students sitting in our classrooms. It's an unsettling thought, and I don't raise it to scare teachers about the students they have. Rather, it serves as a reminder that we as teachers have a role to play in combatting hate. More than just making our students aware of racism, we can do anti-racist work.

It's easy to decry the shooters as "crazy." In the wake of the recent shootings, some educators have called for increased support around mental health and social-emotional learning. While this is critical work, research suggests that the majority of mass shootings are not attributable to mental illness. In fact, roughly 65 percent of the more than 350 mass killers counted by Columbia University forensic psychiatrist Michael Stone showed no evidence of a severe mental disorder.

Even the best SEL programs on the market don't address the deeper roots of hatred we're seeing in our nation. Until we provide focused education about the history and current iterations of racist beliefs at the root of this hatred, we cannot claim we are actively working to solve the problem in our classrooms.

As educators, we don't just teach content; we teach life lessons. Here are changes we can make to ensure we are breaking down racist beliefs and systems of white supremacy in our own classrooms:

1. Educate ourselves about anti-racism work. We can't do this work well with students if we don't understand it ourselves. We must acknowledge that we have all been shaped by a system built on inequality and racism—one that consistently bombards us with stereotypical images of certain cultures and excludes voices from different backgrounds.

Understanding racism and its roots, questioning our own privilege and biases, and slowly dismantling those systems and beliefs internally and in our schools is a life-long process. Online communities like #ClearTheAir and #EduColor that host Twitter chats with important discussions and resources can provide insight into how other educators are grappling with these issues (as well as great ideas for bringing that work to the classroom).

Rethinking Schools provides multiple resources and readings about using schools to break down racial biases in our country. Christopher Emdin's *For White Folks Who Teach in the Hood*, bell hooks' *Teaching to Transgress*, and Cornelius Minor's *We Got This* are a few books that address how to create more equitable education in our classrooms, as well as the internal work teachers must begin to do to get there.

It's also essential to understand racism outside our classrooms. Reading books like Robin DiAngelo's *White Fragility* (with an excellent educator guide), *How to Be an Antiracist* by Ibram X. Kendi, and Beverly Tatum's seminal text *Why Are All the Black Kids Sitting Together in the Cafeteria* is another way to take ownership of our own journeys toward becoming aware and active against racism.

2. Reflect on the voices we're sharing. We can build empathy by listening to and studying other people's stories. Unfortunately, there is very little diversity and inclusion in the stories many of us share in our classrooms. We need to reflect on whose voices we give power to and how we create a more inclusive space with the texts we use.

Online organizations like #DisruptTexts and We Need Diverse Books provide resources and materials about the importance of diversifying the texts in our classrooms. Reflecting on whose viewpoints are given power—in all subjects, including math and science—is an essential way to start breaking down biases and harmful perceptions.

3. Don't be afraid to discuss current events—and ask for help, too. Our classrooms cannot cocoon our students from the real world. We can begin talking through not only the recent violence in our country, but broader instances of systemic oppression related to white supremacy, anti-immigration sentiment, racism, and LGBTQ discrimination. Organizations like Teaching Tolerance and Facing History and Ourselves provide resources for discussing current events and their historical roots.

It is a sad truth that some of us may face resistance from our communities for doing this work. This pushback is often rooted in a fear of disrupting the status quo. By sharing plans and ideas with colleagues in our personal learning network who have more experience teaching these issues, we can navigate these pitfalls together. We should communicate with parents and other teachers to help garner support. We can rely on data and resources to explain the importance of this work to skeptics. These conversations are hard and nuanced, and we can help foster growth in each other by reaching out and asking for help.

The work we do in our classrooms may feel like a small drop in the ocean, but we know that what we teach our students can help turn the societal tide. Teaching

> **Research suggests that the majority of mass shootings are not attributable to mental illness.**

anti-racism may not directly stop a mass shooting, but it can support a cultural shift that helps dismantle racist beliefs in ourselves and each other. If we teach our students to work against white supremacy and racism, we can help create a world that no longer nurtures hatred, but actively challenges the hateful beliefs that lead to targeted violence.

Print Citations

CMS: Torres, Christina. "The Urgent Need for Anti-Racist Education." In *The Reference Shelf: Hate Crimes,* edited by Sophie Zyla, 111–113. Amenia, NY: Grey House Publishing, 2020.

MLA: Torres, Christina. "The Urgent Need for Anti-Racist Education." *The Reference Shelf: Hate Crimes,* edited by Sophie Zyla, Grey Housing Publishing, 2020, pp. 111–113.

APA: Torres, C. (2020). The urgent need for anti-racist education. In Sophie Zyla (Ed.), *The reference shelf: Hate crimes* (pp. 111–113). Amenia, NY: Grey Housing Publishing.

Hate Crime in America Policy Summit

International Association of Chiefs of Police, October 17-20, 2020

Collectively, the recommendations constitute an action agenda to advance understanding of hate crime, prevent hate crime, and improve the effectiveness of our response to this complex and challenging social problem. The agenda sets forth roles and responsibilities for a coordinated, community-wide response by citizens, schools and colleges, police, justice system agencies, social service agencies, and victims.

How Can We Prevent Hate Crime?

Investing in prejudice reduction and violence prevention is vital to reducing the incidence of hate crime. Summit participants were hopeful that communities, schools, and justice system agencies can work together to create and maintain conditions in which prejudice gives way to tolerance and bias-motivated violence is replaced with peaceful problem-solving. Summit participants recommended 18 proactive initiatives to help communities prevent bias-motivated incidents and hate crime.

Increase Public Awareness

An informed citizenry is the cornerstone of our democratic society. Citizen involvement is essential to the success of any program to reduce prejudice and prevent bias-related crimes.

Create multidisciplinary planning processes to develop coordinated approaches to prevent and respond to hate crime. Some communities already engage in crime prevention planning processes that include representatives of business, religious institutions, advocacy groups, public and private schools and colleges, and the full spectrum of justice agencies. Every community should maintain or develop a strategic crime prevention planning process that includes a focus on hate crime, and view planning as an ongoing responsibility, not just a one-time project.

Create local Human Rights Commissions or other forums to promote community harmony and stability. All citizens should be encouraged to talk about their differences and commonalities and to share their visions of safe and healthy communities. HRCs or other organized forums can sponsor community events that bring people together to learn about and celebrate one another and provide multicultural training in many facets of community life.

Focus public attention on issues of prejudice, intolerance, and the ways that hate crime affects community vitality and safety. Community

---

Citizen involvement is essential to the success of any program to reduce prejudice and prevent bias-related crimes.

---

and justice system leaders, particularly police chiefs, must continue to speak out forcefully against intolerance, bigotry, and hate crime, not only in the aftermath of high-profile incidents, but at all times. Citizens must recognize that hate crimes, and even bias-motivated behaviors that are not criminal, victimize not only the targeted individuals or groups, but the entire community. Communities become victims when hate crime erodes mutual respect and civility, and undermines the citizens' sense of well-being and safety.

Develop public information to promote values of tolerance and social equality. Justice agencies, private foundations, and community groups should collaborate to develop hard-hitting, culturally relevant endorsements of the value of tolerance and understanding that can be disseminated through print and electronic means to diverse audiences.

Raise awareness of the goals and activities of organized hate groups. Hate groups are less effective in sowing seeds of social unrest and conflict when their activities (including Internet hate sites) are brought to light. Continuous monitoring of hate group activity is vital for contravening their influence on children, youth, and other groups vulnerable to their toxic diatribe. Their messages of bigotry and intolerance can be countered by community leaders, schools, and justice agencies with truthful information that promotes mutual understanding and honors diversity.

Develop national, regional, and/or state task forces to understand and counter the influence of organized hate groups. Because the influence of many organized hate groups is national or regional, strategies to counter their hate-producing efforts must also be national or regional, and be developed by broad-based coalitions of political, business, religious, community, and justice system leaders. Strategies to contain and counteract the negative influences of hate groups, while respecting their First Amendment rights, require creativity, persistence, and constant vigilance. The United States Department of Justice/United States Attorney Hate Crime Task Force Initiative can serve as a model and a vehicle for coordinated efforts.

Educate Children and Young Adults

Teaching our children to respect differences and celebrate diversity is essential to prevent development of prejudiced attitudes that can lead to hate crime. Because conflict is a fact of human life, children must also be given tools to deal with conflict constructively, to become "peacemakers."

Involve parents in efforts to prevent and intervene against bias-motivated behavior of their children. Parents should be engaged in hate crime prevention in a variety of ways, from helping to design and deliver conflict-resolution and hate crime prevention curricula, to participating in mediation and conflict resolution activities in their children's schools. Schools should consider involving parents of children expressing prejudicial beliefs or behaving in discriminatory ways in interventions to prevent the speech or behavior from escalating into more harmful criminal acts.

Foster a "zero-tolerance" atmosphere in schools and colleges. Written codes of conduct for students, teachers, and other employees should express support for peaceful conflict resolution and clearly delineate the consequences for engaging in bias-motivated behavior. Codes of conduct should be readily available to students, parents of students, faculty, and other employees.

Provide every student and teacher the opportunity to participate in hate crime prevention courses and activities. Hate crime prevention curricula can be used in general and alternative classroom settings, schools experiencing bias crime problems, with student government leaders, in after-school programs, and in teacher training. The Education Development Center, with support of the Office of Juvenile Justice and Delinquency Prevention, has prepared a model curriculum for middle and high school students designed to reduce prejudice and prevent crimes based on intolerance. The U.S. Departments of Education and Justice collaborated to produce a manual that provides guidance to schools and communities to develop school-based hate crime prevention programs.

Incorporate hate crime education into existing curricula. Schools and colleges should encourage faculty to incorporate hate crime education into existing curricula in subject areas such as health, geography, social studies, history, and civics. Studies in these and other areas offer many opportunities to promote tolerance and to illustrate the negative individual and societal impacts of prejudice and bigotry.

Reinforce diversity training and multicultural education at early ages. Multicultural education diminishes reliance on stereotyping, and reduces the chances of miscommunication between members of cultural groups. To develop an appreciation of similarities and differences among groups of people, children and young adults should learn about the many cultures that make up American society.

Provide conflict resolution training to all children. Children should be taught skills essential to peaceful conflict resolution, including active listening, appropriate expression of feelings, negotiation, and interruption of expressions of bias. There are model curricula and approaches appropriate for various age levels and contexts, including New York City's Resolving Conflict Creatively Program (RCCP), peer mediation initiatives, the "peaceable school" approach, as well as parent-led and community-based efforts.

Intervene with students who express discriminatory beliefs before their behavior escalates. Standards for recognizing and responding appropriately to discriminatory expressions and behavior should be clearly articulated and widely disseminated to students, teachers, and parents. Faculty and other staff should be trained to identify early warning signs of risk of hate incidents and crimes. Schools and colleges should offer counseling, mentoring, and educational opportunities for all students who exhibit prejudicial beliefs and behaviors. Efforts of organized hate groups to disseminate information to students or recruit them as members should be carefully monitored.

Educate Community Groups and Leaders

Community leaders and citizen groups should have the skills and knowledge to recognize and actively resist intolerance and hate-motivated actions in their neighborhoods and jurisdictions.

Inform vulnerable groups and individuals about ways to protect themselves from bias-motivated incidents and crime. Individuals or groups that could be a target of hate crime because of race, religion, ethnic/national origin, gender, age, disability, or sexual orientation should be informed about ways to prevent being victimized. Justice system and other professionals should train and counsel potential victims to help them recognize threatening situations and to provide conflict resolution and other coping skills to enable them to deal effectively with bias-motivated behaviors. Vulnerable individuals should be informed about the importance of reporting bias-related incidents and the support that is available for seeking redress of discriminatory actions. Training materials should be published in different languages to reduce language and cultural barriers to reporting.

Provide knowledge and impart skills to recognize and defuse high-risk situations. Community groups and leaders should seek training and support from a coalition of justice system agencies, teachers, social service professionals, and victim advocacy groups to identify patterns of prejudice and discrimination before they escalate into hate incidents or crimes. Coalitions should also train community leaders in techniques for defusing and addressing identified high-risk situations. Professional mediation and conflict resolution services should also be available to support the ongoing prevention efforts of community leaders and neighborhood groups. The Department of Justice Community Relations Service can provide support in this area.

Encourage Strategic Planning and Collaborative Problem-Solving

Ongoing collaboration of citizens, elected officials, and public employees to develop strategic hate crime prevention enhances chances for success. Citizens who participate in governmental decision-making processes are more likely to assume their share of responsibility for specific outcomes and the overall quality of life in their communities.

Develop mechanisms for ongoing problem-solving within local communities. To prevent unresolved racial, ethnic, or other tensions from erupting into hate incidents or crimes, communities should establish coalitions of political, business, religious, and justice system leaders to encourage ongoing dialogue about current problems and recommend collaborative approaches for resolving them. These coalitions could be the same groups that are involved in long-range strategic planning to prevent hate crime.

Encourage responsible and accurate media coverage. The media should be urged to report on hate crimes accurately, to treat victims with dignity and sensitivity, to provide balanced coverage of organized hate group activities, and to highlight community partners' successes in preventing and responding to hate crimes.

Improve accuracy and completeness of information about the incidence of and response to hate crime. Citizens need to know the facts about hate crimes and current responses to them, so they can more effectively prevent hate crime and deal with its impact on communities. Achieving greater accuracy in documenting hate crimes depends to a large extent on developing shared definitions and reducing barriers to comprehensive reporting, as discussed in several recommendations that follow.

How Should We Respond to Hate Crime?

Summit participants reached consensus that the following are effective responses to hate crime:

- The definition of hate crime must be clear and commonly understood.
- Offenders must understand that hate crime will not be tolerated and those who commit it will be apprehended and appropriately sanctioned.
- Victims must be taken seriously and supported in dealing with the social, emotional, physical, and financial impacts of hate crime.
- Justice system practitioners and their community partners must hold hate crime offenders accountable for their actions and provide opportunities for them to broaden their perspectives and change their values.

These general principles helped summit work groups craft 22 policy and program recommendations to guide communities and public agencies toward more effective responses to hate crime.

Develop Shared Definitions of Hate Incidents and Hate Crimes

Prejudicial behavior exists along a continuum including negative speech, discriminatory practices, property damage, physical assault, and murder. Legally, a hate crime is any crime enumerated in a hate crime statute in which a perpetrator is subject to an enhanced penalty if the crime was motivated by bias, as defined by the statute. Hate incidents involve behaviors that, though motivated by bias against a victim's race, religion, ethnic/national origin, gender, age, disability, or sexual orientation, are not criminal acts. Communities and justice agencies should develop a common language for these attitudes and behaviors so that their responses can be consistent, equitable, and effective.

Broaden statutory definitions of hate crimes to eliminate disparities between laws. Disparities between federal and state hate crime laws should be eliminated by supporting new laws, which encompass criminal offenses committed against persons, property, or society, which are motivated in whole or in part by offenders' bias against an individual's or a group's actual or perceived race, religion, ethnicity/national origin, disability, sexual orientation, or, where legally permissible, gender. For example, federal law includes sexual orientation, while some state laws do not.

Clarify the difference between hate incidents and hate crimes. Definitions of reportable incidents (hate crimes) should distinguish hate crimes from hate incidents. Hate incidents, in which an individual or group is subjected to negative or offensive speech or behavior that is not a criminal offense, still harm the sense of safety of victims and communities.

Eliminate Barriers to Hate Crime Reporting

Encourage reporting of all hate incidents and crimes. Citizens should be informed through a variety of sources that reporting crimes as bias-related can result in enhanced penalties for perpetrators and specialized support for victims. Schools and colleges should report all hate crimes occurring on campuses to local police. Law enforcement agencies, school administrators, and other first responders should encourage citizens to report all bias-related incidents to the police, even if these incidents do not constitute hate crimes, so high-risk situations can be tracked and appropriate problem-solving actions can be taken.

Make it safe and easy to report bias-related incidents and crimes. To ensure comprehensive reporting of hate incidents and crimes, victims and witnesses must feel safe from retaliation or stigmatization. Telephone hotlines are one way to encourage community members, including students, to report incidents. Crimes reported on hotlines must be reported to a law enforcement agency to be effectively investigated and prosecuted. Police must ensure that both victims and witnesses feel safe.

Develop and disseminate hate crime reporting protocols. Law enforcement agencies, schools and colleges, medical professionals, and community organizations should collaboratively develop and issue standard operating procedures (SOPs) and memoranda of understanding (MOUs) that detail how and to whom individuals should report hate incidents and crimes. SOPs should include criteria to identify incidents as bias-related and determine whether a crime has occurred. They should include specific procedures for reporting both crimes and incidents. These SOPs should be communicated to citizens and community groups in user-friendly, culturally relevant and language-sensitive formats. Hate crimes should always be reported to the police; other hate incidents may be reported to community organizations and kept in some central repository or database.

Provide Adequate Support to Victims of Hate Incidents and Hate Crimes

Ensure that responses to hate incidents and crimes are swift, thorough and sensitive to the feelings of victims. First responders must obtain accurate information about an incident; conduct a preliminary assessment of physical, emotional, and financial injury to a victim; and reassure victims that their concerns and needs will be addressed. First responders must be prepared to assist victims whose initial emotional reactions to an incident may include rage, terror, and grief. Victims and their families should be immediately referred to victim assistance agencies and other community services when needed.

Develop coordinated community plans to respond to and manage public demonstrations by organized hate groups. Plans should specify the responsibilities of law enforcement agencies, including protection of First Amendment rights, techniques to prevent violence through separation of demonstrators and counter groups, and notification and communications responsibilities. Community groups should partner with justice agencies to develop constructive ways to counter the potential negative impacts of such events and to use demonstrations as opportunities to educate citizens, students, and justice system professionals regarding precipitating factors and effective responses. The Department of Justice Community Relations Service can be an excellent resource for help in designing a peaceful response to hate group marches and gatherings.

Assign organizational responsibility for coordinating and monitoring hate crime response. Every law enforcement agency should fix responsibility for coordinating and monitoring responses to hate crime in a specific individual/operating unit. Other first responder organizations, particularly schools and colleges, should also designate individuals who will ensure that responses to hate incidents and crimes are timely and appropriate.

Accord community recognition to "Good Samaritans" who protect victims of hate incidents or crimes, or who report incidents to appropriate authorities. Individuals who risk their own safety to assist victims of bias crime, as well as those who take the time to report threatening or harmful hate incidents, should be publicly recognized for their efforts.

Provide specialized support to hate crime victims through existing victim assistance programs. Victim assistance programs should individualize support for victims of hate incidents and crimes in recognition of the unique and severe impacts they may suffer. Programs should recognize that hate crimes that involve "only" minor property damage or assaults still may have serious long-term impacts on victims. Programs should partner with schools and community groups to provide ongoing support for all hate crime victims, so victims' alienation from their communities can be ameliorated. Agencies and groups providing ongoing services to hate crime victims should be co-located to permit better coordination.

Establish Mechanisms for Repairing Harms to Communities

Support, console, and assist targeted communities. Hate crimes harm not only individual victims but also the groups and communities of which they are a part. Justice and victim assistance agencies should convene and facilitate community meetings in the aftermath of hate crimes to provide opportunities to express feelings and begin the process of restoring a sense of safety and well-being to community members.

Develop coordinated community incident response plans. Communities should create hate crime response teams that comprise representatives of law enforcement, other justice agencies, schools, health care providers, victim assistance programs, and cultural diversity advocacy groups. These teams should develop policies and procedures to respond to bias-motivated incidents or hate crimes. Communities can turn to the United States Department of Justice/United States Attorney Hate Crime Task Force for guidance.

Ensure that schools and colleges establish processes to respond to bias-related incidents. Schools and colleges are self-contained communities that should support students victimized by hate incidents and crimes, and provide for appropriate school-based disciplinary actions and remedial interventions for student perpetrators.

Engage the media as partners to restore communities to wholeness. Through responsible reporting, the media can play a critical role in defusing community tensions, preventing further bias-motivated incidents in the wake of identified hate crimes, and educating the public to understand and prevent hate crime. Justice agencies and community groups should establish a single point of contact to provide media representatives with accurate information about the nature and impact of hate incidents and crimes while respecting individual victims' rights to privacy and security.

Develop More Effective Sanctions for Hate Crime Perpetrators

Impose enhanced sentences for violent or repetitive hate crime offenders. Most hate crime statutes provide enhanced penalties, usually longer sentences, for crimes determined to be bias-related. These enhancements are particularly appropriate for chronic, violent hate crime offenders who pose a significant and continuing risk to community safety.

Use restorative justice options for first-time nonviolent hate crime offenders. Restorative justice options can promote healing of victims and change offender attitudes, while restoring the trust of the community. They are appropriate whenever victims and communities are willing to hold hate crime offenders accountable for repairing the physical and emotional harm caused by their actions.

Involve parents of juvenile hate crime offenders in post-adjudication sanctions and interventions. Families can have a powerful influence, for better or worse, on the outcomes of correctional interventions for youthful offenders. Involving parents and their children in treatment and education opportunities can teach whole families to practice peaceful conflict resolution and exercise tolerance of individual differences.

Develop strategies to counter the influence of organized hate groups in correctional in institutions. Efforts to change attitudes and behavior patterns of hate crime offenders sentenced to prison may be thwarted by the influence of organized hate groups operating within prisons and jails. Corrections administrators must develop strategies to contain or counter the bias-motivated activities and expressions of these inmate groups.

Enhance Professional Training

Professionals who must respond to hate crimes, assist victims and communities, and impose sanctions and interventions on convicted offenders require ongoing training and technical support. In 1995, a model curriculum for training law enforcement and victim assistance professionals was fashioned by the Education Development Center, with funding from the Office for Victims of Crime and the Bureau of Justice Assistance. A few years before, the FBI published a guide to assist law enforcement agencies with hate crime data collection and training program design. Many other resources can be tapped to help design and implement essential training.

Summit Participants Recommend Four Types of Training

Train first responders, investigators, and leaders. Topics should include the following: recognizing bias-related incidents, utilizing standard criteria to determine bias and assess perpetrator intent, interviewing victims and witnesses, collecting and preserving evidence, referring victims to appropriate community agencies, providing information to prosecutors and the courts, and standardizing documentation of hate incidents/crimes. The U.S. Department of Justice has available four hate crime curriculums that are excellent training resources: Patrol and Responding Officers; Detectives and Investigators; Core Curriculum for Patrol Officers, Detectives, and Command Officers; and Command Officers.

Train victim assistance providers. Topics should include assessing impacts of hate incidents and crimes on victims, reviewing hate crime reporting protocols, exploring the continuum of support options, and engaging community groups in the healing process.

Train judges and prosecutors. Topics should include creative alternative sentencing approaches, outcomes and impacts of all types of sanctions, and treatments for perpetrators. Prosecutors and judges must be fully apprised of community and law enforcement strategies for hate crimes, so subsequent charging and adjudication decisions are consistent.

Provide cross-disciplinary training for all those who respond to hate incidents and crimes. Cross-disciplinary training that involves educators, law enforcement officers, victim assistance providers, court personnel, and correctional officers should promote closer collaboration for response to hate crime.

How Will We Know We Are Succeeding?

Summit participants cited three types of research that are needed to better understand hate crime, its consequences, and promising responses:

- Conduct basic research to shed light on the causes of hate crime and to provide insight into promising ways to deal with the causes.
- Evaluate research to identify the most effective prevention efforts.
- Evaluate research to identify the most effective strategies to heal community harm and reform offenders.

Six recommendations were developed:

Conduct Basic Research

1. **Clearly define expected outcomes of hate crime prevention and response efforts.** Useful program evaluation relies on clear and measurable definitions of outcomes. In addition to reducing the incidence of hate crime (all hate crime or particular offense types targeted by a prevention strategy), positive outcomes could include changes in attitudes of children or community members who participate in hate crime prevention training, improved conflict resolution skills, increased victim satisfaction, enhanced perceptions of safety and well-being, reduced recidivism rates, and positive changes in the behavior or attitudes of offenders.

2. **Define valid measures of expected outcomes.** To assess the impact of prevention and response efforts, outcome measures must be carefully specified and the results interpreted validly. For example, in communities with growing populations, the number of hate crime incidents may increase over time even though prevention and response efforts may be contributing to an overall reduction in the rate of hate crimes. Quantifying changes in other outcomes involving attitudes, values, or perceptions is a challenging evaluation task, but can be accomplished through careful design of survey formats, data collection protocols, and methods of "counting" that ensure uniformity and objectivity.

Evaluate Outcomes of Prevention and Response Efforts

3. **Ensure that all hate incidents and crimes are documented thoroughly and consistently.** To assess correlations among characteristics of victims, perpetrators, and the situations in which hate crimes occur, detailed information about these variables should be routinely collected by first responders and stored in central data repositories accessible to researchers.

4. **Collect data on expected outcomes where particular prevention and intervention efforts are being implemented, over time, across jurisdictions, and in a variety of settings.** By documenting trends in such outcome measures as the rate of reported hate crimes or the recidivism of convicted perpetrators, the long-range impact of prevention and response strategies can be demonstrated. However, in jurisdictions where the rate of hate crime reporting has been low, a desirable short-term or interim outcome may well be to increase the rate of reported hate incidents or crimes. Analyzing differences in trends across jurisdictions and settings may also yield insights about the impacts of contextual factors on outcomes.

5. **Share quantitative and qualitative information about the elements of successful prevention and response programs.** Researchers and program evaluators should collaborate with justice professionals and those who implement prevention and response strategies to design evaluations that will generate information useful for program design, public information campaigns, and professional training efforts. Evaluators must document the qualitative case studies of successful efforts to prevent and respond to bias-motivated incidents. Human-scale stories can enrich the pictures painted by quantitative data, and encourage others to invest in similar efforts in their own communities.

6. **Systematically record characteristics and activities of organized hate groups.** Documenting the extent to which organized hate group activities are linked to hate incidents and crimes is important. Through study of hate group goals, tactics, and impacts, researchers may be able to pinpoint promising ways to counter their influence, both with their members and on the larger society.

Law Enforcement Action Agenda

Law enforcement agencies must assume a central role in implementing the hate crime prevention, response, and performance measurement strategies outlined above. To encourage and enable law enforcement agencies to lead community-wide endeavors, summit participants recommended 12 actions:

- **Establish a "zero-tolerance" atmosphere in every law enforcement agency.** Police leaders and officers must be positive examples for their communities by actively discouraging bias-related behavior or speech in their own organizations. To be leaders in preventing hate crimes, law enforcement professionals must ensure that they exemplify the values of tolerance and peaceful conflict resolution, and that any bias-related behavior by police officers is dealt with swiftly, equitably, and severely.

- **Encourage local jurisdictions to conduct hate crime summits.** Local hate crime summits or focus groups can elicit community views on pressing issues, educate community leaders, and galvanize public support for investing in hate crime prevention and response. Law enforcement agencies can use the IACP summit model to engage community organizations, first responders, schools, and justice system agencies to collaborate closely with police to address hate crimes.

- **Participate in collaborative development of coordinated approaches to prevent and respond to hate crimes.** Law enforcement agencies must be architects of and active participants in ongoing planning processes to enable communities to assess hate crime issues, inventory current policies and practices, and devise strategies to improve prevention and intervention efforts.

- **Sponsor and participate actively in community events, forums, and activities concerning diversity tolerance, bias reduction, conflict resolution, and hate crime prevention.** Police leaders and officers should be an influential presence at public events that encourage community members to talk about differences and commonalities and share visions of safe and healthy communities. Law enforcement leaders must continue to speak out forcefully against intolerance, bigotry, and hate crimes, not only in the aftermath of particular incidents, but at all times.

- **Respond to and support the individual victims of hate crimes and their communities.** Police officers must obtain accurate information about a hate crime or incident; conduct a preliminary assessment of victims' physical, emotional and financial injuries; and reassure victims that their concerns and needs will be addressed comprehensively. Police should encourage members of the community at large to express their feelings and should take action to restore a sense of safety and well being in the community.

- **Employ community policing strategies to prevent and respond to hate crimes.** Community policing principles encourage law enforcement agencies to foster close connections with the communities they serve, and to support officers in creative problem-solving that will prevent or discourage criminal behavior. These principles can readily be applied to the work of preventing hate-motivated incidents and crimes.

- **Continuously investigate, track, and deal appropriately with the activities of organized hate groups.** Continuous intelligence-gathering about hate group activities is a primary responsibility of law enforcement agencies that requires cross-jurisdictional collaboration and significant investment in information systems technology and training. Law enforcement agencies must protect the First Amendment rights of hate groups while simultaneously ensuring the safety and well-being of communities that hate groups attack verbally or in other non-criminal ways.

- **Identify and report all bias-related incidents and hate crimes completely and accurately.** Law enforcement agencies should collaborate with other first responders to specify how and to whom citizens should report bias-related incidents and hate crimes. Detailed information about characteristics of victims, of perpetrators, and the situations in which hate incidents and crimes occur should be routinely collected by police.

- **Ensure that all law enforcement professionals are trained to recognize and respond appropriately to hate crimes.** Police officers must be trained to recognize potential bias-related incidents, use standard criteria for determining bias and assessing perpetrators' intent, interview victims and witnesses, collect and preserve evidence, refer victims to appropriate community agencies, provide information to prosecutors and the courts, and standardize documentation of all hate incidents/crimes.

- **Assist schools and colleges to design and deliver hate crime prevention curricula and to develop response protocols.** Hate crime prevention curricula can be used in general and alternative classrooms, in schools experiencing bias crime problems, with student government leaders, in after-school programs, and in teacher training. The Education Development Center, with support of the Office of Juvenile Justice and Delinquency Prevention, has prepared a model curriculum for middle and high school students designed to reduce prejudice and prevent crimes based on intolerance. The U.S. Departments of Education and Justice collaborated to produce a manual that provides guidance to schools and communities to develop school-based hate crime prevention programs. Police leaders and officers should be involved in planning and delivering such curricula in a wide variety of school and college/university settings. Law enforcement agencies can also assist schools and colleges in developing protocols for recognizing and responding appropriately to hate incidents and crimes.

- **Engage the media as partners in preventing hate crimes and restoring victimized communities.** Law enforcement leaders and their public information officers should encourage the media to report on hate crimes accurately, to treat victims with dignity and sensitivity, to provide balanced coverage of organized hate group activities, and to highlight community successes in preventing and responding to hate crimes.

- **Collaborate in defining measurable outcomes of efforts to prevent and respond to hate crimes.** Police leaders and officers should work with community members and researchers to define standards for success in preventing and responding to hate crimes. Performance measures should focus not only on reducing negative behaviors, but also on enhancing the quality of life in communities. Law enforcement participation in evaluation efforts can help to ensure that research results will be used to continuously improve the effectiveness of prevention and response strategies.

Law enforcement leaders and officers will continue to contribute significantly to stopping violence and preventing hate crimes. However, the work outlined in this report cannot be accomplished solely through the efforts of law enforcement agencies. Implementing summit recommendations requires the continuing collaboration and commitment of community leaders, parents and families, schools, and other public agencies in the ongoing enterprise to create a society of peacemakers.

Print Citations

CMS: "Hate Crime in American Policy Summit." In *The Reference Shelf: Hate Crimes,* edited by Sophie Zyla, 114–127. Amenia, NY: Grey House Publishing, 2020.

MLA: "Hate Crime in American Policy Summit." *The Reference Shelf: Hate Crimes,* edited by Sophie Zyla, Grey Housing Publishing, 2020, pp. 114–127.

APA: International Association of Police Chiefs. (2020). Hate crime in American policy summit. In Sophie Zyla (Ed.), *The reference shelf: Hate crimes* (pp. 114–127). Amenia, NY: Grey Housing Publishing.

Hate in Schools: An In-Depth Look

By Francisco Vara-Orta
Education Week, August 6, 2018

Three swastikas were scrawled on the note found in the girls' restroom, along with a homophobic comment and a declaration: "I Love Trump."

Found inside the backpack of a Latina student, a note that said: Go back to Mexico.

Two other hate-filled incidents—invoking Donald Trump's name and using swastikas—were also reported that same day.

The school: Council Rock High in this mostly white, affluent Philadelphia suburb.

The day: Nov. 9, 2016, the day after the election of President Trump.

Council Rock school district Superintendent Robert Fraser condemned the incidents, but told parents he believed they were isolated events. The acts, he wrote in a letter on Nov. 10, were "inappropriate" and would not be tolerated. But, he emphasized, they were "likely the responsibility of a very small number of individuals whose actions should not damage the reputation of the larger group."

Soon after, the district formed a council on diversity, mostly composed of parents, and took several other steps, including training for school staff to better identify and respond to hate incidents. Despite those efforts, Council Rock High, said some parents and students, continues to have a culture where racist views are sometimes boldly expressed, but oftentimes ferment under the surface.

The hate-fueled incidents at Council Rock in the wake of the divisive 2016 presidential election, and the school's rocky path to addressing them, are not unusual.

Concerns about a rise in hate crimes and bias incidents have surged since the campaign and election of President Trump, who has frequently used coarse language and racist rhetoric when describing immigrants, people of color, and women. In schools, similar worries are echoed by some students, parents, and educators who suggest that Trump's influence has emboldened some children, teenagers, and even school employees to openly espouse hateful views.

To understand how hate, intolerance, and bias are affecting school climate and impacting students and their educators, *Education Week* partnered with the nonprofit news organization ProPublica in a project called Documenting Hate. We analyzed three years of media reports and self-reported incidents of hate and bias in K-12 school settings—many submitted to ProPublica.

In a review of 472 verified accounts, we found that most incidents that took place in schools between January 2015 and December 2017 targeted black and Latino students, as well as those who are Jewish or Muslim.

Most of the incidents—some of which were formally reported to school personnel—involved hate speech, spoken and written. Reports of bodily harm were relatively rare.

The most common words were: "the n-word," various versions of "build the wall" and "go back to [insert foreign country name here, usually Mexico]." The most common hate symbol: swastikas.

The largest number of reports on a single day in K-12 schools: November 9, 2016—the day after Trump's election.

But is it fair to lay all the blame on the words and actions of President Trump for the vitriol spewed in schools?

Anecdotal reports aren't enough to suggest that the president's inflammatory talk has led to increased rates of bullying and new data show that bullying rates held steady in 2017, according to the Youth Risk Behavior Surveillance Survey.

One expert on school climate cautioned school leaders to avoid blaming acts of hate and bullying in the last couple of years on Trump's influence.

"There is usually never just one cause of bullying, so if we scapegoat it on the president, we are overlooking the broader climate issues that were there before and will likely continue if not directly addressed," said Deborah Temkin, who is the director of education research for the nonpartisan Child Trends and previously oversaw federal efforts to combat bullying in the Obama administration.

"How Adults Respond to Incidents Affects the Entire Climate of the School"

In the more than 18 months since the 2016 outburst at Council Rock North, other hateful acts have taken place at the high school and other schools in the district, according to more than a dozen parents and students interviewed by *Education Week*.

When a group of students campaigned last year to change the school's American Indian mascot, someone created an Instagram account to counter with racist alternatives. Among them: a KKK figure, an image of a Latino with the words "Council Rock Tacos," and an image of a black person holding a gun with the words "Council Rock criminals."

Last year, a middle school teacher in the Council Rock district draped a Confederate flag on her classroom wall, while a district contractor showed up at a school during a session of basketball camp with a large Confederate flag hoisted from his truck. After parents on the diversity council reported the flags for being offensive, they were removed.

Schools have long been a venue for bias and harassment, where targeted students can feel threatened and unwelcome and where parents worry about their children's physical safety. And administrators often falter in dealing with the ugliness—in both the immediate aftermath and over the longer-term to confront deeper-seated hate and bias in their school communities.

K-12 leaders must first investigate and identify the motivation for the incidents, Temkin said, and then establish whether there are solutions such as anti-bias training and multicultural education that could address the problem.

"We know how adults respond to incidents affects the entire climate of the school, as in saying that these incidents are not okay and not the norm," Temkin said. "However, there is some assumption on the part of the parents of what a school should do that may not align to what a school should or can do."

Often, Temkin said, school leaders and teachers may feel pressure to discipline those who commit the hateful acts, but doing so can undermine aiming for a more sustainable outcome in trying to push back on the bias itself. The two main areas to focus on should be making sure kids who were targeted feel safe and delving into why the perpetrators of the bias incidents are acting that way.

While data on hate-related incidents in schools is skimpy at best, the U.S. Department of Justice polls students periodically about the issue as part of its National Crime Victimization Survey. In 2015, the most recent school crime survey, more than 25 percent of students reported seeing hate-related graffiti in their schools. That same survey also revealed that the majority of students who reported being a target of hate-related words attend suburban schools.

Public schools in America's suburban communities are increasingly likely to be the most diverse, with majority white student enrollments giving way to an influx of students from a variety of racial, ethnic, and cultural backgrounds.

Schools like Council Rock North High, where 88 percent of students are white, 1.5 percent are black, and 2 percent are Latino.

"I Don't Think My Classmates and Teachers Really Grasp the Pain We Feel"

For Jayla Johnson, 17, who graduated from Council Rock North in June, the post-election spewing of hate and intolerance was not new. The African-American student said she had heard classmates use racial slurs and praise the Ku Klux Klan.

"I don't think my classmates and teachers really grasp the pain we feel," Jayla said. "It runs deep."

Her older sister Janai, who graduated in 2013, had encountered a racist threat written on a wall in a girls' bathroom during her sophomore year: "I'm going to kill all the niggers." The names of black students were listed, Janai's included.

When that happened, school administrators didn't notify Janai's parents, said her mother, Robyn Johnson.

"No one called," she said. "They didn't address it until I addressed it."

The high school of 1,700 students is in Bucks County, about 30 miles from Philadelphia. It has a reputation for strong student achievement. It's in a school district sought after by teachers—for the high-performing students and some of the best salaries in Pennsylvania.

When the cascade of post-Election Day hate incidents struck, Fraser, the superintendent, took several steps to address broader issues of racism and intolerance in the school community. Among the most notable was establishing the diversity council, a voluntary group of parents who were to advise district leaders.

The district's leadership and parent activists—while articulating similar goals—have clashed over how to achieve them. Two major points of disagreement are a lack of diversity in the district's teaching ranks and how to best accommodate transgender students, according to parents on the diversity council.

So less than year after its formation, district officials decided the parent group would no longer be affiliated with the school system.

Fraser declined to be interviewed for this story. He provided a statement listing over two dozen actions the district has taken over the past two years to confront and prevent hateful acts.

"I am committed to ensuring that Council Rock is clearly recognized as a district that not only welcomes diversity of all kinds but celebrates it," Fraser wrote.

In his statement, Fraser cited school climate surveys designed by an external firm that were administered at the beginning of the 2017-18 school year, but no results have been released yet. Teachers have had diversity awareness training and the district has hosted conversations on equity. It has designed cultural competency at every grade level with community social justice groups such as the Peace Center, which has been tracking dozens of bias incidents in the community and helps counsel targeted families.

"We will continue our work in the coming years, as accepting anything less than 100 percent success in this area is unacceptable," Fraser said.

But for the parents of students who were targeted by the earlier incidents, the district's overall response has been too slow and defensive, said Kim Xantus, an Asian-American parent who serves on the diversity council.

While the principal and staff at her children's elementary school have been proactive on fostering conversations about race, such efforts have been sporadic districtwide and left to students or parents to often lead the charge, Xantus said.

Jayla, similarly frustrated, was motivated to start a diversity club for students on campus. Late last year, she testified in Washington, before U.S. Rep. Brian Fitzpatrick, a Republican, about her experiences with racism and prejudice in school.

But in many places, it is intimidating for students to report being harassed or bullied because of their race, ethnicity, or family's immigration status.

In Carbon Hill, Ala., three students—all of them African-American girls who are about to start their sophomore year—say they were repeatedly harassed at school during their freshmen year by five white male upperclassmen.

In a high school that is 96 percent white, these students say they were called the n-word and sexually charged slurs by the boys on multiple occasions during the 2017-18 school year. They've had fake money thrown at them during lunch. One of the boys threatened to kill the girls by hanging, their parents said.

Keisha King, whose daughter has been one of the main targets of the harassment, says it feels like times have regressed compared to her experience at Carbon Hill High 18 years ago, when she also was one of the few black students. All three families said the aggressive nature of the behavior prompted them to speak out and seek help from the NAACP.

Even though King said that some of the boys were suspended, she still feels the district hasn't taken her concerns about safety seriously. The students harassing her daughter are slated to return to campus in the fall.

After weighing whether she could move her family to Birmingham—an hour away—so that her daughter could attend another school, King recently decided that for now they would stay. Miracle, King's daughter, confided to her that she didn't want to run away from the problem nor abandon her classmates who feel isolated.

Jason Adkins, the superintendent of Walker County schools where Carbon Hill is located, said in an interview that he believed the school had taken care of the parents' concerns about their daughters' safety. He declined to speak specifically about the discipline measures taken against the boys, citing student privacy. But he did address what he thinks should be done in such circumstances.

"We exist to intervene in those situations where people can not intervene for themselves and need a little help, from somebody that can make a difference," Adkins said. "First and foremost, there should always be an investigation. Hopefully, most of the time, we then do what we should do as a school system and do something toward helping improve the situation. I am sure that we do make mistakes, and that doesn't always happen, but it should."

Adkins, who recently lost a re-election campaign to remain superintendent in Walker County, said he would reach out again to the girls and their families before school starts to make sure their concerns were addressed more thoroughly. "We need to examine working on the school's culture and asking, 'how do we go about embracing people from various backgrounds?'"

"It's Hard to Believe in a Way It's Still Around and Becoming More Prevalent"

Jewish organizations such as the Anti-Defamation League have reported that anti-Semitic incidents in general have soared to their highest levels in two decades in the U.S. over the last couple of years.

The ADL has an anti-bias education program that's in more than 70 schools in New England, mostly in Massachusetts. It focuses on high school students training younger peers, particularly in middle school.

While anti-Semitic incidents took place in schools dotting the nation, *Education Week* found at least 73 incidents occurred in schools in Massachusetts during the 2015-2017 period that it analyzed. The ADL, however, reported 93 incidents occurring in Massachusetts schools alone in 2017, up from 50 in 2016.

One of those occurred in 2016 at Marblehead High School, in the Boston area. Students circulated on Snapchat an image of a swastika made from pennies that was photographed in a chemistry lab.

"For me, who has direct heritage tied to the Holocaust, including hearing stories from my grandmother during [World War II] of what our family and friends experienced, seeing these reminders of how members of our families died just thrown around on social media, is painful," said Talia Ornstein, a 17-year-old student at Marblehead High. "It's hard to believe in a way it's still around and becoming more prevalent."

Her classmate, Sophia Spungin, 16, said the incident felt "like a direct attack as it's the symbol signifying hatred toward a particular group. Plain and simple, it's not okay."

After the incident, students at Marblehead worked to raise money to bring in the ADL's anti-bias program, which extends beyond addressing anti-Semitism to other forms of discrimination.

Some teachers say they must play a frontline role in combatting intolerance. One of those teachers is Jennifer Goss, who designed a course on the Holocaust and other genocides in world history at Robert E. Lee High School in Staunton, Va., where many of her students are white. Goss has taught her course for nearly 15 years, but she said interest has grown among her students, as well as her fellow teachers in recent years, something she attributes to the heightened cultural tensions in the country.

"Initially when I started teaching the class I was using examples of anti-Semitic graffiti that were from 10 years ago," Goss said. "And sadly, I can go onto most major news outlets today and find examples from just a couple of weeks ago."

"I'm Not in School with Her, I Can't Protect Her"

The pervasive use of social media to spread messages of hate can leave communities feeling pummeled.

Many of the bias reports *Education Week* reviewed included the use of Instagram and Snapchat. Parents interviewed in various cities said they usually find out about hate-related incidents from their children or social media.

In another case of racist speech spreading like wildfire on social media, seven students at Bel Air High School in Bel Air, Md., used the occasion of the school's "Scrabble Day" to spell out the n-word with letters written on their T-shirts. A photo went viral on social media in the following days.

Jahneen Keatz, an African-American mother whose daughter Jenea is a junior at the high school, said she got a robocall from the principal who said there had been an "incident" and students had been disciplined. But the principal offered no other details. Keatz finally found out what happened when another black parent saw the image on social media and called her.

After community outrage, the Harford County school district started some diversity initiatives at the high school, where 79 percent of students are white, according to state data.

Bel Air school officials declined to be interviewed, but Laurie Namey, the district's supervisor of equity and cultural proficiency, sent a statement that listed their efforts, including at the high school campus where "students directly involved in the incident took part in a restorative lesson focused on the historical and current social impact" of the slur used.

Jenea, 15, has become a vocal activist against racism since last fall's incident, said her mother. But Keatz said she worries about her daughter's safety.

"My daughter will tell you, I check in with her every day," Keatz said. "I want her to know that she has a voice and my only job is to teach her how to use it productively, to hopefully evoke change. But as a parent, as a mother…there is some worry. Because I'm not in school with her, I can't protect her."

These conversations are inescapable for families of color, said Karsonya Wise Whitehead, a professor of communication, African, and African-American studies at Loyola University Maryland who is often is tapped to speak to audiences after a bias incident occurs in their community.

This school year, that call came from her own backyard, after a cluster of affluent private schools in Baltimore, including the school her own sons attend, started a social media firestorm after photos of students and alumni dressed in racist Halloween costumes circulated online.

According to the *Baltimore Sun*, one photo showed a graduate of Boys' Latin School of Maryland dressed in an orange jumpsuit with the name "Freddie Gray" on the back, referring to the African-American man who died from injuries while in police custody in 2015 and who became a prominent symbol in the greater Black Lives Matter movement. A second photo, from a different party, depicted two teens from Gilman School and Roland Park Country School dressed in orange jumpsuits with a racial slur in the caption, the *Sun* reported.

One of the schools, Roland Park, brought in Whitehead to talk to all students about how hurtful and racist the images were and to lead a discussion about diversity, inclusion, and taking "ownership over our words and actions" with the predominately upper-class, white student body, she said.

Whitehead has found that sometimes it's parents—not school administrators—who are the most reluctant to address incidences of bigotry.

"Sometimes the complaint is, my child is too young," Whitehead said. "Or it seems like you're stuffing this down our throat. Or I can't believe we have to deal with this again."

Whitehead's oldest son Kofi is a student at the all-male Gilman, one of the private schools involved in the Halloween scandal. He will be the vice president of the school's Black Student Union next year.

"After the incident, I talked with my parents, trying to figure out how to make my white classmates understand what it means to be black and male in America," he said. "There are days when I do not completely understand it myself."

"I Tell Them to Be Proud of Who We Are and What We Bring to the Community"

In rural Perry, Iowa, the Latino student population has grown a lot in the past 20 years due in part to the meat processing plants and other industries that employ many immigrants from Mexico. Perry High School, once mostly white, is now half white and half Latino, said Principal Dan Marburger. Most of the school's Latino students are U.S.-born with Mexican-born parents.

But in a region that's still predominately white, Perry High's Latino students have been the targets of hate speech—especially in the realm of high school sports.

During a basketball game in February 2016, the Perry Hall team—most of its players were Latino—heard chants of "Trump! Trump! Trump!" when they ran onto the court to start the game. The taunts came from about a dozen students from the opposing high school, Marburger said.

In statements to their communities and in media interviews, both Marburger and the opposing school's principal immediately condemned the actions. But those taunts followed a pattern that has been common when teams play Perry High, Marburger said. He's seen Perry referred to as "little Mexico" on Snapchat, heard soccer players report that people at games shout "hey, where's your green card?" and had fans from opposing teams wear sombreros.

Most of his students of Mexican descent have "been in our communities forever and were born here," Marburger said. "Neighboring schools don't know that. They just see that, 'Hey, there's a couple brown kids out on the court. Let's start chanting that stuff.'"

"We have to talk about race every year with our kids at different times," Marburger said. "I tell them to be proud of who we are and what we bring to the community. Then, we also deal with it straight-up with other schools when we do hear it."

When hate incidents happen, Marburger says school leaders "need to get out in front of it," and be proactive, both with students and the broader community. But often, these types of incidents aren't handled that way. Two of the districts contacted by *Education Week* for this story, for example, declined to speak directly with a reporter, sending carefully worded statements instead.

"This Conversation Does Not Need to Be about Blame, Shame, or Judgment"

While many of the reported incidents were peer-to-peer hate speech, teachers and school support staff have also been the source of bigoted statements.

Marialis Vasquez, who graduated from her New Jersey high school in 2017, said a white male teacher told her and her classmates that he agreed with Donald Trump that Mexicans are bad for the country, calling them "pigs" and "lazy" the day after the election in 2016. The high school, Vasquez said, has a predominately Latino student population. Although she is from the Dominican Republic, Vasquez took the teachers' remarks on Mexicans as derogatory for all Latinos.

"When people talk about Latinos, they talk about all of us as a whole," said Vasquez, who reported the incident to the school's principal, but declined to identify the school or names of personnel out of fear of retribution.

"I just remember him saying in front of the class—it wasn't a full apology—that he wouldn't speak about his beliefs any more in the class," Vasquez recalled. "And that was it."

Hate speech and bigoted ideas coming from a teacher or school official can result in a different type of long-term damage for students that arguably rivals trauma similarly inflicted by their peers.

> **The two main areas to focus on should be making sure kids who were targeted feel safe and delving into why the perpetrators of the bias incident are acting that way.**

"We have some initial evidence that if you are being discriminated against by your peers, that is more likely to affect kind of your social and emotional well-being," said Aprile Benner, a University of Texas at Austin professor who conducts research on the development of low-income students and students of color. "If you are being discriminated by educators, it is more likely to influence academics, not surprisingly."

In interviews, both parents and teachers stressed the importance of recruiting teachers of color as an important solution to stemming a tide of bigotry and intolerance. While black and Latino students benefit from having teachers with a shared experience, white students have much to learn from educators from different backgrounds than their own.

One such network pushing to expand the ranks of diverse teachers—Teaching While Muslim—was founded by New Jersey teachers Nagla Bedir and Luma Hasan.

In the hate incident reports *Education Week* reviewed, Muslim students, particularly girls, are often targeted. One reason: Wearing a hijab, the traditional religious head cover for Muslim girls and women.

Bedir said she and Hasan created the group because Muslim teachers often feel alone when either they or their Muslim students face discrimination in schools. The duo works with other Muslim and non-Muslim educators to hold workshops throughout the country to help combat Islamophobia. They have a blog where Muslim students, parents, and teachers can describe their experiences in school, and list resources such as lesson plans and curriculum guides on anti-bias education.

"We want to also highlight that, and make sure that people don't just see Muslims as one monolithic group," said Bedir.

Others echoed Bedir, quick to remind educators that minority groups within themselves have intracultural differences important to take into account when designing inclusion initiatives.

Among the hate and bias incidents that *Education Week* reviewed, some white students expressed a curiosity as to why white pride groups are shunned, and expressed feeling left out of diversity work. In a handful of instances, white students said they were bullied for expressing support for Trump, usually in districts with more racial diversity.

In one urban school district—Denver—leaders have embraced such questions and are exploring "whiteness" as part of its broader work around diversity and inclusion. Twenty-five percent of the district's students are white, while 75 percent of its teachers are white.

"We really start off with the understanding that everyone has bias, and it doesn't make you a racist," said Allen Smith, the Denver district's chief of culture, equity, and leadership, who is black. "This conversation does not need to be about blame, shame, or judgment, which does ease the tension a little bit, and gives permission for people to talk."

He brought in Jennifer Harvey, a professor of ethics and religion at Drake University in Des Moines, Iowa, to speak to students and district employees about institutional racism and white privilege. Harvey said the term "white privilege" is often off-putting, but she believes the concept behind it is true—that people who are white have had major advantages, over people of color in how American society functions.

Harvey explained that while it's "always dangerous to be too general" when analyzing a cultural group, there are important observations to keep in mind when talking to white students and educators about white privilege.

Some white students may never really think about their own identity in terms of race, so don't see racism as their problem, she said. And in highly diverse communities, like Denver, white students may see themselves as "onlookers" to the bigger discussions around diversity.

"There's a lot of white guilt that then ends up causing white youth to vacate the race conversation altogether," said Harvey, who is white. "Or the push (for diversity) ends up, more terrifyingly, turning into resentment towards their peers of color."

In Council Rock North High School, a discussion of white privilege triggered some staff members to leave in protest during a diversity training session, according to parents on the diversity council. Those who left felt the term ignored their lower economic class roots, parents heard.

Dealing with bias remains a work in progress in the Council Rock district.

Kathia Monard-Weissman, who is Latina and has two elementary-aged children in Council Rock's schools, said a core group of eight parents serve as the executive board, each of whom oversees committees made up of other parents. Students attend the council's meetings, along with other family members. As many as 100 people have come to the council's meetings.

At a gathering in late May at a public library in Newtown, a dozen parents discussed their concerns, more than 18 months since the post-election cascade of hate incidents.

Among them:

- Some school employees who think that dealing with bigotry should not be a top priority given the small number of minority students;

- Some white parents who say the district is failing to prepare white students for living and working in diverse communities; and,

- Fears that students of color and their families will avoid Council Rock's schools because they don't feel welcome.

"The community's changing and we have to prepare kids," said Lori Perusich, a Jewish mother of two Council Rock students who serves on the council. "We have to realize what's at stake here if we don't act now. And we're not going away."

Print Citations

CMS: Vara-Orta, Francisco. "Hate in Schools: An In-Depth Look." In *The Reference Shelf: Hate Crimes,* edited by Sophie Zyla, 128–138. Amenia, NY: Grey House Publishing, 2020.

MLA: Vara-Orta, Francisco. "Hate in Schools: An In-Depth Look." *The Reference Shelf: Hate Crimes,* edited by Sophie Zyla, Grey Housing Publishing, 2020, pp. 128–138.

APA: Vara-Orta, F. (2020). Hate in schools: An in-depth look. In Sophie Zyla (Ed.), *The reference shelf: Hate crimes* (pp. 128–138). Amenia, NY: Grey Housing Publishing.

Political Correctness and Anti-Jewish Bias Mar First Draft of California's Ethnic Studies Curriculum

By Evan Gerstmann
Forbes, **August 15, 2019**

In the near future, all California high school students will probably have to take ethnic studies courses before they graduate. That's fine in theory but the process so far has been marred by political bias, extreme hostility to Israel, and not coincidentally, a complete white-washing of anti-Semitism in America.

The first draft of the California ethnic studies curriculum was recently released to the public with the comment period ending on August 15. Its glossary is almost a parody of political correctness. It calls for students to learn such terms as "Herstory" in which "The prefix 'her' instead of 'his' is used to disrupt the often androcentric nature of history." But even this term is now considered politically incorrect so students will also be taught about "Hxrstory," which is "used to describe history written from a more gender inclusive perspective. The 'x' is used to disrupt the often rigid gender binarist approach to telling history."

Under the draft curriculum, students will also be taught about "Heteropatriarchy—a system of society in which men and heterosexuals (especially heterosexual men) are privileged, dominant, and hold power" and "Cisheteropatriarchy—a system of power that is based on the dominance of cisheterosexual men."

Students will also be taught about racism, sexism and Islamophobia. However, one term that they will not be taught is "anti-Semitism." Although the curriculum's glossary makes room for all the terms mentioned here, anti-Semitism is nowhere to be found. This is particularly amazing because there are more Jewish people living in California than almost anywhere else in the world and hate crimes against them are up sharply.

In fact, hate crimes against Jews are more common in America than hate crimes against Muslims—nearly five times as common. But you would never know it from the draft standards. As noted, they discuss Islamophobia but not anti-Semitism. They have a robust section discussing anti-Arab stereotypes but not anti-Semitic stereotypes. The silence about hate and hate crimes against Jews is deafening.

Given the large number of Jewish Californians and all the hate crimes directed against them, what might account for this willful silence? Looking at the draft standards as a whole, the answer is obvious: it is extreme hostility to Israel. The

> **The silence about hate and hate crimes against Jews is deafening.**

academic left, the folks who embrace terms such as "Cisheteropatriarchy," largely sees Israel as an oppressor state and believes that the very idea of a Jewish homeland is inherently oppressive.

Given that these are supposed to be standards for teaching students about various ethnicities of Californians, one would think that the Israeli-Palestinian conflict, which is a foreign policy issue, would not be a part of the curriculum. But the drafters found plenty of room to bring it up anyway and consistently in a manner that vilifies Israel.

For example, the draft curriculum discusses the "Boycott, Divest, Sanction (BDS)" movement against Israel. This would seem to have little to do with the study of ethnicity in California. Nonetheless, it is included and described in a way that one-sidedly demonizes Israel: "Boycott, Divestment and Sanctions (BDS) —is a global social movement that currently aims to establish freedom for Palestinians living under apartheid conditions. Inspired by tactics employed during the South African anti-apartheid movement, the Palestinian-led movement calls for the boycott, divestment, and sanctioning of the Israeli government until it complies with International law."

Comparing Israel to South Africa is as one-sided as a curriculum can get. The curriculum is even more one-sided since it mentions nothing about any of the reasons that Israel remains in the West Bank, such as legitimate fear that the West Bank will fall under Hamas control if Israel withdraws. Hamas is a terrorist organization that regularly launches rockets at Jewish civilian's homes and schools and diverts international aid to build terrorist tunnels. Although polling data of Palestinians shows that Hamas is as likely to win an election as the Palestinian Authority, the draft curriculum does not see fit to even mention its existence. This one-sided curriculum is propaganda, not education.

Critics of Israel often bristle at the idea that they are promoting anti-Semitism. And it is, of course, possible to criticize Israeli policies without being an anti-Semite. But this egregious draft curriculum shows yet again how hatred of Israel leads even intelligent people to downplay anti-Semitism. Acknowledging the global breadth and depth of anti-Semitism might be seen as justifying the need for a Jewish state to protect Jews from violence and oppression. This would complicate the narrative that a Jewish state is a form of apartheid, which is how the draft curriculum describes it.

To be clear, this is a draft, not a final product. At a press conference on Wednesday, California State Superintendent of Public Instruction Tony Thurmond stated, "Jews are being attacked at this time in synagogues. Acts of hate are happening against the Jewish people. They must be included."

Nonetheless, it is important to ask how such a biased document has gotten this far. If one looks at the fact that the same document ignores anti-Semitism and also demonizes Israel, it is difficult to ignore the link between these two attitudes. If a person thinks that the world's only Jewish state is an unredeemed villain and that it hides behind the excuse of anti-Semitism to justify its existence as a Jewish state, of course, that person is going to be more likely to ignore evidence of anti-Semitism. The demonization of Israel and the white-washing of anti-Semitism in the same document is not a coincidence. Not only should the draft be drastically altered, but Californian's should be demanding that process for creating it be reformed as well.

Print Citations

CMS: Gerstmann, Evan. "Political Correctness and Anti-Jewish Bias Mar First Draft of California's Ethnic Studies Curriculum." In *The Reference Shelf: Hate Crimes,* edited by Sophie Zyla, 139–141. Amenia, NY: Grey House Publishing, 2020.

MLA: Gerstmann, Evan. "Political Correctness and Anti-Jewish Bias Mar First Draft of California's Ethnic Studies Curriculum." *The Reference Shelf: Hate Crimes,* edited by Sophie Zyla, Grey Housing Publishing, 2020, pp. 139–141.

APA: Gerstmann, E. (2020). Political correctness and anti-Jewish bias mar first draft of California's ethnic studies curriculum. In Sophie Zyla (Ed.), *The reference shelf: Hate crimes* (pp. 139–141). Amenia, NY: Grey Housing Publishing.

Justice Department Commemorates 10th Anniversary of Matthew Shepard and James Byrd, Jr., Hate Crimes Prevention Act

U.S. Department of Justice, October 16, 2019

In commemoration of the tenth anniversary of the enactment of the Matthew Shepard and James Byrd, Jr., Hate Crimes Prevention Act, the Department of Justice today announced technical assistance resources to fight hate crimes across the country, including development of a new hate crimes training curriculum for law enforcement, and a hate crimes outreach and engagement program for communities entitled United Against Hate: Cultivating Community Partnerships.

"Hate crimes are especially reprehensible because of the toll they take on families, communities, and our nation as a whole. Precisely because they are fueled by bias against specific people and groups, they also are a grave affront to America's foundational principles and ideals," said Attorney General William P. Barr. "That is why the Department of Justice is committed to using every tool at its disposal to combat crimes motivated by this kind of intolerance. The measures announced at today's commemoration of the tenth anniversary of the Hate Crimes Prevention Act will strengthen our ability to identify and prosecute those who perpetrate these unconscionable acts of hatred."

"The tenth anniversary of the Shepard-Byrd Act reminds us of the Act's continued importance. Today Department of Justice officials, law enforcement, and other Americans have come together to highlight both the substantial efforts we have made to combat, prevent, and prosecute hate crimes, and the critical work still to be done," said Assistant Attorney General Eric Dreiband for the Civil Rights Division.

A year ago this month, in October 2018, the Department's Hate Crimes Enforcement and Prevention Initiative convened a law enforcement roundtable on hate crimes. The day and a half–long event, highlighted in a forthcoming report, brought law enforcement and other leaders from around the country together with Department of Justice officials to explore successful practices and challenges in identifying, reporting, and tracking hate crimes. At the roundtable, it was announced that technical assistance through the Collaborative Reform Initiative for Technical Assistance Center (CRI-TAC)a partnership with the International Association of Chiefs of Police and nine leading law enforcement leadership and labor organizations, funded through the Office of Community Oriented Policing Services

(COPS Office), would be extended to help state, local, and tribal law enforcement with hate crimes prosecution and prevention.

The Department today announced that the COPS office is supporting the development of a new hate crimes curriculum through CRI-TAC. This important training will focus on law enforcement response, investigation, and reporting of hate crimes consistent with the Administration's guidance. The course when developed and made available will be focused on increasing the capacity and competency to investigate and accurately report hate crimes, and pursuing the best option for prosecution of perpetrators.

At last year's roundtable, law enforcement emphasized the single most important tool the federal government could provide would be training to improve investigating and reporting of hate crimes to state, local, and tribal law enforcement.

"The training is directly responsive to the requests from the field that we heard at the Initiative's Law Enforcement Roundtable, and embodies our philosophy of 'by the field, for the field,'" said COPS Director Phil Keith.

In addition to the hate crimes training, the Department is also launching a two-phase hate crimes outreach and engagement program. The outreach program "United Against Hate: Cultivating Community Partnerships," aims to address the underreporting of hate crimes to law enforcement. In phase two of the outreach program the U.S. Attorney's Offices will have the opportunity to facilitate trainings across the country, convening a wide array of community groups, such as advocacy organizations, educators, and local leaders (including religious leaders) to discuss the impact of hate crimes and explore strategies to build trust with federal, state, local, and tribal law enforcement.

In recent years, the Department has strengthened its hate crimes prosecution program and increased training of federal, state, and local law enforcement officers to ensure that hate crimes are identified and prosecuted to the fullest extent possible. Over the past 10 years, the Department of Justice has charged more than 330 defendants with hate crimes offenses, including more than 70 defendants total during FY 2017, 2018, and 2019. During this three-year time period, the Department has obtained convictions of more than 65 defendants for hate crimes incidents with some cases still pending.

Hate crimes prosecutions are often high profile and their impact is felt nationally and sometimes internationally. This year, the Department's hate crimes prosecutors have handled several high-profile investigations and criminal prosecutions, including cases in Charlottesville, VA, Pittsburgh, PA, and Jeffersontown, KY.

In southern California, after a shooter killed one and wounded three others at the Chabad of Poway Synagogue, and set fire to the Dar-ul-Arqam Mosque in Escondido, the Department secured a 113-count indictment that included numerous hate crimes charges. And in Dallas, Texas, the Department secured a

> **Hate crimes prosecutions are aften high profile and their impact is felt nationally and internationally.**

guilty plea from a man for kidnapping and conspiracy charges for his involvement in a scheme to single out men because of their sexual orientation. The defendant conspired with others to use Grindr, a social media platform, to lure gay men to areas around Dallas for robbery, carjacking, kidnapping, and violent hate crimes.

"The FBI's mission is simple but profound: to uphold the Constitution and protect the American people. It's why battling hate crime is one of the FBI's top priorities," said FBI Director Christopher Wray. "Hate crime strikes at the very heart of our society, targeting people in our communities based solely on who they are. The FBI will not allow this threat to cast a shadow over our safety and our security. We'll continue to work with our law enforcement partners and use every tool at our disposal to prevent and investigate acts of hate and protect the American people."

"Prosecuting hate crimes is critical to keeping our community safe. When one member of a group in the community is the victim of a hate crime, all members carry with them a fear that they too may be targeted because of who they are," said U.S. Attorney for the District of Columbia Jessie K. Liu, Chair of the Attorney General's Advisory Committee. "The Department of Justice will use every tool at its disposal to protect the people of the United States from these cowardly crimes."

The Department offers a variety of training and outreach programs to work with local communities and organizations and law enforcement to find, identify, investigate, and prosecute hate crimes cases all over the country. These programs include state and local law enforcement trainings, roundtable and panel discussions, stakeholder telephone conferences, and hate crime summits.

"For example, in Fiscal Year 2019, the Community Relations Service (CRS) facilitated 19 Protecting Places of Worship forums and 10 Hate Crime Forums across the United States where law enforcement and other experts shared best practices with community groups working to prevent and respond to hate crimes," said Gerri Ratliff, CRS Deputy Director.

Print Citations

CMS: "Justice Department Commemorates 10th Anniversary of Matthew Shepard and James Byrd, Jr., Hate Crimes Prevention Act." In *The Reference Shelf: Hate Crimes*, edited by Sophie Zyla, 142–144. Amenia, NY: Grey House Publishing, 2020.

MLA: "Justice Department Commemorates 10th Anniversary of Matthew Shepard and James Byrd, Jr., Hate Crimes Prevention Act." *The Reference Shelf: Hate Crimes*, edited by Sophie Zyla, Grey Housing Publishing, 2020, pp. 142–144.

APA: U.S. Department of Justice. (2020). Justice Department commemorates 10th anniversary of Matthew Shepard and James Byrd, Jr., Hate Crimes Prevention Act." In Sophie Zyla (Ed.), *The reference shelf: Hate crimes* (pp. 142–144). Amenia, NY: Grey Housing Publishing.

5
The Role of the Media and Big Tech

Photo by Michal Klajban, via Wikimedia.

The New Zealand Christchurch Mosque, above, was the scene of a shooting that killed 51 people, which was streamed live on social media. It is the most notorious example of live-streaming a violent hate crime. If white supremacist groups were treated as terrorist organizations, they would be banned from major social media sites.

The Connected Society

Many of us carry a cell phone or tablet with us all day, every day. We have become accustomed to instant updates on a variety of subjects, and often see eyewitness videos of events that go viral before the authorities even arrive on the scene.

Digital Footprints Aid FBI Agents and Law Enforcement

Along with vehicles and residences, a perpetrator's social media activity is now searched after a hate crime. Text messages, photos, location tracking from cell phone data, and postings of criminal activity plans provide much-needed information to law enforcement. The posting of a manifesto, which often includes motive for a crime, and affiliation with a hate group, are gathered as evidence. Home and work computers are often seized, and postings are also removed in order to prevent copycat crimes and glorifying the criminal with media exposure.

The United States has a long history of hate. Today, it has re-surfaced in an intense and disturbing way. Reasons for the current rise in hate crimes and mass shootings include mental illness, the internet, guns, and rhetoric of political leaders. Copycat crimes are not new but have become a growing concern after each new hate crime occurs or a manifesto or video is released to social media.

Role of Journalists

Cherlan George of the Ethical Journalism Network defines hate speech as "any expression that vilifies an identifiable group—a race, religious community, or sexual minority, for example—and thus prompts harm to members." George acknowledges that hate speech presents a major challenge to journalism as it is often difficult to differentiate censorship from deleting hate speech. George claims that many media organizations cannot afford to thoroughly review their platforms on a regular basis.

Mainstream media finds itself deciding not only what to report but also having to fact-check newsworthy stories and statistics. There is a fine line between providing a platform to extremists and reporting controversial news that makes for popular stories. The June 2016 Orlando nightclub shooting that took the lives of 49 individuals is noted for spawning hate speech by religious leaders and other commentators stating that the victims got what they deserved. George states: "Like covering crime, corruption and the abuse of political power, covering hate campaigns calls on journalism's highest principles and deepest skills."[1]

Will the Haters Please Step Forward?

Journalist Issie Lapowsky covered a congressional hearing on hate crimes in 2019 in response to the Christchurch massacre in New Zealand, in which shooter Brenton

Tarrant posted live footage online which spread quickly on Facebook, YouTube, and other social media platforms.

Lapowsky noted, "YouTube even had to disable comments on the House Judiciary Committee's livestream of the hearing because it filled up with so much filth." She said that talk about hate crimes and white nationalism became a four-hour squabble over who's most hated, and who's doing the hating, in America. No consensus or answers resulted. Representative Mary Gay Scalon said the only thing accomplished was "pitting minority groups against each other. The haters . . . got their way and the tech giants that have allowed those hatemongers to fester and find each other got off scot free." Facebook and Google representatives took part in the hearing as did members of other organizations. Candace Owens of the conservative group Turning Points USA stated "the real hatred is coming from Democrats and gave tech companies cover for their role in stoking hate." Eileen Hershenov, senior vice president of the Anti-Defamation League, said that moderating content on one site may drive individuals to other platforms where their violent threats can be less visible to authorities and more dangerous.[2] Tarrant chose his plans based on the hope that it would create conflict in the United States. His message to white nationalists used paintings, writings, songs, dances, poetry, and memes.[3]

Social media and online platforms, not just ways to share inspiration and good news, turned into catalysts of hate. Zachary Laub in an article for the Council on Foreign Relations raises many concerns with online platforms, including attacks on minorities, inflammatory speech, and violent acts: "At their most extreme, rumors and invective disseminated online have contributed to violence ranging from lynchings to ethnic cleansing." Social media has offered opportunities for individuals inclined toward racism, misogyny, or homophobia to find ways to reinforce their views and violent tendencies. Algorithms lead to sites that are misleading, contain conspiracy theories, or are radicalizing. Laws and standards vary worldwide, and there are a limited amount of content moderators. Mark Zuckerberg of Facebook "called for global regulations to establish baseline content, electoral integrity, privacy, and data standards." Facebook admitted some responsibility for its platform inciting violence against the Rohingya community in Myanmar in 2015, resulting in the forced emigration to Bangladesh of 700,000 members of the minority Muslim group. Facebook has since banned some organizations from its platform and agreed to increase fluent moderators.

In the United States social media platforms are protected by the Communications Decency Act of 1996, which exempts them from liability for their users' content. In the European Union, tech companies have agreed to review user-flagged posts, removing those in violation within twenty-four hours. The European Commission, in a 2019 review, saw this happen in three-quarters of cases. Similar laws for removing content within twenty-four hours exist in India, Japan, and Germany.

Laub says, "Cases of genocide and crimes against humanity could be the next frontier of social media jurisprudence, drawing on precedents set in Nuremberg and Rwanda." He cites the conviction of a publisher in the post-Nazi Germany Nuremberg trials and of two media executives by the UN International Criminal

Tribunal in the case of Rwanda for the crime of "direct and public incitement to commit genocide." Prosecutors are looking at Myanmar and social media for similar charges.[4]

Social Media Solutions

Daniel Byman and Christopher Meserole in "How Big Tech Can Fight White Supremacist Terrorism" write that "from a technical and moral point of view, white supremacist content is no different from jihadi content" and the initial step in restricting the spread of hate online is to "treat all ideologies the same." ISIS was banned in 2014 from posting on many major sites due to its official designation as a terrorist organization. Tech companies and those running social media platforms have hired skilled content monitors to identify terrorist content and distinguish it from legitimate political speech. The Global Internet Forum to Counter Terrorism was started by the major tech companies in 2017. Facebook employs 200 terrorism analysts and more than 15,000 content monitors to monitor more than two billion users globally. Do tech companies have the responsibility to publish listings of extremists and organizations? Such listings might make it easier for smaller tech companies, who don't have the same resources, to know what to ban. Increased transparency will also help governments and the public evaluate if tech companies are striking the right balance between allowing free speech and preventing hate crimes.[5]

Works Used

Byman, Daniel, and Christopher Meserole. "How Big Tech Can Fight White Supremacist Terrorism." *Foreign Affairs*. Aug 15, 2019. https://www.foreignaffairs.com/articles/united-states/2019-08-15/how-big-tech-can-fight-white-supremacist-terrorism.

George, Cherlan. "Hate Speech: A Dilemma for Journalists the World Over." *Ethical Journalism Network (EJN)*. https://ethicaljournalismnetwork.org/resources/publications/ethics-in-the-news/hate-speech.

Kirkpatrick, David D. "Massacre Suspect Traveled the World but Lived on the Internet." *New York Times*. Mar 15, 2019. https://www.nytimes.com/2019/03/15/world/asia/new-zealand-shooting-brenton-tarrant.html.

Lapowsky, Issie. "In Congressional Hearing in Hate, the Haters Got Their Way." *Wired*. Apr 9, 2019. https://www.wired.com/story/house-hearing-hate-crimes-white-nationalism/.

Laub, Zachary. "Hate Speech on Social Media: Global Comparisons." *Council on Foreign Relations*. Jun 7, 2019. https://www.cfr.org/backgrounder/hate-speech-social-media-global-comparisons.

Notes

1. George, "Hate Speech: A Dilemma for Journalists the World Over."
2. Lapowsky, "In Congressional Hearings in Hate, the Haters Got Their Way."
3. Kirkpatrick, "Massacre Suspect Traveled the World but Lived on the Internet."

4. Laub, "Hate Speech on Social Media: Global Comparisons."
5. Byman and Meserole, "How Big Tech Can Fight White Supremacist Terrorism."

How Journalists Cover Mass Shootings: Research to Consider

By Denise-Marie Ordway
Journalist's Resource, **August 6, 2019**

After covering a major tragedy such as a mass shooting, it's helpful for editors and reporters to review their work. What did they do well? What were their shortcomings and oversights? How did their coverage impact audiences, communities and victims' families? And just as important: How can the newsroom do a better job next time?

Unfortunately, in the case of mass shootings, some news outlets might have to deal with a next time.

To help guide newsrooms in their conversations about how they cover mass shootings, we've gathered a sampling of research that examines news coverage from several angles, including how journalists portray shooters of different races and religious backgrounds. We've included two studies that look specifically at how the *New York Times* covers mass shootings and which factors—for example, the location of a shooting or the perpetrator's motivation for killing—affect how much time and resources the newspaper dedicates to each event. This collection of research has been updated since it was originally posted in December 2018.

Media Coverage and Firearm Acquisition in the Aftermath of a Mass Shooting

Porfiri, Maurizio, et al. *Nature Human Behavior*, 2019.

For this study, researchers examined the relationship between news coverage of mass shootings and firearm purchases in the U.S. They find a "potential causal link" between news articles about gun control policies in the aftermath of a mass shooting and increased gun sales. The researchers also find that firearm acquisition increases nationally as well as in states with the weakest firearm laws. "Many firearm control advocates regard the aftermath of a mass shooting to be a fertile policy window: as people's attention is captured by these gruesome incidents, more restrictive policies might gain traction among policymakers, and legislatures may become more amenable to change," write the authors, led by New York University professor Maurizio Porfiri. "However, this increased attention may elicit a parallel reaction, in which people may fear that their access to firearms will be soon restrained and, thus, opt to purchase firearms before this happens."

The researchers analyzed information on mass shootings that they collected from a database created by the investigative news outlet *Mother Jones*. They looked at 69 mass shootings that occurred in public locations between 1999 and 2017, excluding any that were connected to gang activity or armed robberies. They also examined media coverage of firearm laws and regulations provided by the *New York Times* and the *Washington Post* during that time period. Because there is no national registry or record of gun acquisition in the U.S., Porfiri and his colleagues used federal weapons background check numbers as a proxy for gun acquisition. They examined monthly data on background checks conducted between January 1999 and December 2017.

What they found was that federal weapons background checks spiked after a mass shooting. "The highest number of background checks at the national level (n = 2,171,293) was recorded in December 2012, which follows the Sandy Hook Elementary School shooting," they write. They also note that news coverage was most concentrated in January 2013, in the aftermath of the Sandy Hook massacre. "The number of background checks increases with the number of mass shootings, and both of these variables increase with relevant media output," they write.

Can a Non-Muslim Mass Shooter Be a "Terrorist"?: A Comparative Content Analysis of the Las Vegas and Orlando Shootings

Elmasry, Mohamad Hamas; el-Nawawy, Mohammed. *Journalism Practice*, 2019.

Researchers analyzed news coverage of mass shootings in Las Vegas in 2017 and Orlando in 2016 to determine whether there are differences in the way journalists portrayed the two perpetrators—an American Muslim of Afghani origin and a white, non-Muslim American. They found big differences. Among them: "The Orlando shooting, carried out by a Muslim, was allotted more coverage despite the fact that it produced nine fewer fatalities than the Las Vegas shooting, perpetrated by a white non-Muslim," the authors write. "The analysis also showed that the examined newspapers were more likely to employ a 'terrorism' frame in their coverage of the Orlando shooting than in their coverage of the Las Vegas shooting; link the Orlando mass shooting with the global war on terrorism; and to humanize Stephen Paddock, the white perpetrator of the Las Vegas shooting."

Mohamad Hamas Elmasry, an assistant professor at the University of North Alabama, and Mohammed el-Nawawy, a professor at the Queens University of Charlotte, looked at how the *Los Angeles Times* and the *New York Times* framed the two shootings. They chose these news outlets, they write, "because of their status as elite American newspapers capable of setting the agenda for other American news outlets, and also because they represent the two largest media markets in the United States and the East and West coasts of the country, respectively." They studied the newspapers' coverage during the week following each shooting, analyzing a total of 190 news articles and editorials.

Elmasry and el-Nawawy explain that their findings suggest the Muslim shooter's religious and ethnic identities might have prompted more news coverage. The

Muslim perpetrator was called a "terrorist" in about 38% of articles about the Orlando shooting. The non-Muslim perpetrator was labeled a "terrorist" in 5% of articles about the Las Vegas shooting. Meanwhile, about 55% of articles focusing on the Orlando massacre described the perpetrator as a "gunman," compared with more than 80% of articles about the Las Vegas killings.

The researchers warn that differences in how the two shooters were framed could reinforce fears of Islam and Muslims. Also, they write that the "downplaying of white male identity in violent crimes carried out by white men may prevent the public's learning about the potential threat of white male shooters."

A Comparative Analysis of Media Coverage of Mass Public Shootings: Examining Rampage, Disgruntled Employee, School, and Lone-Wolf Terrorist Shootings in the United States

Silva, Jason R.; Capellan, Joel A. *Criminal Justice Policy Review*, forthcoming.

This paper focuses on differences in how journalists cover different types of mass shootings and whether these differences have changed over time. The authors also pose the question: Are newsrooms intentionally emphasizing certain kinds of mass shootings?

To gain insights, the authors compiled a database of mass shootings that happened in public spaces between 1966 and 2016, placing them into one of four categories: school, disgruntled employee, lone-wolf terrorist and rampage. The researchers—Jason Silva of the John Jay College of Criminal Justice and Joel Capellan of Rowan University—consider a mass public shooting to be "an incident of targeted violence where an offender had killed or attempted to kill four or more victims on a public stage." A firearm is the primary weapon used in these attacks, which aren't connected to profit-driven crime such as drug trafficking or gang violence.

Silva and Capellan find that 19% of the 314 shootings identified occurred at schools, including college campuses, and 32% involved disgruntled employees who targeted their current or former place of work. Meanwhile, 13% were "lone-wolf terrorist" shootings in which the perpetrator acted alone, motivated by ideological extremism. The remaining 34%, labeled "rampage" shootings, are those that don't fall into the other three categories. The authors also examined the *New York Times'* print coverage of mass public shootings over the same 50-year period.

What their analyses reveals is that even though school shootings and those perpetrated by lone-wolf terrorists make up a combined 32% of all mass public shootings, they received 75% to 80% of the *Times'* total coverage of mass shootings. Conversely, disgruntled employee and rampage shootings make up a combined 68% of all mass public shootings but received 15% to 20% of the news coverage. Silva and Capellan point out that, over time, school and lone-wolf terrorist shootings consistently received a larger number of news articles and words compared with rampage and disgruntled employee shootings. "It is important to note," the authors write, "that lone-wolf terrorists experienced the highest growth in news coverage between 1966 and 2016. In the 1970s and 1980s, lone-wolf terrorist shootings received an average of 10 to 15 articles, but by the 1990s, news salience increased to 30 articles, and by [the] 2010s, these ideologically motivated shootings received more than 40 articles on average."

The authors suggest the *Times* may be purposely giving more attention to school and lone-wolf terrorist shootings. "This study finds the disproportionate amount of coverage given to school and lone-wolf terrorist incidents is not warranted, given their relative threat to public safety," they write. The emphasis on these two types of mass shootings, Silva and Capellan write, "may serve to (a) potentially distort public anxiety and perceptions of risk and (b) drive into the public policy agenda a range of measures that may be ineffective and even counterproductive in preventing such incidents." They add that "the relative dearth in coverage of other types of mass shootings (disgruntled employee and rampage violence) threatens to undermine policy and preventive responses."

Mental Illness, the Media, and the Moral Politics of Mass Violence: The Role of Race in Mass Shootings Coverage

Duxbury, Scott W.; Frizzell, Laura C.; Lindsay, Sade L. *Journal of Research in Crime and Delinquency*, 2018.

Three researchers from Ohio State University examined news coverage of mass shootings to see how journalists portray perpetrators of different races. A key finding: Stories about white or Latino shooters were much more likely to suggest that mental illness was to blame than stories involving black perpetrators.

"The odds that White shooters will receive the mental illness frame are roughly 19 times greater than the odds for Black shooters," Scott Duxbury and his colleagues write. "The odds that a Latino shooter will receive the mental illness frame are roughly 12 times greater when compared to Blacks."

The researchers analyzed news articles written about mass shootings between January 1, 2013 and December 31, 2015. They used *News Bank* and *Lexis Nexis* to conduct a national search for articles that mention or allude to the race of the perpetrator and the motive or an explanation for the killings. The researchers only examined shootings with four or more victims, excluding the perpetrator.

The research team also discovered that when journalists reported or insinuated that a white shooter was mentally ill, they tended to "establish the offender as a good person suffering from extreme life circumstances." This happened only sometimes when the shooter was Latino and almost never when the shooter was black.

"Blacks in the mental illness subsample never receive testament to their good character nor do the media ever claim that the shooting was out of character," the authors explain. "Further … the media only frame White shooters as coming from a good environment."

When journalists reported a mass shooting was gang related, perpetrators generally were people of color. In these stories, the researchers found that journalists usually referenced the shooters' criminal histories and portrayed them as public menaces. For example, when people made statements about the shooters, journalists quoted them as saying such things as, "Everyone is relieved that this individual is off the street" and "He is part of some kind of new generation that is absolutely heartless."

Covering Mass Murder: An Experimental Examination of the Effect of News Focus—Killer, Victim, or Hero—on Reader Interest

Levin, Jack; Wiest, Julie B. *American Behavioral Scientist*, 2018.

Jack Levin, a professor emeritus at Northeastern University, and Julie B. Wiest, a sociologist at West Chester University, conducted an electronic survey of 212 adults, aged 35 to 44 years, to gauge their interest in reading different kinds of news coverage of a school shooting. They found that people were much more interested in reading a story that focused on the actions of a courageous bystander than those focusing on the shooter or his victims.

For the study, Levin and Wiest presented survey participants with different versions of the same news story. In all three versions, the photos, font sizes, layout, main headline and pull-out quote were identical. But one story focused on the killer. One focused on a victim. And one story focused on a "hero student who stopped the attack."

Nearly 73% of participants chose to read the hero story after the first paragraph. Meanwhile, 55.7% chose to read the story that focused on the killer beyond the first paragraph. Of those assigned to read the article that focused on the victim, 52.2% opted to read past the first paragraph.

"Subjects' greater interest in the hero-focused story may be interpreted as an information-seeking behavior, as it presumably would provide information about how to stop a mass murderer and avoid future victimization," the authors write. "Although all stories suggested a certain threat, those that focused on the killer and victim offered uncertain solutions ... which may explain why they were less interesting to subjects."

The researchers note that coverage focusing on courageous bystanders could prompt positive copycat behavior. "If the copycat phenomenon applies to increasing the prevalence of mass killers, why would it not also apply to increasing the prevalence of heroes who take an active role in ending a mass murder?" they write.

The researchers also found that people who reported feeling anxious or afraid that they or someone they love could become victims of a mass murder were more interested in reading stories about mass shootings than individuals who said they felt little or no fear.

Levin and Wiest write that their findings provide lessons for journalists.

Although there is some evidence that sensational and shocking coverage of crime events may increase news consumption (likely by way of inducing fear), news outlets that employ such tactics may not be giving consumers what they want," they write. "It seems clear that news consumers seek crime stories that reduce uncertainty, offer practical solutions, and include relevant contextual information that suggests the possibility of an effective response to violence.

Covering Mass Shootings: Journalists' Perceptions of Coverage and Factors Influencing Attitudes

Dahmen, Nicole Smith; Abdenour, Jesse; McIntyre, Karen; Noga-Styron, Krystal E. *Journalism Practice*, 2018.

This study, led by faculty at the University of Oregon's School of Journalism and Communication, examines journalists' attitudes about news coverage of mass shootings in the U.S. Among the main takeaways: Journalists, by a small margin, agreed that coverage is "sensational" and most agreed that the way newsrooms cover these events "is an ethical issue." Meanwhile, journalists generally did not acknowledge a connection between mass shooting coverage and copycat shooters—a connection found in previous research.

"Most journalists were in favor of perpetrator coverage and did not believe it glamorized suspected perpetrators," the authors write. "Most news workers likely do not want to believe that their work contributes to further carnage and suffering, despite evidence showing that fame-seeking mass shooters and a contagion effect do, in fact, exist."

The researchers surveyed 1,318 journalists from newspapers with a circulation of 10,000 or more, asking them how strongly they agree or disagree with certain statements. About half of the people who participated were reporters while almost 26% were editors, 14.5% were photographers or videographers and 2.4% were columnists. Most—60%—were men and 89.4% were white.

Nicole Dahmen and her colleagues find that age is a powerful predictor of how journalists feel about mass shooting coverage. "Older journalists held a more favorable opinion of the state of mass shooting coverage, more strongly supported coverage of perpetrators, and were less receptive to the idea that mass shooting coverage is an ethical issue," they write.

They also discovered that editors had a more positive view of coverage than reporters and photographers and that white journalists had a much higher opinion of it than journalists of other races. "Non-white respondents were more likely to be critical of mass shooting coverage," the researchers write.

Mass Shootings and the Media: Why All Events Are Not Created Equal

Schildkraut, Jaclyn; Elsass, H. Jaymi; Meredith, Kimberly. *Journal of Crime and Justice*, 2017.

For this study, researchers analyzed one large national newspaper's coverage of mass shootings to see how factors such as victim counts, the location of a shooting and the shooter's race affect the newsworthiness of each event. Here's the gist of what they learned: "Race/ethnicity and victim counts are the most salient predictor of whether or not a shooting was covered, with perpetrators of Asian and other descent and those events with higher victim counts generating more prominent coverage (measured as higher article and word counts), whereas incidents occurring in locations other than schools yielded less coverage," they write.

The research team, led by Jaclyn Schildkraut of State University of New York at Oswego, examined the *New York Times'* coverage of

> **How did the coverage impact audiences, communities, and victims' families? How can the newsroom do a better job next time?**

90 mass shootings between 2000 and 2012. The team only included mass shootings in which victims and locations were targeted at random or "for their symbolic value." Researchers excluded shootings connected to gang violence and militant or terrorist activities.

The team found considerable variation in coverage. For nearly 78% of shootings, coverage was limited to fewer than five articles. Half the shootings received fewer than 1,500 words. Almost 60% of all the articles the *Times* printed about mass shootings during this period focused on five incidents: the attempted assassination of Congresswoman Gabrielle Giffords in 2011 and shootings at Virginia Tech in 2007, the Fort Hood military base in 2009, Sandy Hook Elementary School in 2012 and a Century 16 movie theater in Aurora, Colorado in 2012.

Schildkraut and her colleagues found that when the shooter was Asian or from "other" racial groups—a category that includes Middle Eastern, Indian, Native American and multiracial people—the *Times* published more and longer stories about the incident than when the shooter was white. The analysis also revealed that shootings occurring in the Northeast garnered more attention than those in the South, which, historically, has tended to be more violent.

The Media's Coverage of Mass Public Shootings in America: Fifty Years of Newsworthiness

Silva, Jason R.; Capellan, Joel A. *International Journal of Comparative and Applied Criminal Justice*, 2018.

This study also looks at variation in the *New York Times'* coverage of mass shootings, but over a longer period—50 years. Jason Silva of the John Jay College of Criminal Justice and Joel Capellan of Rowan University analyzed 3,510 articles written about 314 mass shootings that occurred in the U.S. between 1966 and 2016. For the purposes of their research, they defined a mass shooting as "an incident of targeted violence where an offender has killed or attempted to kill four or more victims on a public stage." Gang-related shootings were excluded.

Silva and Capellan also found a lot of variation in the *Times'* coverage. Three quarters of the shootings drew little coverage—fewer than four articles and fewer than 4,028 words each. Meanwhile, 68% of all articles the newspaper wrote about mass shootings during those five decades focused on 15 incidents, starting with the University of Texas tower shooting in 1966. The Columbine High School shooting in 1999 received the most coverage of any of the shootings, followed by the Sandy Hook shooting in 2012. The *Times* published a total of 503 articles about the Columbine massacre and 248 on Sandy Hook.

Some of the other big takeaways: Massacres at schools, government buildings and religious institutions got more coverage than those occurring at businesses. Shooters of Middle Eastern descent received more coverage than shooters of other races. For example, the *Times* covered 90% of shootings involving a Middle Eastern perpetrator, 74.3% of shootings with a white perpetrator and 60% of shootings with a Latino perpetrator. Shootings motivated by ideological extremism were much more likely to be covered than those that were not.

"Eight of the top 15 cases were ideologically motivated," Silva and Capellan write. "The finding that Middle Eastern perpetrators are more newsworthy also suggests the overrepresentation of jihad-inspired mass public shootings in media coverage of the phenomenon."

Print Citations

CMS: Ordway, Denise-Marie. "How Journalists Cover Mass Shootings: Research to Consider." In *The Reference Shelf: Hate Crimes*, edited by Sophie Zyla, 151–158. Amenia, NY: Grey House Publishing, 2020.

MLA: Ordway, Denise-Marie. "How Journalists Cover Mass Shootings: Research to Consider." *The Reference Shelf: Hate Crimes*, edited by Sophie Zyla, Grey Housing Publishing, 2020, pp. 151–158.

APA: Ordway, D.-M. (2020). How journalists cover mass shootings: Research to consider. In Sophie Zyla (Ed.), *The reference shelf: Hate crimes* (pp. 151–158). Amenia, NY: Grey Housing Publishing.

In Congressional Hearing on Hate, the Haters Got Their Way

By Issie Lapowsky
Wired, April 9, 2019

Tuesday's House Judiciary Committee hearing on the rise of hate crimes and white nationalism devolved into a four-hour squabble over who's most hated, and who's doing the hating, in America. The members of the committee and some of the eight witnesses who sat before them battled over whether anti-semitism or anti-black hate is most deserving of their attention, and whether it's white supremacists or Muslims or Democrats or the President who harbor the most hate. Meanwhile, in cyberspace, the comment section on the YouTube livestream of the hearing filled up with so much filth that YouTube had to shut it down.

Like so many congressional hearings before it, the committee failed to reach any meaningful bipartisan consensus or elicit illuminating answers from the representatives from Facebook and Google who sat before them. Instead, by the time it ended, it seemed the hearing had succeeded in doing just one thing, and that is, as Representative Mary Gay Scanlon (D-Pennsylvania) put it, pitting minority groups against each other. The haters, in other words, got their way—and the tech giants that have allowed those hatemongers to fester and find each other got off scot free.

The impetus for the hearing was, of course, the recent mass shooting in Christchurch, New Zealand, in which an apparent white supremacist, deeply steeped in alt-right internet culture, slaughtered 50 people at two mosques, and broadcast the attack on Facebook Live. That video spread far and wide on Facebook, YouTube, and other platforms, leaving tech companies helpless to stop its spread. As a result, among the witnesses at Tuesday's hearing were representatives from Facebook and Google who work on the platforms' content policies.

It seemed possible that such an obvious tragedy, which so clearly exposed how tech platforms have become a honeypot for hate and violence, might prompt even a deeply divided Washington to seek real answers about what to do about it. But that was too much to hope for.

Some of the day's witnesses came armed with facts about the scope of the problem. There was Eileen Hershenov, senior vice president of the Anti-Defamation League, who explained that over the past decade white supremacists have committed more than 50 percent of all domestic extremism-related murders. Over the past year, they've accounted for more than three-quarters of them. Others, like Mohammad Abu-Salha, came to tell their stories. In 2015, Abu-Salha's two daughters and son-in-law were shot and killed at home in Chapel Hill, North Carolina, a gruesome murder that Abu-Salha believes was driven by anti-Muslim sentiment.

Content moderation can sometimes drive people spewing hate to other platforms, where their threats of violence are less visible to law enforcement.

The alleged shooter is still awaiting trial for first-degree murder in what investigators initially said was a parking dispute. "There's no question in our mind this tragedy was born of bigotry and hate," Abu-Salha said, choking up at times as he spoke.

Candace Owens, a conservative commentator with the group Turning Points USA, said in her opening remarks that the real hatred is coming from Democrats and gave tech companies cover for their role in stoking hate. "They blame Facebook. They blame Google. They blame Twitter. Really, they blame the birth of social media, which has disrupted their monopoly on minds," Owens said of Democrats. "They called this hearing, because they believe if it wasn't for social media, voices like mine would never exist."

Owens accused Democrats of "manipulating statistics" on hate crimes, a notion Hershenov was quick to dismiss, and said that if the left really cared about cracking down on white nationalism, they would hold a hearing on the far-left group antifa, which Owens said chased her out of a Philadelphia restaurant.

As all this unfolded, the tech industry representatives—Neil Potts of Facebook and Alexandria Walden of Google—mostly sat back, fielding overly simple questions about whether Facebook allows people to report hate or how YouTube spots videos that violate its policies. Even those committee members who seemed serious about holding tech companies accountable lacked the time needed to pin the companies down on, for instance, whether they have historically policed white supremacist content as fiercely as they've monitored, say, ISIS content. And if not, why not?

Hershenov, meanwhile, raised the important point that content moderation can sometimes drive people spewing hate to other platforms where their threats of violence are less visible to law enforcement, and possibly, more dangerous. But Potts wasn't asked to answer for how Facebook plans to police these very threats in the future, when, if CEO Mark Zuckerberg stays true to his recent promises, all Messenger, WhatsApp, and Instagram direct messages will be encrypted. Nor were either of the techies on the panel asked about whether their companies are watching platforms like Gab and 8Chan, which Hershenov described as "digital white supremacist rallies," for signs of what new hateful content might be headed for their sites. And while, in a meta moment, Chairman Jerry Nadler read aloud from a Washington Post story about the hateful YouTube comments on the committee's very own livestream, no one stopped to ask Walden about YouTube's broader issues moderating comments of all kinds.

On Wednesday, the Senate Judiciary Committee will have a chance to follow up on some of these questions in another hearing with Potts and Twitter's director of public policy Carlos Monje, Jr. But if the hearing's title is any indication—Stifling

Free Speech: Technological Censorship and the Public Discourse—it's all but guaranteed to be another good day for the haters.

Print Citations

CMS: Lapowsky, Issie. "In Congressional Hearings in Hate, the Haters Got Their Way." In The Reference Shelf: Hate Crimes, edited by Sophie Zyla, 159–161. Amenia, NY: Grey House Publishing, 2020.

MLA: Lapowsky, Issie. "In Congressional Hearings in Hate, the Haters Got Their Way." The Reference Shelf: Hate Crimes, edited by Sophie Zyla, Grey Housing Publishing, 2020, pp. 159–161.

APA: Lapowsky, I. (2020). In congressional hearings in hate, the haters got their way. In Sophie Zyla (Ed.), The reference shelf: Hate crimes (pp. 159–161). Amenia, NY: Grey Housing Publishing.

A Campus Murder Tests Facebook Clicks as Evidence of Hate

By Issie Lapowsky
Wired, May 23, 2017

Investigators say they still don't know why Sean Urbanski, a 22-year-old University of Maryland student, walked up to 23-year-old Richard Collins III, a US Army lieutenant just days shy of college graduation, and fatally stabbed him at a campus bus stop this weekend. What they do say they know is that Collins, who was visiting a friend at UMD and did not appear to know Urbanski, was black, and that Urbanski belonged to a Facebook group called Alt-Reich: Nation, a haven of white supremacist content.

"Suffice to say that it's despicable," UMD police chief David Mitchell said, at a press conference, of the now deleted Alt-Reich: Nation group. "It shows extreme bias against women, Latinos, members of the Jewish faith, and especially African Americans."

In addition to the local police department's ongoing homicide investigation, the FBI is looking into whether Collins' murder also amounts to a hate crime. The judges and jury of the internet have quickly reached a guilty verdict, but law enforcement is less sure. "We need something probably more than just a Facebook posting," said Angela Alsobrooks, prosecutor for Prince George's County, Maryland, during a press conference Monday.

Digital breadcrumbs have become key pieces of evidence for investigators in the age of social media, but they've also put a unique strain on the legal system, forcing courts to grapple with new questions about the relative significance of a Facebook post, a "Like," a follow, a tweet. It's natural for the public to want to level the harshest punishment on a person who could kill a stranger in cold blood, particularly when that killer lurked in the internet's darkest corners and may have been motivated by racial hatred. But in Urbanski's case, investigators, and eventually the courts, will have to carefully decide how much weight they can really put on a person's online allegiances and whether mere membership in such a hateful online group constitutes evidence of intent to commit a hate crime.

"These are not questions the law has had to answer before," says Neil Richards, a professor of First Amendment and privacy law at Washington University School of Law. "We don't want to permit a system in which merely reading something or associating with other people can be used as strong evidence that you hold the views of the people you hang out with or the things you read."

Critical Evidence

So far, investigators have revealed little about Urbanski's relationship to the Alt-Reich: Nation page. John Erzen, a spokesperson for the Office of the State Attorney for Prince George's County, declined to tell Wired whether Urbanski had ever posted suspicious content in the group. "It's one of many aspects of the investigation right now," he said.

Meanwhile, Matthew Goodman, one of the founders of Alt-Reich: Nation, told the New York Times that he "never saw [Urbanski] comment or like anything" on the page. He also denied that the group had any ties to white supremacy, despite its collection of overtly racist memes.

Barring more evidence revealing some racial animus on Urbanski's part, legal experts say Facebook group membership alone won't be enough to bring a hate crime case against him. "From an investigator's point of view, it's a hot lead," says Dan Rhynhart, chair of commercial litigation at Blank Rome, who has used social media evidence in his cases. "But without more, you'd have a hard time getting that into evidence."

In fact, Rhynhart anticipates such evidence might lead to a pretrial hearing to determine whether it should be considered prejudicial, and therefore withheld from the trial altogether. "That could be the critical piece of evidence that everyone argues about," Rhynhart says.

Joining an online group is a far more passive act than, say, posting a message on Facebook. The latter, says Eric Goldman, codirector of the High Tech Law Institute at Santa Clara University, is a form of communication no different from a written letter, and is therefore subject to the same standards of admissibility of evidence. "We ask questions like: Is it relevant? Is it subject to privacy restrictions? Is it credible? Can we authenticate the evidence?" Goldman says. "Many of those questions apply, with minimal change, to social media."

But joining a Facebook group or, say, following white supremacist Richard Spencer on Twitter doesn't map so easily to those standards. If anything, Goldman says, hanging a hate crime charge on membership in an online hate group would run up against First Amendment rights. "It would be chilling the right of association," he says.

Social Responsibility

The Supreme Court has set some precedent regarding the tenuous balance between First Amendment freedoms and civil rights protections, Richards says. In R.A.V. v. City of St. Paul (1992), authorities charged a group of Minnesota teens who burned a cross on a black family's lawn under a local ordinance that bans symbols that arouse "anger, alarm or resentment in others on the basis of race, color, creed, religion or gender." The Supreme Court unanimously struck down the ordinance, arguing that the law banned only intolerant viewpoints. "You can't punish only racist speech," Richards says. "The First Amendment tries to bridge this uneasy tension between liberty and equality, but American law tends to err on the side of protecting liberty."

In other words, unless investigators discover more evidence of Urbanski's explicit racial bias—and they well may—it's unlikely that the grieving online masses who have already convicted him of a

> **The courts will have to carefully decide how much weight they can really put on a person's online allegiances and whether mere membership in such a hateful online group constitutes evidence of intent to commit a hate crime.**

hate crime in their minds will get the kind of justice they crave.

Still, while they may be unable to change the way the law works, they can still pressure companies like Facebook to more aggressively monitor hateful content on their platforms. "It raises the question of why Facebook allows groups like this to exist," says Mary Anne Franks, who teaches criminal law at the University of Miami School of Law. "You can't blame a Facebook group for the acts of one probably unhinged person, but what possible benefit does a group like this actually serve?"

The First Amendment may protect the freedom of assembly, but as a private company, Franks notes, "Facebook can do, frankly, whatever it wants." Whether prosecutors ultimately charge Urbanski with a hate crime or not, it's important that investigators have at least shined a light on the the existence of these groups, Franks says. "We should take it at least as seriously as we do ISIS groups and propaganda."

Facebook, for its part, recently announced it would hire 3,000 new content moderators this year to review abusive content that Facebook users flag. But the fundamental challenge of policing the internet will remain: One Alt-Reich: Nation has fallen, but another Facebook group with the same name has already risen to take its place.

Print Citations

CMS: Lapowsky, Issie. "A Campus Murder Tests Facebook Clicks as Evidence of Hate." In The Reference Shelf: Hate Crimes, edited by Sophie Zyla, 162–164. Amenia, NY: Grey House Publishing, 2020.

MLA: Lapowsky, Issie. "A Campus Murder Tests Facebook Clicks as Evidence of Hate." The Reference Shelf: Hate Crimes, edited by Sophie Zyla, Grey Housing Publishing, 2020, pp. 162–164.

APA: Lapowsky, I. (2020). A campus murder tests Facebook clicks as evidence of hate. In Sophie Zyla (Ed.), The reference shelf: Hate crimes (pp. 162–164). Amenia, NY: Grey Housing Publishing.

The Media Botched the Covington Catholic Story

By Caitlin Flanagan
The Atlantic, **January 23, 2019**

On Friday, January 18, a group of white teenage boys wearing MAGA hats mobbed an elderly Native American man on the steps of the Lincoln Memorial, chanting "Make America great again," menacing him, and taunting him in racially motivated ways. It is the kind of thing that happens every day—possibly every hour—in Donald Trump's America. But this time there was proof: a video. Was it problematic that it offered no evidence that these things had happened? No. What mattered was that it had happened, and that there was video to prove it. The fact of there being a video became stronger than the video itself.

The video shows a man playing a tribal drum standing directly in front of a boy with clear skin and lips reddened from the cold; the boy is wearing a MAGA hat, and he is smiling at the man in a way that is implacable and inscrutable. The boys around him are cutting up—dancing to the drumbeat, making faces at one another and at various iPhones, and eventually beginning to tire of whatever it is that's going on. Soon enough, the whole of the video's meaning seems to come down to the smiling boy and the drumming man. They are locked into something, but what is it?

Twenty seconds pass, then 30—and still the boy is smiling in that peculiar way. What has brought them to this strange, charged moment? From the short clip alone, it is impossible to tell. Because the point of the viral video was that it was proof of racist bullying yet showed no evidence of it, the boy quickly became the subject of rage and disgust. "I'd be ashamed and appalled if he was my son," the actress Debra Messing tweeted.

A second video also made the rounds. Shot shortly after the event, it consisted of an interview with the drummer, Nathan Phillips. There was something powerful about it, something that seemed almost familiar. It seemed to tell us an old story, one that's been tugging at us for years. It was a battered Rodney King stepping up to the microphones in the middle of the Los Angeles riots, asking, "Can we all get along? Can we get along?" It was the beautiful hippie boy putting flowers in the rifle barrels of military policemen at the March on the Pentagon.

In the golden hour at the Lincoln Memorial, the lights illuminating the vault, Phillips stands framed against the light of the setting sun, wiping tears from his eyes as he describes what has happened—with the boys, with the country, with land itself. His voice soft, unsteady, he begins:

As I was singing, I heard them saying, "Build that wall, build that wall." This is indigenous land; we're not supposed to have walls here. We never did … We never had a wall. We never had a prison. We always took care of our elders. We took care of our children … We taught them right from wrong. I wish I could see … the [young men] could put that energy into making this country really great … helping those that are hungry.

It was moving, and it was an explanation of the terrible thing that had just happened—"I heard them saying, 'Build that wall.'" It was an ode to a nation's lost soul. It was also the first in a series of interviews in which Phillips would prove himself adept—far more so than the news media—at incorporating any new information about what had actually happened into his version of events. His version was all-encompassing, and he was treated with such patronizing gentleness by the news media that he was never directly confronted with his conflicting accounts.

When the country learned that Phillips was—in addition to being, as we were endlessly reminded, a "Native elder"—a veteran of the Vietnam War, the sense of anger about what had happened to him assumed new dimensions. That he had defended our country only to be treated so poorly by these MAGA-hatted monsters blasted the level of the boys' malevolence into outer space.

The journalist Kara Swisher found a way to link the horror to an earlier news event, tweeting:

> And to all you aggrieved folks who thought this Gillette ad was too much bad-men-shaming, after we just saw it come to life with those awful kids and their fetid smirking harassing that elderly man on the Mall: Go fuck yourselves.

You know the left has really changed in this country when you find its denizens glorifying America's role in the Vietnam War and lionizing the social attitudes of the corporate monolith Procter & Gamble.

Celebrities tweeted furiously, desperate to insert themselves into the situation in a flattering light. They adopted several approaches: old-guy concern about the state of our communities ("Where are their parents, where are their teachers, where are their pastors?": Joe Scarborough); dramatic professions of personal anguish meant to recenter the locus of harm from Phillips to the tweeter ("This is Trump's America. And it brought me to tears. What are we teaching our young people? Why is this ok? How is this ok? Please help me understand. Because right now I feel like my heart is living outside of my body": Alyssa Milano); and the inevitable excesses of the temperamentally overexcited: ("#CovingtonCatholic high school seems like a hate factory to me": Howard Dean).

By Saturday, the story had become so hot, and the appetite for it so deep, that some news outlets felt compelled to do some actual reporting. This was when the weekend began to take a long, bad turn for respected news outlets and righteous celebrities. Journalists began to discover that the viral video was not, in fact, the Zapruder film of 2019, and that there

The Black Hebrew Israelites had come to the Lincoln Memorial with the express intention of verbally confronting the Native Americans.

were other videos—lots and lots of them—that showed the event from multiple per-spectives and that explained more clearly what had happened. At first the journal-ists and their editors tried to patch the revelations onto the existing story, in hopes that the whole thing would somehow hold together. CNN, apparently by now aware that the event had taken place within a complicating larger picture, tried to use the new information to support its own biased interpretation, sorrowfully reporting that early in the afternoon the boys had clashed with "four African American young men preaching about the Bible and oppression."

But the wild, uncontrollable internet kept pumping videos into the ether that allowed people to see for themselves what had happened.

The New York Times, sober guardian of the exact and the nonsensational, had cannonballed into the delicious story on Saturday, titling its first piece "Boys in 'Make America Great Again' Hats Mob Native Elder at Indigenous Peoples March."

But the next day it ran a second story, with the headline "Fuller Picture Emerges of Viral Video of Native American Man and Catholic Students."

How had the boys been demilitarized from wearers of "Make America Great Again" hats to "Catholic students" in less than 24 hours?

O, for a muse of fire.

It turned out that the "four African American young men preaching about the Bible and oppression" had made a video, almost two hours in length, and while it does not fully exonerate the boys, it releases them from most of the serious charges.

The full video reveals that there was indeed a Native American gathering at the Lincoln Memorial, that it took place shortly before the events of the viral video, and that during it the indigenous people had been the subject of a hideous tirade of racist insults and fantasies. But the white students weren't the people hurling this garbage at them—the young "African American men preaching about the Bible and oppression" were doing it. For they were Black Hebrew Israelites, a tiny sect of people who believe they are the direct descendants of the 12 tribes of Israel, and whose beliefs on a variety of social issues make Mike Pence look like Ram Dass.

The full video reveals that these kids had wandered into a Tom Wolfe novel and had no idea how to get out of it.

It seems that the Black Hebrew Israelites had come to the Lincoln Memorial with the express intention of verbally confronting the Native Americans, some of whom had already begun to gather as the video begins, many of them in Native dress. The Black Hebrew Israelites' leader begins shouting at them: "Before you started worshipping totem poles, you was worshipping the true and living God. Be-fore you became an idol worshipper, you was worshipping the true and living God. This is the reason why this land was taken away from you! Because you worship ev-erything except the most high. You worship every creation except the Creator—and that's what we are here to tell you to do."

A young man in Native dress approaches them and gestures toward the group gathering for its event. But the Black Hebrew Israelites mix things up by throwing some dead-white-male jargon at him—they are there because of "freedom of the speech" and "freedom of religion" and all that. The young man backs away. "You have to come away from your religious philosophy," one Black Hebrew Israelite yells after him.

A few more people in Native costume gather, clearly stunned by his tirade. "You're not supposed to worship eagles, buffalos, rams, all types of animals," he calls out to them.

A Native woman approaches the group and begins to challenge its ideology, which prompts the pastor's coreligionists to thumb their Bibles for relevant passages from Proverbs and Ecclesiastes. He asks the woman why she's angry, and when she tells him that she's isn't angry, he responds, "You're not angry? You're not angry? I'm making you angry." The two start yelling at each other, and the speaker calls out to his associates for Isaiah 58:1.

Another woman comes up to him yelling, "The Bible says a lot of shit. The Bible says a lot of shit. The Bible says a lot of shit."

Black Hebrew Israelites believe, among other things, that they are indigenous people. The preacher tells a woman that "you're not an Indian. Indian means 'savage.'"

Men begin to gather with concerned looks on their face. "Indian does not mean 'savage,'" one of them says reasonably. "I don't know where you got that from." At this point, most of the Native Americans who have surrounded—"mobbed"?—the preacher have realized what the boys will prove too young and too unsophisticated to understand: that the "four young African American men preaching about the Bible and oppression" are the kind of people you sometimes encounter in big cities, and the best thing to do is steer a wide berth. Most of them leave, exchanging amused glances at one another. But one of the women stays put, and she begins making excellent points, some of which stump the Black Hebrew Israelites.

It was heating up to be an intersectional showdown for the ages, with the Black Hebrew Israelites going head to head with the Native Americans. But when the Native woman talks about the importance of peace, the preacher finally locates a unifying theme, one more powerful than anything to be found in Proverbs, Isaiah, or Ecclesiastes.

He tells her there won't be any food stamps coming to reservations or the projects because of the shutdown, and then gesturing to his left, he says, "It's because of these ... bastards over there, wearing 'Make America Great Again' hats."

The camera turns to capture five white teenage boys, one of whom is wearing a MAGA hat. They are standing at a respectful distance, with their hands in their pockets, listening to this exchange with expressions of curiosity. They are there to meet their bus home.

"Why you not angry at them?" the Black Hebrew Israelite asks the Native American woman angrily.

"That's right," says one of his coreligionists, "little corny-ass Billy Bob."

The boys don't respond to this provocation, although one of them smiles at being called a corny-ass Billy Bob. They seem interested in what is going on, in the way that it's interesting to listen to Hyde Park speakers.

The Native woman isn't interested in attacking the white boys. She keeps up her argument with the Black Hebrew Israelites, and her line of reasoning is so powerful that it throws the preacher off track.

"She trying to be distracting," one of the men says. "She trying to stop the flow."

"You're out of order," the preacher tells the woman. "Where's your husband? Let me speak to him."

By now the gathering of Covington Catholic boys watching the scene has grown to 10 or 12, some of them in MAGA hats. They are about 15 feet away, and while the conflict is surely beyond their range of experience, it also includes biblical explication, something with which they are familiar.

"Don't stand to the side and mock," the speaker orders the boys, who do not appear to be mocking him. "Bring y'all cracker ass up here and make a statement." The boys turn away and begin walking back to the larger group.

"You little dirty-ass crackers. Your day coming. Your day coming ... 'cause your little dusty asses wouldn't walk down a street in a black neighborhood, and go walk up on nobody playing no games like that," he calls after them, but they take no notice. "Yeah, 'cause I will stick my foot in your little ass."

By now the Native American ceremony has begun, and the attendees have linked arms and begun dancing. "They just don't know who they are," one of the Black Hebrew Israelites says remorsefully to another. Earlier he had called them "Uncle Tomahawks."

The boys have given up on him. They have joined the larger group, and together they all begin doing some school-spirit cheers; they hum the stadium-staple opening bars of "Seven Nation Army" and jump up and down, dancing to it. Later they would say that their chaperones had allowed them to sing school-spirit songs instead of engaging with the slurs hurled by the Black Hebrew Israelites.

And then you hear the sound of drumming, and Phillips appears with several other drummers, all of them headed to the large group of boys. "Here come Gad!" says the Black Hebrew Israelite excitedly. His religion teaches that Native Americans are one of the 12 tribes of Israel, Gad. Apparently he thinks that his relentless attack on the Native Americans has led some of them to confront the white people. "Here come Gad!" he says again, but he is soon disappointed. "Gad not playing! He came to the rescue!" he says in disgust.

The drummers head to the boys, and keep playing. The boys, who had been jumping to "Seven Nation Army," start jumping in time to the drumming. Phillips takes a step toward the group, and then—as it parts to admit him—he walks into it. Here the Black Hebrew Israelites' footage is of no help, as Phillips has moved into the crowd.

Now we may look at the viral video—or, as a CNN chyron called it, the "heartbreaking viral video"—as well as the many others that have since emerged, none of which has so far revealed the boys to be chanting anything about a wall or about making America great again. Phillips keeps walking into the group, they make room for him, and then—the smiling boy. One of the videos shows him doing something unusual. At one point he turns away from Phillips, stops smiling, and locks eyes with another kid, shaking his head, seeming to say the word no. This is consistent with the long, harrowing statement that the smiling boy would release at the end of the weekend, in which he offered an explanation for his actions that is consistent with the video footage that has so far emerged, and revealed what happened to him in the 48 hours after Americans set to work doxing him and threatening his family with violence. As of this writing, it seems that the smiling boy, Nick Sandmann, is the one person who tried to be respectful of Phillips and who encouraged the other boys to do the same. And for this, he has been by far the most harshly treated of any of the people involved in the afternoon's mess at the Lincoln Memorial.

I recommend that you watch the whole of the Black Hebrew Israelites' video, which includes a long, interesting passage, in which the Covington Catholic boys engage in a mostly thoughtful conversation with the Black Hebrew Israelite preacher. Throughout the conversation, they disrespect him only once—to boo him when he says something vile about gays and lesbians. (Also interesting is the section at the very end of the video, in which—after the boys have left—the Black Hebrew Israelites are approached by some police officers. The preacher had previously spent time castigating police and "the penal code," so I thought this would be a lively exchange, but the Israelites treat the cops with tremendous courtesy and gratitude, and when they leave the pastor describes them as "angels." So let that be a lesson about the inadvisability of thinking you can predict how an exchange with a Black Hebrew Israelite will end up.)

I have watched every bit of video I can find of the event, although more keep appearing. I have found several things that various of the boys did and said that are ugly, or rude, or racist. Some boys did a tomahawk chop when Phillips walked into their group. There is a short video of a group that seems to be from the high school verbally harassing two young women as the women walk past it. In terms of the school itself, Covington Catholic High School apparently has a game-day tradition of students painting their skin black for "black-out days," but any attempt by the school to cast this as innocent fun is undercut by a photograph of a white kid in black body paint leering at a black player on an opposing team.

I would not be surprised if more videos of this kind turn up, or if more troubling information about the school emerges, but it will by then be irrelevant, as the elite media have botched the story so completely that they have lost the authority to report on it. By Tuesday, the New York Times was busy absorbing the fact that Phillips was not, apparently, a Vietnam veteran, as it had originally reported, and it issued a correction saying that it had contacted the Pentagon for his military record, suggesting that it no longer trusts him as a source of reliable information.

How could the elite media—the New York Times, let's say—have protected themselves from this event, which has served to reinforce millions of Americans' belief that traditional journalistic outlets are purveyors of "fake news"? They might have hewed to a concept that once went by the quaint term "journalistic ethics." Among other things, journalistic ethics held that if you didn't have the reporting to support a story, and if that story had the potential to hurt its subjects, and if those subjects were private citizens, and if they were moreover minors, you didn't run the story. You kept reporting it; you let yourself get scooped; and you accepted that speed is not the highest value. Otherwise, you were the trash press.

At 8:30 yesterday morning, as I was typing this essay, the New York Times emailed me. The subject line was "Ethics Reminders for Freelance Journalists." (I have occasionally published essays and reviews in the Times). It informed me, inter alia, that the Times expected all of its journalists, both freelance and staff, "to protect the integrity and credibility of Times journalism." This meant, in part, safeguarding the Times' "reputation for fairness and impartiality."

I am prompted to issue my own ethics reminders for the New York Times. Here they are: You were partly responsible for the election of Trump because you are the most influential newspaper in the country, and you are not fair or impartial. Millions of Americans believe you hate them and that you will casually harm them. Two years ago, they fought back against you, and they won. If Trump wins again, you will once again have played a small but important role in that victory.

Print Citations

CMS: Flanagan, Caitlin. "The Media Botched the Covington Catholic Story." In The Reference Shelf: Hate Crimes, edited by Sophie Zyla, 165–171. Amenia, NY: Grey House Publishing, 2020.

MLA: Flanagan, Caitlin. "The Media Botched the Covington Catholic Story." The Reference Shelf: Hate Crimes, edited by Sophie Zyla, Grey Housing Publishing, 2020, pp. 165–171.

APA: Flanagan, C. (2020). The media botched the Covington catholic story. In Sophie Zyla (Ed.), The reference shelf: Hate crimes (pp. 165–171). Amenia, NY: Grey Housing Publishing.

Hate Speech on Social Media: Global Comparisons

By Zachary Laub

Council on Foreign Relations, June 7, 2019

A mounting number of attacks on immigrants and other minorities has raised new concerns about the connection between inflammatory speech online and violent acts, as well as the role of corporations and the state in policing speech. Analysts say trends in hate crimes around the world echo changes in the political climate, and that social media can magnify discord. At their most extreme, rumors and invective disseminated online have contributed to violence ranging from lynchings to ethnic cleansing.

The response has been uneven, and the task of deciding what to censor, and how, has largely fallen to the handful of corporations that control the platforms on which much of the world now communicates. But these companies are constrained by domestic laws. In liberal democracies, these laws can serve to defuse discrimination and head off violence against minorities. But such laws can also be used to suppress minorities and dissidents.

How Widespread Is the Problem?

Incidents have been reported on nearly every continent. Much of the world now communicates on social media, with nearly a third of the world's population active on Facebook alone. As more and more people have moved online, experts say, individuals inclined toward racism, misogyny, or homophobia have found niches that can reinforce their views and goad them to violence. Social media platforms also offer violent actors the opportunity to publicize their acts.

Social scientists and others have observed how social media posts, and other online speech, can inspire acts of violence:

- In Germany a correlation was found between anti-refugee Facebook posts by the far-right Alternative for Germany party and attacks on refugees. Scholars Karsten Muller and Carlo Schwarz observed that upticks in attacks, such as arson and assault, followed spikes in hate-mongering posts.

- In the United States, perpetrators of recent white supremacist attacks have circulated among racist communities online, and also embraced social media to publicize their acts. Prosecutors said the Charleston church shooter, who killed nine black clergy and worshippers in June 2015, engaged in a "self-learning process" online that led him to believe that the goal of white supremacy required violent action.

- The 2018 Pittsburgh synagogue shooter was a participant in the social media network Gab, whose lax rules have attracted extremists banned by larger platforms. There, he espoused the conspiracy that Jews sought to bring immigrants into the United States, and render whites a minority, before killing eleven worshippers at a refugee-themed Shabbat service. This "great replacement" trope, which was heard at the white supremacist rally in Charlottesville, Virginia, a year prior and originates with the French far right, expresses demographic anxieties about nonwhite immigration and birth rates.

- The great replacement trope was in turn espoused by the perpetrator of the 2019 New Zealand mosque shootings, who killed forty-nine Muslims at prayer and sought to broadcast the attack on YouTube.

- In Myanmar, military leaders and Buddhist nationalists used social media to slur and demonize the Rohingya Muslim minority ahead of and during a campaign of ethnic cleansing. Though Rohingya comprised perhaps 2 percent of the population, ethnonationalists claimed that Rohingya would soon supplant the Buddhist majority. The UN fact-finding mission said, "Facebook has been a useful instrument for those seeking to spread hate, in a context where, for most users, Facebook is the Internet."

- In India, lynch mobs and other types of communal violence, in many cases originating with rumors on WhatsApp groups, have been on the rise since the Hindu-nationalist Bharatiya Janata Party (BJP) came to power in 2014.

- Sri Lanka has similarly seen vigilantism inspired by rumors spread online, targeting the Tamil Muslim minority. During a spate of violence in March 2018, the government blocked access to Facebook and WhatsApp, as well as the messaging app Viber, for a week, saying that Facebook had not been sufficiently responsive during the emergency.

Does Social Media Catalyze Hate Crimes?

The same technology that allows social media to galvanize democracy activists can be used by hate groups seeking to organize and recruit. It also allows fringe sites, including peddlers of conspiracies, to reach audiences far broader than their core readership. Online platforms' business models depend on maximizing reading or viewing times. Since Facebook and similar platforms make their money by enabling advertisers to target audiences with extreme precision, it is in their interests to let people find the communities where they will spend the most time.

Users' experiences online are mediated by algorithms designed to maximize their engagement, which often inadvertently promote extreme content. Some web watchdog groups say YouTube's autoplay function, in which the player, at the end of one video, tees up a related one, can be especially pernicious. The algorithm drives people to videos that promote conspiracy theories or are otherwise "divisive, misleading or false," according to a *Wall Street Journal* investigative report. "YouTube may be one of the most powerful radicalizing instruments of the 21st century," writes sociologist Zeynep Tufekci.

YouTube said in June 2019 that changes to its recommendation algorithm made in January had halved views of videos deemed "borderline content" for spreading misinformation. At that time, the company also announced that it would remove neo-Nazi and white supremacist videos from its site. Yet the platform faced criticism that its efforts to curb hate speech do not go far enough. For instance, critics note that rather than removing videos that provoked homophobic harassment of a journalist, YouTube instead cut off the offending user from sharing in advertising revenue.

How Do Platforms Enforce Their Rules?

Social media platforms rely on a combination of artificial intelligence, user reporting, and staff known as content moderators to enforce their rules regarding appropriate content. Moderators, however, are burdened by the sheer volume of content and the trauma that comes from sifting through disturbing posts, and social media companies don't evenly devote resources across the many markets they serve.

A ProPublica investigation found that Facebook's rules are opaque to users and inconsistently applied by its thousands of contractors charged with content moderation. (Facebook says there are fifteen thousand.) In many countries and disputed territories, such as the Palestinian territories, Kashmir, and Crimea, activists and journalists have found themselves censored, as Facebook has sought to maintain access to national markets or to insulate itself from legal liability. "The company's hate-speech rules tend to favor elites and governments over grassroots activists and racial minorities," ProPublica found.

Addressing the challenges of navigating varying legal systems and standards around the world—and facing investigations by several governments—Facebook CEO Mark Zuckerberg called for global regulations to establish baseline content, electoral integrity, privacy, and data standards.

Problems also arise when platforms' artificial intelligence is poorly adapted to local languages and companies have invested little in staff fluent in them. This was particularly acute in Myanmar, where, Reuters reported, Facebook employed just two Burmese speakers as of early 2015. After a series of anti-Muslim violence began in 2012, experts warned of the fertile environment ultranationalist Buddhist monks found on Facebook for disseminating hate speech to an audience newly connected to the internet after decades under a closed autocratic system.

Facebook admitted it had done too little after seven hundred thousand Rohingya were driven to Bangladesh and a UN human rights panel singled out the

---

The same technology that allows social media to galvanize democracy activists can be used by hate groups seeking to organize and recruit.

company in a report saying Myanmar's security forces should be investigated for genocidal intent. In August 2018, it banned military officials from the platform and pledged to increase the number of moderators fluent in the local language.

How do Countries Regulate Hate Speech Online?

In many ways, the debates confronting courts, legislatures, and publics about how to reconcile the competing values of free expression and nondiscrimination have been around for a century or longer. Democracies have varied in their philosophical approaches to these questions, as rapidly changing communications technologies have raised technical challenges of monitoring and responding to incitement and dangerous disinformation.

United States. Social media platforms have broad latitude, each establishing its own standards for content and methods of enforcement. Their broad discretion stems from the Communications Decency Act. The 1996 law exempts tech platforms from liability for actionable speech by their users. Magazines and television networks, for example, can be sued for publishing defamatory information they know to be false; social media platforms cannot be found similarly liable for content they host.

Recent congressional hearings have highlighted the chasm between Democrats and Republicans on the issue. House Judiciary Committee Chairman Jerry Nadler convened a hearing in the aftermath of the New Zealand attack, saying the internet has aided white nationalism's international proliferation. "The President's rhetoric fans the flames with language that—whether intentional or not—may motivate and embolden white supremacist movements," he said, a charge Republicans on the panel disputed. The Senate Judiciary Committee, led by Ted Cruz, held a nearly simultaneous hearing in which he alleged that major social media companies' rules disproportionately censor conservative speech, threatening the platforms with federal regulation. Democrats on that panel said Republicans seek to weaken policies dealing with hate speech and disinformation that instead ought to be strengthened.

European Union. The bloc's twenty-eight members all legislate the issue of hate speech on social media differently, but they adhere to some common principles. Unlike the United States, it is not only speech that directly incites violence that comes under scrutiny; so too does speech that incites hatred or denies or minimizes genocide and crimes against humanity. Backlash against the millions of predominantly Muslim migrants and refugees who have arrived in Europe in recent years has made this a particularly salient issue, as has an uptick in anti-Semitic incidents in countries including France, Germany, and the United Kingdom.

In a bid to preempt bloc-wide legislation, major tech companies agreed to a code of conduct with the European Union in which they pledged to review posts flagged by users and take down those that violate EU standards within twenty-four hours. In a February 2019 review, the European Commission found that social media platforms were meeting this requirement in three-quarters of cases.

The Nazi legacy has made Germany especially sensitive to hate speech. A 2018 law requires large social media platforms to take down posts that are "manifestly illegal" under criteria set out in German law within twenty-four hours. Human Rights Watch raised concerns that the threat of hefty fines would encourage the social media platforms to be "overzealous censors."

New regulations under consideration by the bloc's executive arm would extend a model similar to Germany's across the EU, with the intent of "preventing the dissemination of terrorist content online." Civil libertarians have warned against the measure for its "vague and broad" definitions of prohibited content, as well as for making private corporations, rather than public authorities, the arbiters of censorship.

India. Under new social media rules, the government can order platforms to take down posts within twenty-four hours based on a wide range of offenses, as well as to obtain the identity of the user. As social media platforms have made efforts to stanch the sort of speech that has led to vigilante violence, lawmakers from the ruling BJP have accused them of censoring content in a politically discriminatory manner, disproportionately suspending right-wing accounts, and thus undermining Indian democracy. Critics of the BJP accuse it of deflecting blame from party elites to the platforms hosting them. As of April 2018, the New Delhi–based Association for Democratic Reforms had identified fifty-eight lawmakers facing hate speech cases, including twenty-seven from the ruling BJP. The opposition has expressed unease with potential government intrusions into privacy.

Japan. Hate speech has become a subject of legislation and jurisprudence in Japan in the past decade, as anti-racism activists have challenged ultranationalist agitation against ethnic Koreans. This attention to the issue attracted a rebuke from the UN Committee on the Elimination of Racial Discrimination in 2014 and inspired a national ban on hate speech in 2016, with the government adopting a model similar to Europe's. Rather than specify criminal penalties, however, it delegates to municipal governments the responsibility "to eliminate unjust discriminatory words and deeds against People from Outside Japan." A handful of recent cases concerning ethnic Koreans could pose a test: in one, the Osaka government ordered a website containing videos deemed hateful taken down, and in Kanagawa and Okinawa Prefectures courts have fined individuals convicted of defaming ethnic Koreans in anonymous online posts.

What Are the Prospects for International Prosecution?

Cases of genocide and crimes against humanity could be the next frontier of social media jurisprudence, drawing on precedents set in Nuremberg and Rwanda. The Nuremberg trials in post-Nazi Germany convicted the publisher of the newspaper *Der Stürmer*; the 1948 Genocide Convention subsequently included "direct and public incitement to commit genocide" as a crime. During the UN International Criminal Tribunal for Rwanda, two media executives were convicted on those grounds. As prosecutors look ahead to potential genocide and war crimes tribunals for cases such as Myanmar, social media users with mass followings could be found similarly criminally liable.

Print Citations

CMS: Laub, Zachary. "Hate Speech on Social Media: Global Comparisons." In *The Reference Shelf: Hate Crimes,* edited by Sophie Zyla, 172–177. Amenia, NY: Grey House Publishing, 2020.

MLA: Laub, Zachary. "Hate Speech on Social Media: Global Comparisons." *The Reference Shelf: Hate Crimes,* edited by Sophie Zyla, Grey Housing Publishing, 2020, pp. 172–177.

APA: Laub, Z. (2020). Hate speech on social media: Global comparisons. In Sophie Zyla (Ed.), *The reference shelf: Hate crimes* (pp. 172–177). Amenia, NY: Grey Housing Publishing.

How Big Tech Can Fight White Supremacist Terrorism: It Has the Tools—It Just Needs to Use Them

By Daniel Byman and Christopher Meserole
Foreign Affairs, August 15, 2019

On the morning of August 3, Patrick Crusius uploaded a 2,300-word manifesto to 8chan, an online forum popular with white nationalists. Within seconds, byte-sized packets bearing the anti-immigrant screed would cross borders the world over, wending their way from El Paso, Texas, to the Philippines, where 8chan is based. News of what Crusius did next would travel even wider. Armed with an AK-47, the recent college dropout stormed a Walmart not far from the Mexican border, killing 22 and wounding as many more. His self-professed goal: to kill as many Mexicans as possible.

The carnage in El Paso, coupled with a separate mass shooting in Dayton, Ohio, that night, prompted renewed debate over how to respond to online hate. As political pressure mounted, U.S. President Donald Trump borrowed a page from the Obama playbook and convened a "tech summit" on extremism. On August 9, White House officials hosted representatives from major technology companies—Amazon, Google, Facebook, Twitter, Microsoft, and others—and discussed potential ways of disrupting extremist recruitment and coordination online.

The summit will likely be remembered as yet another missed opportunity. Trump's administration may be more willing than Obama's to challenge the technology sector, but it has opted to fight the wrong battle, and its efforts risk making the problem worse. Consider the administration's reported plan to grant the Federal Communications Commission (FCC) broad new authority to regulate social media companies. The authority would not help the FCC force technology companies to more aggressively police their platforms for extremist accounts and content. Rather, the FCC, by virtue of an executive order called Protecting Americans from Online Censorship, would seek to ensure that social media companies aren't "biased" against conservatives. With Trump's rhetoric and language often indistinguishable from that of avowed white nationalists, such a measure would make it more difficult for technology companies to counter extremism online.

As the Trump administration dithers, the threat only continues to grow. The horrific attack in El Paso was the latest performance of a troublesome new script, one in which white nationalists, radicalized online, post their fealty to the movement before carrying out a kind of gamified violence designed to be quickly celebrated and shared on the Internet before being repeated anew. The script was written in Norway, where in 2011 Anders Breivik posted a massive manifesto before killing 77 people, primarily youths at a summer camp for a left-leaning political party. Earlier this year, Brenton Tarrant published his manifesto on 8chan before gunning down 51 worshippers at a mosque and Islamic Center in Christchurch, New Zealand. In a horrific twist, Tarrant broadcast video of the attack in real time on Facebook Live. Despite Facebook's efforts to block the video, it spread like wildfire—it was uploaded, often in modified form, over a million times on Facebook and countless more on sites such as 8chan and Reddit.

In terms of its global reach and lethality, white nationalist terrorism has grown increasingly reminiscent of the jihadi movement. It has also, like the jihadi movement, used the Internet and social media to recruit and radicalize members, disseminate propaganda, and broadcast images and video of its violence. What can tech companies—and governments—do to stop it?

Treat White Nationalism Like Jihadism

Balancing the right to free expression online with the need to monitor and disrupt extremist use of the Internet is by no means a uniquely American problem. In the aftermath of the Christchurch attack, for example, New Zealand Prime Minister Jacinda Ardern worked with France and other major technology companies to launch the Christchurch Call in May. Building on the digital counterextremism efforts of the EU and other bodies (including the Aqaba Process, launched by Jordan in 2015), the Christchurch Call brought tech companies and governments together to commit to "eliminate terrorist and violent extremist content online."

From a technical and moral point of view, white supremacist content is no different from jihadi content.

The Christchurch Call was an admirable start, but, like the Aqaba Process, it is long on good intentions and short on specifics. Thankfully, there are concrete steps that technology companies can take to curb the spread of online hate.

The first step should be to treat all hateful ideologies the same. Until very recently, Facebook and other social media companies have focused far more on jihadi content than on white nationalist and other forms of far-right content. This is largely a legacy of the struggle against the Islamic State (ISIS). When the group emerged in 2014, Facebook and other companies tried to preemptively block ISIS content and remove users associated with it and other international terrorist groups. At the same time, they wanted to reassure constituencies dedicated to free speech. They were able to strike this balance because the U.S. government had officially designated ISIS as a terrorist group, giving the companies a legal rationale for restricting ISIS-related content. The U.S. government does not similarly designate domestic terrorist groups.

From a technical and moral point of view, however, white supremacist content is no different from jihadi content—if social media companies can block one, they can block the other. So far, they have avoided doing so because they fear blowback from conservatives. As extremism expert J. M. Berger notes, "Cracking down on white nationalists will … involve removing a lot of people who identify to a greater or lesser extent as Trump supporters, and some people in Trump circles and pro-Trump media will certainly seize on this to complain they are being persecuted."

Yet such crackdowns work. By taking down individual jihadi accounts, identifying and blocking common types of jihadi propaganda, and cooperating with law enforcement, companies such as Facebook, Twitter, and YouTube have reduced jihadi groups' online presence. They can do the same to white nationalists. These efforts are not required by law, and especially in the United States, civil libertarians might join racists in opposing them. But the tech firms are private companies and can legally remove hateful content from their platforms without falling afoul of the First Amendment.

Second, tech companies should begin hiring more—and more highly trained—content moderators. Although companies such as Facebook and Google increasingly rely on artificial intelligence to flag problematic content, they also employ thousands of contactors to review those decisions. Facebook alone employs more than 200 terrorism analysts in-house and contracts with over 15,000 content moderators worldwide. This number, however, is not commensurate with the scale of the problem—there are well over two billion Facebook users. In Myanmar, for example, Facebook has struggled to moderate violent content in part because it has too few moderators who speak Burmese.

The quality of content moderators is even more important than their quantity. Effective moderation requires the ability to distinguish between terrorist content and legitimate forms of political speech. This, in turn, requires a large team of analysts with both an in-depth knowledge of terrorism and a wide array of local and regional expertise who can set globally consistent policies. And these moderators must have the language, cultural, and analytical skills necessary to apply those policies quickly and accurately around the world. Attracting moderators with the right qualifications means that companies will have to not only pay them better but also provide them with more prestige and respect than they currently receive.

Tech companies must also improve information sharing across platforms. Most small and early-stage companies lack the resources to invest in counterterrorism expertise and therefore struggle to identify extremist groups and content on their platforms. In 2017, Google, Facebook, and other major companies created the Global Internet Forum to Counter Terrorism. In part, the rationale behind the forum was to share information on suspected terrorist activity and prevent dangerous content from migrating across platforms. After the New

> White supremacist content is no different from jihadi content—if social media companies can block one, they can block the other.

Zealand attacks, for example, Facebook "hashed" the original video, essentially giving it a digital fingerprint that allowed Facebook and other companies to more easily identify it. Earlier this month, the company also open-sourced an algorithm that smaller companies and organizations can use to identify terrorist imagery.

These steps are welcome, but more could be done. Most obviously, Facebook and others could publish the full list of extremist organizations and individuals that are banned from their platforms, along with brief explanations for each decision. Such a move would make it far easier for smaller companies without in-house terrorism expertise to assess whether to block specific groups and individuals, too.

Don't Let the Problem Fester

We can't know if technology companies are getting the balance right if we don't know what they're doing, so improving transparency and publicizing metrics for content regulation is another important step. Facebook claims that it is doing its best to counter extremist content, but this claim is difficult to evaluate without comprehensive data—and Facebook is one of the better companies in terms of reporting. In addition to reporting the number of accounts taken down or the amount of content blocked, major companies should list the number of user-flagged content problems and how long it takes them to respond. They should also report their false-positive rate: if Facebook takes down millions of videos, what percentage of those were actually legitimate content (for instance, a news organization that uses a clip of the El Paso manifesto or the Christchurch video)? Such reporting would help ensure that companies do not overreact to hateful content, allowing better judgments as to when legitimate speech might be suppressed, which methods of tagging content are most effective, and whether AI algorithms are effective.

Finally, although calls to ban live-streaming and other media formats are unrealistic, Facebook and other companies can put limits on them in ways that do not impede their core function. In the aftermath of the Christchurch shooting, for instance, Facebook instituted a "one-strike" policy that prevents users who engage with terrorist content in specific ways—for example, by sharing a statement from a terrorist group without adding any context—from using Facebook Live. Likewise, in a bid to cut down on disinformation and extremist propaganda in India, Facebook has placed limits on the number of people users can forward messages to on WhatsApp. Restrictions like these do not meaningfully compromise the free expression of most Facebook users, yet they also make it significantly harder to broadcast and share terrorist attacks in real time. Other social networks and file-sharing services should follow suit.

Reforms such as these will not be a panacea. Yet without them the problem will only grow. At the time of the White House summit last Friday, Crusius was the last known white nationalist to follow Tarrant's model. By the next evening he no longer was. On Saturday, a young Norwegian man uploaded his own anti-immigrant message to 8chan, praising Tarrant and Crusius by name. Later that night, he entered a mosque outside Oslo armed with a handgun and two "shotgun-like weapons" and opened fire.

Print Citations

CMS: Byman, Daniel, and Christopher Meserole. "How Big Tech Can Fight White Supremacist Terrorism: It Has the Tools—It Just Needs to Use Them." In *The Reference Shelf: Hate Crimes,* edited by Sophie Zyla, 177–182. Amenia, NY: Grey House Publishing, 2020.

MLA: Byman, Daniel, and Christopher Meserole. "How Big Tech Can Fight White Supremacist Terrorism: It Has the Tools—It Just Needs to Use Them." *The Reference Shelf: Hate Crimes,* edited by Sophie Zyla, Grey Housing Publishing, 2020, pp. 177–182.

APA: Byman, D., & Meserole, C. (2020). How big tech can fight white supremacist terrorism: It has the tools—it just needs to use them. In Sophie Zyla (Ed.), *The reference shelf: Hate crimes* (pp. 177–182). Amenia, NY: Grey Housing Publishing.

Bibliography

ADL. "Gun Violence and Mass Shootings." Updated Aug 2019. ADL website. https://www.adl.org/education/resources/tools-and-strategies/table-talk/gun-violence-mass-shootings.

Beirich, Heidi. "The Year in Hate: Rage Against Change." Southern Poverty Law Center (SPLC). Feb 20, 2019. https://www.splcenter.org/fighting-hate/intelligence-report/2019/year-hate-rage-against-change.

Bendery, Jennifer. "157 Republicans Just Opposed Renewing the Violence Against Women Act." *Huffington Post*. Updated Apr 5, 2019. https://www.huffpost.com/entry/republicans-oppose-violence-against-women-act_n_5ca68295e4b047edf957b5e1?fbclid=IwAR19LNFLFZVqXlaLkyWdk1WXVf9Ae8gJZqFgGmU7RKuNK0SV_hFeQqv8P8Q.

Booker, Cory. "Cory's Plan to Confront Hate Crimes and White Supremacist Violence." Cory 2020. https://corybooker.com/issues/national-security/combat-hate/.

Brudholm, Thomas, and Birgitte Schepelern Johnansen. "Hate, Politics, Law— Critical Perspectives on Combating Hate." *International Network for Hate Studies (INHS)*. May 12, 2019. https://internationalhatestudies.com/hate-politics-law-critical-perspectives-on-combating-hate/.

Byman, Daniel, and Christopher Meserole. "How Big Tech Can Fight White Supremacist Terrorism." *Foreign Affairs*. Aug 15, 2019. https://www.foreignaffairs.com/articles/united-states/2019-08-15/how-big-tech-can-fight-white-supremacist-terrorism.

Costello, Maureen, and Coshandra Dillard. "Hate at School Report." *Teaching Tolerance*. https://www.tolerance.org/magazine/publications/hate-at-school-report.

Crime Museum. "Ku Klux Klan." https://www.crimemuseum.org/crime-library/hate-crime/ku-klux-klan/.

Crime Museum. "Matthew Shepard." https://www.crimemuseum.org/crime-library/hate-crime/matthew-shepard.

Everytown for Gun Safety. "Disarm Hate: The Deadly Intersection of Guns and Hate Crimes." https://everytownresearch.org/wp-content/uploads/2019/05/Disarm-Hate-HATE-CRIMES-FACT-SHEET-051619A.pdf.

Federal Bureau of Investigation. "2018 Hate Crime Statistics Released." https://www.fbi.gov/news/stories/2018-hate-crime-statistics-released-111219.

Federal Bureau of Investigation. "A Byte Out of History: Mississippi Burning." https://archives.fbi.gov/archives/news/stories/2007/february/miburn_022607.

Federal Bureau of Investigation. "What We Investigate: Hate Crimes." https://www.fbi.gov/investigate/civil-rights/hate-crimes.

First Amendment. National Constitution Center. https://constitutioncenter.org/interactive-constitution/amendment/amendment-i.

Frazin, Rachel. "FBI Chief Says Racist Extremists Fueling One Another, Making Connections Overseas." *The Hill*. Oct 30, 2019. https://thehill.com/policy/national-security/468195-wray-domestic-racially-motivated-violent-extremists-are-connecting.

Gearty, Robert, and Don Gentile. "Michael Griffith Dies Fleeing a White Mob in Howard Beach in 1986." *The Daily News*. Dec 21, 1986. https://www.nydailynews.com/new-york/nyc-crime/michael-griffith-died-fleeing-white-mob-howard-beach-1986-article-1.2917533

George, Cherian. "Hate Speech: A Dilemma for Journalists the World Over." *Ethical Journalism Network (EJN)*. https://ethicaljournalismnetwork.org/resources/publications/ethics-in-the-news/hate-speech.

Goodwyn, Wade. "Texas Executes Man Convicted in 1998 Murder of James Byrd Jr." *NPR*. Apr 24, 2019. https://www.npr.org/2019/04/24/716647585/texas-to-execute-man-convicted-in-dragging-death-of-james-byrd-jr.

Hilleary, Cecily. "Rise in Hate Crimes Alarms Native American Communities." *VOA News*. Jun 5, 2017. https://www.voanews.com/usa/rise-hate-crimes-alarms-native-american-communities.

"The History of Diversity Training & Its Pioneers." *Diversity Officer Magazine*. https://diversityofficermagazine.com/diversity-inclusion/the-history-of-diversity-training-its-pioneers/.

Human Rights Campaign. "Civil Rights Leaders Respond to the Orland Nightclub Tragedy." Jun 12, 2016. Video. https://www.hrc.org/videos/civil-rights-leaders-respond-to-the-orlando-nightclub-tragedy.

Human Rights Campaign. "Hate Crimes Timeline." https://www.hrc.org/resources/hate-crimes-timeline.

Human Rights Campaign. "Questions and Answers: The Matthew Shepard and James Byrd, Jr. Hate Crimes Prevention Act. Hate Crimes." Feb 1, 2010. https://www.hrc.org/resources/questions-and-answers-the-matthew-shepard-and-james-byrd-jr.-hate-crimes-pr.

Institute for Democracy, Education, and Access. "Executive Summary—School & Society in the Age of Trump." *UCLA/IDEA Publications*. Mar 2019. https://idea.gseis.ucla.edu/publications/files/executive-summary-school-and-society-in-the-age-of-trump/view.

International Association of Chiefs of Police. "Action Agenda for Community Organizations and Law Enforcement to Enhance the Response to Hate Crimes." Apr 1, 2019. https://www.theiacp.org/resources/document/action-agenda-for-community-organizations-and-law-enforcement-to-enhance-the.

Katz, Brigit. "The U.S. Finally Made Lynching a Federal Crime." *SmartNews*. *Smithsonian*. Dec 21, 2018.: https://www.smithsonianmag.com/smart-news/after-200-failed-attempts-us-has-made-lynching-federal-crime-180971092/.

Kennedy, Randall. "Is the Cure of Censorship Better than the Disease of Hate Speech?" *Knight First Amendment Institute*. Apr 9, 2018. https://knightcolumbia. org/content/cure-censorship-better-disease-hate-speech.

Kirkpatrick, David D. "Massacre Suspect Traveled the World but Lived on the Internet." *New York Times*. Mar 15, 2019. https://www.nytimes.com/2019/03/15/ world/asia/new-zealand-shooting-brenton-tarrant.html.

Lapowsky, Issie. "In Congressional Hearing in Hate, the Haters Got Their Way." *Wired*. Apr 9, 2019. https://www.wired.com/story/house-hearing-hate-crimes-white-nationalism/.

Laub, Zachary. "Hate Speech on Social Media: Global Comparisons." *Council on Foreign Relations*. Jun 7, 2019. https://www.cfr.org/backgrounder/hate-speech-social-media-global-comparisons.

Learning First Alliance. "Resources Addressing Hate and Harassment in Schools." https://learningfirst.org/page/resources-addressing-hate-and-harassment-in-schools.

Levin, Brian. "Global Terrorism: Threats to the Homeland, Part 1." Center for the Study of Hate and Extremism, Department of Criminal Justice, California State University, San Bernardino. Sep 10, 2019. https://csbs.csusb.edu/sites/csusb_csbs/files/GLOBAL%20TERRORISM-%20cong%20BL2%2091019.pdf.

Levin, Brian, and Kevin Grisham. "Special Status Report Hate Crime in the United States 20 State Compilation of Official Data." Center for the Study of Hate and Extremism, California State University, San Bernardino, CSUSB. 2016. https://csbs.csusb.edu/hate-and-extremism-center/data-reports/original-reports-hate-and-terrorism-center-staff.

Levin, Brian, and Lisa Nakashima. "Report to the Nation: 2019: Factbook on Hate & Extremism in the U.S. & Internationally." Center for the Study of Hate and Extremism, California State University, San Bernardino. Jul 2019. https://www. hsdl.org/c/just-released-report-to-the-nation-on-hate-and-extremism/.

Levin, Jack, and Jack McDevitt. "Hate Crimes." In *Encyclopedia of Peace, Violence, and Conflict*. 2nd ed., Academic Press, 2008. https://jacklevinonviolence.com/articles/HateCrimesencyc92206FINAL.pdf.

Matthew Shepard Foundation. "Erase Hate in Business." https://www.matthewshepard.org/business-allies/.

Mervosh, Sarah. "Principal Who Tried to Stay 'Politically Neutral' about Holocaust Is Removed." *New York Times*, Jul 8, 2019. https://www.nytimes.com/2019/07/08/ us/spanish-river-william-latson-holocaust.html.

Onn, Melissa. United Kingdom Parliament, House of Commons Hansard. "Misogyny as a Hate Crime." Vol. 637. Mar 7, 2018. https://hansard.parliament.uk/ Commons/2018-03-07/debates/92236C51-2340-4D97-92A7-4955B24C2D74/ MisogynyAsAHateCrime#contribution-452DE3BC-B238-48C0-8D21-0198B5348C5B.

Povich, Elaine S. "The Holocaust: States Require Education about It as Anti-Semitism, Hate Crimes Surge." *USA Today*. Jul 15, 2019. https://psmag.com/news/a-florida-principals-reassignment-raises-questions-about-the-quality-of-holocaust-education.

Roser, Max, and Mohamed Nagdy. "Genocides in the 20th Century." *Our World in Data*. https://ourworldindata.org/genocides.

"Rwanda Genocide: 100 Days of Slaughter." *BBC News*. Apr 4, 2019. https://www.bbc.com/news/world-africa-26875506.

Schoen Consulting. "The Conference on Jewish Materials Claims Against Germany." Feb 23-27, 2018. http://www.claimscon.org/wp-content/uploads/2018/04/Holocaust-Knowledge-Awareness-Study_Executive-Summary-2018.pdf.

Southern Poverty Law Center. "Hate at School: Something Ugly Is Happening in America's Schools. And It's Not Going Away." May 2, 2019. https://www.splcenter.org/20190502/hate-school.

Torres, Christina. "The Urgent Need for Anti-Racist Education." *Education Week Teacher*. Aug 14, 2019. https://www.edweek.org/tm/articles/2019/08/14/the-urgent-need-for-anti-racist-education.html.

U.S. Census Bureau. "New Census Bureau Report Analyzes U.S. Population Projections." Mar 3, 2015. https://www.census.gov/newsroom/press-releases/2015/cb15-tps16.html.

U.S. Department of Justice. "Attorney General William P. Barr Delivers Keynote Speech at the U.S. Department of Justice's Summit on Combatting Anti-Semitism." Jul 15, 2019. https://www.justice.gov/opa/speech/attorney-general-william-p-barr-delivers-keynote-speech-us-department-justices-summit.

U.S. Department of Justice. "Hate Crime Laws: About Hate Crimes." https://www.justice.gov/crt/hate-crime-laws.

U.S. Department of Justice. Office of Justice Programs, Bureau of Justice Statistics. "Special Report. Hate Crime Victimization, 2004-2015." Jun 2017. https://www.bjs.gov/content/pub/pdf/hcv0415.pdf.

U.S. Department of Justice. "State Specific Information." https://www.justice.gov/hatecrimes/state-specific-information.

Vara-Orta, Francisco. "Swastikas on Bathroom Stalls. Chants of 'Build the Wall.' Notes That Say 'Go Back to Mexico.' Hate in Schools." *Education Week*. Aug 6, 2018. https://www.edweek.org/ew/projects/hate-in-schools.html.

Websites

California State University, San Bernardino (CSUSB), Center for the Study of Hate and Extremism
https://csbs.csusb.edu/hate-and-extremism-center

The Center for the Study of Hate and Extremism at California State University is a nonpartisan research and policy center offering aid and information.

Crime Museum
www.crimemuseum.org

The Crime Museum is an resource on law enforcement, crime history, and forensic science opened in 2008 in Washington D.C. The Crime Library provides online resources on statistics, law and punishment, and the history of hate crimes along with a variety of crime-related topics.

Department of Justice (DOJ) Hate Crimes
www.justice.gov/hatecrimes

The U.S. Department of Justice was established in 1870 with a mission of the law enforcement, defending U.S. interests: ensuring public safety, providing leadership in preventing and controlling crime, seeking punishment for guilty parties, and ensuring fair justice for Americans. The website offers news reports, articles, research and case reports, statistics, and information on prevention.

Everytown for Gun Safety
www.everytownresearch.org

Everytown for Gun Safety is an independent, nonpartisan organization founded by Michael Bloomberg that strives to research gun violence in order to improve understanding, reduce the instances of gun violence in America, develop evidence-based policies, and offer the knowledge gained through research to courts and the public.

Federal Bureau of Investigation: Civil Rights
www.fbi.gov/investigate

The Federal Bureau of Investigation (FBI) was established in 1908 and began efforts to protect civil rights and fight the Ku Klux Klan (KKK) in 1918. The FBI has evolved into a national security organization working around the globe to uphold the U.S. Constitution and protect from terrorism, espionage, counterintelligence, cyber- and high-technology crimes, public corruption, terrorism, civil rights, organized crime, human trafficking, international human rights violations, and other major criminal threats. The FBI, working with law enforcement agencies, prosecutors, nongovernment organizations, and community and minority groups provides assistance, support, training, leadership, and community outreach. They are the primary agency investigating violations of civil rights statutes and protecting citizens and noncitizens.

Human Rights Campaign

www.hrc.org

The Human Rights Campaign and Human Rights Campaign Foundation are America's largest civil rights organization working on LGBTQ equality; and increasing understanding and inclusive policies and practices and education of the public

International Association of Chiefs of Police (IACP)

www.theiacp.org

The IACP is a worldwide association for police leaders started in 1893 with a headquarters in Alexandria, Virginia. IACP includes over 30,000 members in 160 countries that are committed to advancing the safety of communities and speaking out on behalf of law enforcement.

International Network for Hate Studies (INHS)

www.internaionalhatestudies.com

The INHS is a cross-jurisdictional, interdisciplinary, and international network established in 2013 by academics to facilitate sharing information on the study of hate and hate crimes. The key aims and objectives are information sharing, public policy engagement, collaboration in research, and understanding hate. Links are available for network member websites, an online library of publications, antihate initiatives, a blog, and events.

Our World in Data

www.ourworldindata.org

Research, reports, and data on major problems faced by the world including poverty, disease, hunger, climate change, war, existential risks, and inequality. Our World in Data is based at the University of Oxford at the Oxford Martin Programme on Global Development.

Pew Research Center

www.pewresearch.org

Pew Research Center is a nonprofit, nonpartisan, and nonadvocacy organization conducting polling, providing research and analysis of politics, policy, journalism, media, science, technology, religion, public life, Hispanic trends, U.S. and global trends, among others.

ProPublica, Documenting Hate

www.propublica.org

ProPublica is an independent, nonprofit newsroom producing investigative articles on issues of abuse of power and betrayals of public trust. *ProPublica* is working on collecting and verifying reports of hate crime and building a data base of hate and bias incidents.

Southern Poverty Law Center (SPLC)

www.splcenter.org

The Southern Poverty Law Center was founded in 1971 by civil rights attorney's Morris Dees and Joseph Levin Jr. working to protect the civil rights of those facing discrimination, abuse, or exploitation. The SPLC monitors activities of over 1,600 hate and extremist groups across the country, publishes investigative reports, and trains law enforcement officers. The Teaching Tolerance program founded in 1991 offers free resources to educator's working with grades kindergarten through high school to emphasize social justice and antibias to create inclusive diverse communities.

Teacher Education Week

www.edweek.org

Education Week is an online resource for editorial projects, news, information, and analysis in precollegiate education. The acquisition of the TV company Learning Matters Inc. allows for visual storytelling, TV broadcasting, and web-based videos.

Index